'Seasoned' for Family and Friends

notionpress.com

Contemporary Recipes with an Old World Flavour and Reminiscences and Vignettes of Life in Provincial India

'Seasoned' for Family and Friends

Morvarid Fernandez

Notion Press

Old No. 38, New No. 6
McNichols Road, Chetpet
Chennai - 600 031

First Published by Notion Press 2016

ISBN 978-1-946204-35-6

Cover Design and Illustrations by Annushka Hardikar

In Memory of my beloved Parents

Sheila and Farrokh Irani

My beloved Grandmother Una Maud Ferguson

and

Kairus

"Say not in grief he is no more — but live

in thankfulness that he was"

*Jewish Proverb

Contents

Acknowledgements

Writing a cookbook is not just about tapping the keys on your computer. It involves food, the cooking and eating of it, and more, much more! A cookbook only turns meaningful when family and friends get involved, to savour and appraise and hopefully ask for more! So David and Katrina, thank you for your constructive criticism that forced me to do better, for your unstinting encouragement and support. I will always be grateful to our many guests at the Hermitage, who have visited us over the years, and have unwittingly been at the receiving end of some of my experiments with food!

What joyfulness in the kitchen when the dishes come back empty!

I would like to thank my dear niece, Vashti for taking time off to read my book chapter by chapter and for giving me such valuable feedback, my brother Raian for his support and excellent ideas. My dear cousin Kayandokth for the stories and reminiscences we shared – thank you. Finally, I am ever so grateful to my extended family for being who they are and for making life such an incredible journey!

Tushna, thank you for checking and proofreading 'Seasoned,' for every comma you added and every comma removed! Your help is much appreciated. Annushka, I wish to thank you for understanding 'Seasoned' so perfectly and illustrating it so beautifully.

I want to thank the Karnataka State Divisional Archives Office in Mysore for permission to view the Palace Maramath files, and to Mr. K. S Chandrasekhar family friend, for all his help.

Finally, all of you at Notion Press who have contributed to making this book a reality, thank you for everything, working with you has been a fulfilling experience, greatly appreciated.

1. The Hermitage

The sounds of the jungle change subtly through the day but seasonal differences are unambiguous and sharply defined. Monsoon mornings begin with the call of the peacock, summer days break with those of the jungle fowl, while the early birdsong of a winter visitor warms a chilly morning. During the monsoons, the drumming of the rain enhances the timbre of the amphibian choir that sings night and day. In peak summer, you just cannot ignore the serpent eagles screaming overhead, nor the countless cicadas for whom silence is meaningless. These are some of the jungle sounds that intermingle with the mundane everyday sounds of our household, the whistle of a pressure cooker, the clatter of teacups, the roll of the curry stone, or Dhakliya chopping wood. In the background, you can hear the farmhands at work, the hum of a water pump, and David on his tractor.

We live on a farm, David my husband, my daughter Katrina and I; deep in the jungles of the Western Ghats of Peninsular India, we call it The Hermitage. We moved here in 1981 and have lived here ever since. Our daughter Katrina was born in 1983 and is now a conservation biologist, assiduously studying the magnificent biodiversity that surrounds us.

Some years ago, we started a small family run guesthouse, and many visitors from around the world have stopped by to experience life in a jungle environment. Some are fleeting encounters, many stay longer coming back time and again to build long and lasting friendships. Nevertheless, everyone who had passed this way has touched and enriched our lives and for this, we are truly grateful. I spend a lot of time in my kitchen because I do all the cooking, and the recipes in this book are for the uncomplicated, straightforward meals that I cook our guests. However, my recipes aren't perfect, and I should like you to think of them as mere ideas to expand and experiment with, to work on and improve.

I had no desire to write a conventional cookbook but preferred it to be as straightforward and uncomplicated as my recipes. Therefore, you won't find surreal photo-shopped photographs of food, elaborate Master Chef Compositions, or cut and dried recipes with calorie counts. Instead, I thought to write a home cook's handbook, and because I live on a farm, you will find instead, home-grown tips on country living, and plenty of stories!

I grew up with stories. My grandmother would read me one every night even after I learnt to read myself. Hidden among the recipes in the book you will find stories. I hope you will enjoy them; they are about growing up in the sixties and seventies in small town India. Life in boarding school, still other stories about weird and wonderful experiences in rural and provincial living, and life on the farm through the eighties and beyond. Most relate to food in some way or the other! I hope that while you cook, patiently waiting for that final whistle to blow, the milk to boil, or those eggs to coddle you could perhaps read a story or two. I am sure we will both meet, through the food and the stories, and discover that our lives, no matter how far apart, are not very different.

2. Recipes Across Borders

Cooking should be a fulfilling and enjoyable experience, rather than a tedious, stressful chore you have to endure. To achieve this, what better way to go than creativity and inventiveness? Celebrate and treasure a good recipe, but finally, the dish that sits on the table is an interpretation and the result of the hands that cooked it. Borrow ingredients across borders and meld them into your style of cooking using them to play new and unconventional roles. Turn the mundane into the outstanding with the addition of an exotic and mysterious element ingeniously used! Turn your everyday cookery on its head by using familiar ingredients but in different and unusual ways. The recipes in this book include ingredients from around the world, your local Asian, Middle Eastern or specialty store are sure to stock most of them. If not you can always source them online.

We truly forget how to provide for ourselves. It is hard to ignore the hard sell of modern retail, huge conglomerates, and supermarkets that relentlessly tell us what we should eat, what's best for us, and reassure us that taking unhealthy shortcuts in the kitchen is intelligent thinking. The commercial food system has besmirched our taste buds with artificial sweeteners, flavour enhancers, harmful preservatives and with unhealthy additions of hormones and antibiotics. Let's shop for healthy ingredients at an organic store, shun G. M, and pick heirloom over a hybrid. Let's grow our herbs in a pot on the balcony and exercise in a vegetable garden instead of a gym. Let's promise to use those leftovers and to fill our store cupboard with homemade pickles, jams, and jellies. Let's take responsibility for sourcing our healthy food.

I strive to make my kitchen a happy place, reminding myself that even the simple chores of cleaning and washing, can be calming and restful. At sundown, when our hens begin to roost, when my feet ache and my back need a rest when the cattle come home, and the last of the dishes have been washed and put away, I think, what better place to spend the day, than in a kitchen?

No aerosol can replicate the aroma that wafts gently through

Biscuits in the oven just beginning to brown

A pot of brewing South Indian coffee

Dark, roasting spices

Deep fried chillies

Ambe Mohar[1] as it bubbles and spits in it's hot water bath

No finer colour palette than

Squid ink the colour of jet

The pristine white of a daikon radish

The rainbow colours of Swiss chard

The intense yellow of an Indian egg

Crisp freshly picked salad greens

During the sixties and seventies, magazines for the homemaker often carried a column called 'Household Hints,' or something to that effect. Readers sent in their entries, some of the suggestions were bizarre probably causing the harried homemaker far more problems than they solved, but the best entries won prizes. My mother cut out the 'hints' she thought the best and stuck them on the inside covers of all her scrapbooks. Here are some of them!

Add a teaspoon of all-purpose flour to the hot oil in a pan before frying your eggs, stops them from sticking and breaking if they aren't very fresh.

To prevent your fried fish from sticking or breaking first dry roast a tablespoon or two of sea salt in your pan, wipe clean and then proceed as per plan.

To get more juice out of a lemon steep it in boiling water for five minutes. A fruitful idea, especially if like me, you impatiently pluck them too green!

To cut super thin slices of bread for those sandwiches, keep dipping your knife into a bowl of hot water.

Before baking your jacket potatoes, steep them in hot water for half an hour.

Have a great day cooking!

1. Ambe Mohar a delightful heirloom variety of rice.

3. Soups

Broccoli and Curry Leaf Soup with Almonds

Makes 5 or 6 nutty mugs full

You require the following:

500 grams fresh broccoli florets

75 grams white onion

800ml homemade chicken or vegetable stock [or water with three soup cubes[2]]

250 ml milk

¼ cup almonds

50 grams Parmesan or Cheddar cheese

1 teaspoon fennel seed

3 to 4 sprays curry leaves[3]

1 tablespoon butter

1 tablespoon vegetable oil

Salt and pepper to taste

Chop the broccoli into pieces, tip into a pan with the curry leaves and with just enough stock or water to cover, cook until tender. Set aside to cool and then blend until smooth. Heat the oil and butter in a pot; add the fennel and brown half a minute. When done add the finely minced onion and fry until translucent and soft, then add the broccoli, the remaining stock, and mix well. Season to taste and simmer for a few minutes. Meanwhile, roughly grind the almonds and grate the cheese, add the almonds to the soup and mix well. Finish with the milk adding just enough to thin down the soup. When ready to serve heat through, but do not bring to the boil, serve individually with a sprinkling of cheese on top.

---

2. The quantity should depend on the size of the soup cube.

3. Use mature curry leaves, tender young leaves will not give enough flavour.

Carrot Soup with Black Sesame Seed

Enough for 6

Serve with a bowlful of lettuce, rocket or watercress

You require the following:

500 grams deep orange carrots

100 grams orange sweet potato

50 grams finely chopped onion

3 to 4 cloves of garlic crushed

3 cups vegetable or meat stock

1 cup hot milk [or a little more to thin if required]

1/3 cup fresh cream

1 tablespoon dried summer savoury

1 tablespoon black sesame seeds

1 teaspoon caraway seeds

50 grams butter

2 tablespoons Asian sesame oil

Peel and grate the carrots and sweet potato. Gently heat the butter in a heavy-bottomed frying pan, add the crushed garlic and cook for half a minute. Next tip in the carrots and sweet potato, and fry until well coated with the butter and lightly softened. Then transfer to a vessel, add enough of the stock just to cover the vegetables and simmer on medium heat until done. Cool and process in a blender until smooth. Meanwhile, heat the oil in a pan, add the caraway seed and fry lightly but do not burn. Next, add the finely chopped onions and the summer savoury and cook until the onions are a light brown, add the carrot and sweet potato puree and cook 2 minutes. Then put in the remaining stock and simmer for a few moments more. Just before serving, roast the black sesame seeds on a griddle. Heat the soup and add the hot milk, then take off the heat. Lightly beat the cream and add to the soup, mix well and pour into individual bowls and sprinkle the sesame seed on top.

My Home Town

When my parents first settled in Mysore[4] in 1951, they lived in a charming old homestead called 'Bloomfield.' It is also, where I spent the first three years of my life, but consequently, I have very faint recollections of what it was really like. My maternal grandmother Una Maud Fergusson also lived with us and resided in the outhouse right at the back. It was haunted! The ghost was apparently a young woman with a broken heart, who ended her life by jumping into the well located just outside the outhouse door. At night, she would recline at the foot of my grandmother's bed or nudge her while she knelt to say the Lord's Prayer.

In 1959, my family moved to Krupalaya, a splendid two storied mansion two houses away from Bloomfield. Though I had just turned three, I can recall the servants walking across to our new home with our rosewood pelmets slung across their shoulders and the crimson drawing room curtains billowing behind them. Probably built in 1900[5] Krupalaya like Bloomfield and the other houses on the street were Palace properties. Before we moved in, Krupalaya was the official residence of the Huzur Secretary to H. H. The Maharaja of Mysore and was at various times occupied by Sadeg Z. Shah, H. N. Pallegar and J. B. Mallaradhya. Our home was originally called 'Home Craft,' Sadeg Z. Shah requested a change of name in the early '20's, and he suggested 'Krupalaya' - the house of blessings.[6]

And the 'House of Blessings' it was indeed, all twenty-two thousand square feet of it. Set in just under an acre of garden it was fortified by magnificent flowering trees. Coral pink cassia, the ephemeral but remarkable Jacaranda, and the rusty shield bearer with its copper pods and carpet of fallen yellow flowers. Just outside the green wooden gate, in the sweltering heat of summer, a scorching streak of orange and red appeared when the gul mohar flowered. Opposite Krupalaya was Vasantha Mahal the palace guesthouse for His Highness's personal guests. Behind us was the palace garage with its incomparable fleet of custom-built cars, and flanked on the left by The Retreat, the home of the late maharani's aunt. Adjoining the palace garage was the headquarters of the palace band, where Mr. D' freese was the bandmaster. There were spirited practice sessions in the mornings and while Colonel Bogey was inescapable, Sousa's many signature pieces floated by intermingled with the rolling of a tonga's[7] wheels, a bicycle bell or the blast of an occasional horn.

4. Mysore is a historic township in Karnataka, South India just a three-hour drive away from the capital city of Bangalore. It was the capital city of the princely rulers of the Wodeyar dynasty.
5. This inference is made from the fact, that when fire destroyed the old Mysore Palace in 1897, construction of palace properties in Mysore was mostly restricted to within the fort area.
6. Source: Palace Maramath, Karnataka State Divisional Archives, Mysore.
7. Tonga an Indian pony trap.

I moved into my new nursery on the first floor of Krupalaya on Sunday afternoon the 26th of April 1959. My brother Raian was due shortly, sometime in mid-June but the nursery was large enoughfor both of us, with plenty of room to spare for my brother Kairus who arrived in 1963. My parents[8] had their suite just next door to the nursery. My grandmother lived downstairs in a beautiful set of rooms leading off from the drawing room, and opening onto the garden.

The family ate in the breakfast room, a very functional sort of place; it's where you threw down your school bag, gossiped with the servants, and made phone calls. The day's menu discussed, where marketing money changed hands, and also where my brother's and I negotiated our way through the holidays, daily life centred on the breakfast room.

The dining room at Krupalaya in apricot and green was my mother's masterpiece. A beautiful room with rosewood furniture treasured Bohemian cut glass, sets of crockery in the dozens, and on the walls the 'oils' of two very artistically gifted grand aunts Alice and Emma. The adjacent drawing room is where we often spent the evenings, Marlene Dietrich on the turntable, the heavy crimson curtains lifting gently in the breeze. The upright Bluthner stood silently [my mother no longer played], and in an alcove alongside was the carved opium table, surrounded by books with names that are now mostly forgotten Corelli, Buck, Haggard.

Krupalaya, like most traditional Mysore homes, had a large service area at the back of the house bounded on all sides by trees, bull's heart, silk cotton, neem, and mango. Everyone parked their sturdy black bicycles under the wood apple tree. The fruit, hard, dull brown and unappealing was nevertheless sent off to Poona to help treat a dear aunt's stomach ulcers. I loved to loiter around the back of the house; it's where the servants hung out, and I was often an eyewitness to their minor politics as they played out. It is where the vessels were washed, the masala's ground, and the dogs gave birth. Here, clothes were sometimes hung out to dry, where the coalman deposited his sack on the first of every month, and visiting drivers sat around for a smoke, while their memsahib's gossiped inside. Mid morning every Sunday, the dhobi and his donkeys arrived. Tethered and glad to be unburdened of the weeks washing, they stood, and like me were also mute spectators, to life as it went on at the back of Krupalaya.

---

8. My father was an industrialist, and along with his uncle Rustom Mama, set up the Ideal Jawa [Later Yezdi] Motorcycle Factory in Mysore in 1960. Commercial production began in 1961 in technical collaboration with Jawa of Czechoslovakia.

Cream of Drumstick Soup with Pesto

Enough for 3 or 4

You require the following:

400 ml thick drumstick pulp [approximately ten long drumsticks][9]

75 grams red or white onion

300 ml vegetable or chicken stock

150 ml thick coconut milk

1 teaspoon white pepper powder

1 teaspoon cumin powder

1 sprig curry leaves

1 tablespoon mint

2 tablespoon fresh coriander leaves

2 tablespoons olive oil or vegetable oil of your choice

Rock salt or sea salt to taste

A little cream and mint leaves to garnish [optional]

For the Pesto:

2 cups tightly packed fresh basil leaves

1 or 2 mild green chillies deseeded

3 or 4 fat cloves of garlic

4 tablespoons olive oil, or use any other mild vegetable oil

2 tablespoons Parmesan cheese finely grated

9. Drumsticks have a short shelf life; choose those that are fresh, plump and less than two days old. Soup making requires a lot of pulp, therefore, choose traditional varieties of drumstick with their smaller seeds, rather than modern hybrids.

To make the pesto:

Wash the basil well; place in a food processor with the other ingredients and process to form a thick, smooth paste, season to taste.

Prepare the drumsticks[10] and with a pinch of salt and enough water to cover them, cook until well done. Remove from the heat and cool. Retain one cup of the cooking water. Split open the drumstick and with a spoon, scoop out the pulp and the seeds. Chop the onion finely. Heat the oil in a pot, add the onion, curry leaves and fry on a medium heat. Add the pepper powder and cumin powder. When the onions are a light brown, add the drumstick pulp and cook for about 3 minutes, then add the cup of cooking water. Continue to cook for 3 minutes more. Cool and process in a blender. Tip the puree back into a pot and place on medium heat adding the chicken or vegetable stock. Add the chopped coriander and mint. Cook on a slow fire until the herbs are well blended. Just before you are ready to serve, add the coconut milk and heat through but do not boil. Top each serving with a dollop of cream and a sprig of mint and serve the pesto separately in a small bowl.

10. See page 263 on how to prepare the drumsticks.

A Short Family Brief

The Iranis living in India, are Zoroastrians, an ethnoreligious community, who fled from their native country Iran due to religious persecution during the 19th and 20th centuries. Though we share the same religion with the Parsees [who left Persia more than 1200 years ago], culturaly, socially and linguistically we are distinct. My paternal Grandfather Khudamorad Irani and his Father Jamshed and Mother Shirine e anok came from Moubarakhai in Yazd. When he and his family journeyed to India on donkey back, sometime around 1895, he was probably 12 to 14 years old. The journey took two years, and a journal would have been a fascinating read. Sadly, neither my grandfather nor his parents were literate, and so the stories have been lost forever. Not much is known about my grandfather's early life, but for the greater part of it, he earned a living washing dishes and cleaning tables in the 'Irani' restaurants across Bombay. He met my paternal Grandmother Mothibai whose family incidentally also owned an Irani restaurant; he later married her on the 21st of March 1919.

My paternal grandparents and their five children lived for the most of their lives in Poona oscillating between prosperity and penury, often running away from creditors to obscurity in places such as Talegaon. On one such exodus, Nergis Fui [my aunt] met her future husband Adershir; he was the truck driver who helped them move. Besotted not only by her beauty but also by her indomitable spirit, he promised never to forget her and one day to return.

Eventually, prosperity came to stay. A fine home at No. 42 Sassoon Road, a model A Ford, the purchase of land and a booming family business. Proudly driving his brand new car down the street one day, my grandfather near ran over a dog, terrified that the influential Parsee owners would corner him; he concealed his car for a whole six months until finally, his cloud of apprehension blew away!

My mother was of mixed ancestry. My maternal grandmother Una Maud was of Dutch descent and came from a large family based in Agra. Her father, red haired Peter Glendower Kouwen, born in 1842 was a telegraph dispatcher. He died of a ruptured appendix. Peter's, father William Kouwen was Superintendent of the Fire Engineers of Fort St. George, at Madras, and lived to the ripe old age of ninety. Una Maud's mother was Sarah Ann Scattergood of whom we know very little, other than the fact that she was an excellent cook, I have a handwritten recipe of hers for Sooji Halva. I had it framed and it hangs on my kitchen wall. The family tree however does trace her lineage to John Scattergood and Arrabella Forbes who married in 1706 at Fort St. George, Madras.

My maternal grandfather was Irish. My Great Great Grandparents were John Ferguson [a weaver] and Wilhelmina Mc ILreath from Hill Hall, in the Parish of Drumbeg, County Antrim. Their son James served in the Duke of Cornwall's Light Infantry. After seven years in the Army and five in the reserves, he was discharged a Lance Corporal at Belgaum in 1894. He returned to Ireland for a short spell, living at 5 Low Road, Lisburn, County Antrim where he worked as a bleacher. However, India beckoned, and he was back, working as a driver on the MSM[11] railways that had its headquarters in Egmore, Madras. Unfortunately, he died young of ptomaine poisoning allegedly contracted from contaminated beer.

My Great Grandparents, James and Jane Constance Gager, had six sons, of which the third Egbert George, my grandfather was born in Belgaum. Trained as a doctor, he served in Mesopotamia WW1. He married my grandmother Una Maud, a nurse by profession and together they raised four daughters.

Posted all over India during his military service George and his family finally settled in Poona. Aunts Ollie and Ethel [Una's sisters] joined the family group. A few years later Granny Jane Constance Ferguson arrived around 1937. Having brought up six boys, she was very strict, and often cautioned her four naughty granddaughters, 'If you were one of mine, you would be beaten and vinegar and brown paper applied'! There is a story that tells of how one day, while sewing in the garden, Granny Constance dropped her needle and asked my mother to find it. She did, and when Granny Constance complimented her on her excellent eyesight, my mom who had just turned six replied, 'I am like god I can see everything'!

11. MSM: The Madras and Southern Mahratta Railway, was a railway company founded on the 1st of January 1908, and operated from Madras in South India. Brought about by the merger of two railroads, the Madras Railway, and the Southern Mahratta Railway. Finally, in April 1951, it merged with the South Indian Railway, and the Mysore state railway to form The Southern Railway.

Smoked Mulligatawny Soup with Kaffir Lime Leaves 4 to 5 servings

It is usual to serve Mulligatawny Soup meatless, using just the stock as a base for the soup. My mulligatawny is a rural version, where discarding real meat and bone would be a sacrilege.

You require the following:

500 grams mutton or beef on the bone
150 ml thick coconut milk
1 sprig curry leaves
1 large mild red chilly
6 peppercorns
1 teaspoon turmeric powder
2 tablespoons ghee
Salt and pepper to taste
300 ml water [approximately]
75 grams red onions
1 tablespoon ginger paste
2 tablespoons coriander seed
2 tablespoons gram dhal
1 tablespoon shredded kaffir lime leaves
Sliced lime to serve

Clean and wash the meat well, place in a pressure cooker with a little salt and just enough water to cover and cook until done. Cool and set aside until required. Meanwhile, roast the gram dhal, the peppercorns, and the red chilli and coriander seeds on a griddle until the colour of the spices change slightly. When done grind to a fine paste with the ginger, turmeric, and a little water.

Melt the ghee in a pot, add the curry leaves and finely chopped onion and fry until a light golden brown. Add the ground masala, fry until the raw smell disappears. Put in a little of the meat stock now and then as the onions and masala begin to dry out. Next, add the mutton and remaining stock and bring once to a boil, then lower the heat and simmer for 10 minutes. Half an hour before you serve, smoke the soup with the ingredients given below. Reheat the soup, add the coconut milk and the kaffir lime leaves and simmer for two minutes more. Serve hot with slices of lime and a small bowl of white basmati or jasmine rice.

To smoke the soup you require the following ingredients:

3 or 4 lime leaves or 6 to 8 curry leaves crushed
4 to 6 black peppercorns
1 teaspoon coriander seed roughly pounded

Smoking the soup is a simple process. Smoke the soup following the procedure on page 68.

Oriental Mushroom Soup with Fenugreek [Kasuri Methi]

Makes 6 servings

You require the following:

5 large shitake mushrooms [caps only]

½ cup dried black fungus

½ cup dried white fungus

200 grams onions

6 cloves garlic

1 small knob galangal or ginger

4 to 5 young spring onions

1 teaspoon Szechuan pepper crushed

3 to 4 dried red cascabel chillies[12] [deseeded if you like]

1/3 cup well packed dried fenugreek[13]

6–7 cups strong vegetable or meat stock

3 tablespoons vegetable oil

Salt to taste

Soak the mushrooms and fungi separately in hot water until rehydrated. Clean them thoroughly. Slice the mushroom caps into pieces. Soak the chillies in warm water to soften them. Thinly slice the onions, crush the garlic, mince the ginger or galangal, and chop the spring onions. Heat the oil in a pot and add the galangal or ginger, the garlic, and the chillies, fry half a minute then add the onions, and cook them until they change colour to a light brown. Add the crushed Szechuan pepper and cook for another minute or two. Next, put in the mushrooms and stir well, tip in the spring onions and adding a little of the stock, cook the mushrooms until they soften. When done pour in the rest of the stock, season to taste and simmer for 10 to 15 minutes. Finally, add the dried fenugreek and simmer five minutes more, then turn off the heat. Serve with a bowl of soba[14] noodles.

---

12. Cascabel chillies are very popular in the state of Tamil Nadu and readily available.
13. *See page 283.
14. Japanese soba noodles are made from buckwheat.

Spinach and Mascarpone with Bishop's Weed

Makes 5 to 6 cups

Bishops weed or ajwain is the key player in this soup. Crush the seeds in the palm of your hand to release the aroma of its fragrant oil before adding it to the pot. The quarter teaspoon recommended below is a conservative one; I usually end up adding a little more, however, be cautious too much of the Bishop can be overwhelming!

You require the following:

500 grams spinach weighed in after cleaning[15]
50 grams red or white onions
1 teaspoon garlic paste
1/4 teaspoon Bishops weed [ajwain]
3 vegetable or chicken soup cubes or to taste[16]
250 ml of water to thin the soup [approximately]
200 grams mascarpone or any full fat soft cream cheese[17]
250ml milk
4 spring onions
2 tablespoons fresh mint
2 tablespoons butter
1 tablespoon olive oil
Salt and pepper to taste

Bring the mascarpone to room temperature. Rinse the spinach and then drain thoroughly. Chop the greens and tip into a pot with one tablespoon of butter and 50 ml of water, cover the pan with a well fitting lid and place on low heat. Cook for 3 to 4 minutes until the spinach has wilted a little then lift off the lid and give the spinach a good stir. Replace the lid and continue to cook the spinach until done. Remove from the heat and set aside to cool and then puree in a food processor.

Meanwhile, mince the onions, and finely chop the spring onions and mint. Place a pot on medium heat and add the remaining butter and oil, put in the Bishops weed and cook for half a minute, then add the onions and fry them until they change colour and become translucent. Next, tip in the garlic and spring onions and continue to cook adding a little water if the onions begin to dry out. Crush the soup cubes and add to the pot blending them well into the onions. After a minute or two put in the spinach puree and the mint, mix well and cook for a further 5 minutes until the soup heats through. Remove the pot from the stove, add the mascarpone or cream cheese, and stir gently. Place the pot back on the stove and heat until the cheese has completely melted, add the milk and season to taste with the salt and pepper and serve immediately.

---

15. Use the spinach stalks as well, discarding only those that are tough and fibrous.
16. Soup cubes come in different sizes, the strength of the cubes will be a guide as to how much you require.
17. Be sure to use full fat cream cheese, low fat cream cheese does not melt very well.

The Servant Corps

My bewildered husband David once remarked that my mother and her retinue of servants should theoretically come under the 'Factory's Act. ' Admittedly, there were many, but they were like extended family with a relationship that was truly symbiotic. Now decades later, in times that have changed, there are recollections and reminiscences, about the cooks and the bearers, malis and drivers, those that swept and others that cleaned; and the ayahs, whose gentle hands rocked our cradles. Time has obscured some of the names and faces have faded, but the memories are strong and alive.

One treasured snapshot is Maria pounding spices under the shade of the Yellow Silk cotton tree. Inseparable cumin and coriander, shards of white glistening coconut, delicately roasted poppy seeds, freshly unearthed ginger and luminous unblemished turmeric. Her dexterous hands would rhythmically roll the coal black grinding stone until finally the spices mingled and came together as fragrant compositions in dark orange or burnt umber, yellow ochre and jade.

Our cook Patrick gave Maria her orders. He was a man of few words; his speech as clipped as the starched whites he wore, held up with his narrow black leather belt. Marie was his wife and kitchen help. Neither was very even tempered. Largely, because Patrick's strangulated hernia dulled his days and Maria, perhaps, because she had to live with Patrick.

Louisa also had a close bond with the Yellow silk cotton tree[18]. Leafless in summer, the tree would shed its heavily ribbed brown capsules concealing a multitude of black seeds within the silky cotton. Louisa was ayah to my brother Kairus. With Spats the Welsh Border Collie by her side and her snuff-box in hand, she spent her free time collecting the capsules, releasing the seeds and gathering the cotton into piles. At sundown, with her day's work done she would bring out the board of Pallanguzhi[19], quickly dropping the shells into the shallow cups. Silently we would play in the dull evening light until Krishna called out that it was dinnertime.

There was no evening walk for the dogs to Kuppana's garden on Tuesdays; it was Krishna's day off. Quiet and dignified, as dependable as a rock. The heavy black bakelite phone in the breakfast room with the din of a bicycle bell was his to answer, informing all those who wanted to know if 'Master was in or out. ' There was also tall, dark, lanky Das;

18. Cochlospermum gossypium.
19. Pallanguzhi is a traditional South Indian board game. It takes two to play, a wooden board and cowries [shells] or seeds.

the two bearers worked together for decades. Through the day, they would polish the brass, churn ice cream, and serve us our meals. At sundown, it was time to fix my father's Scotch.

As a driver and mechanic but mostly as my dad's trusted valet, Krupalaya was Ramu's first and only job. He preferred those great Americans [but was so small in stature, he needed an extra cushion to look out over the top], but willingly compromised and maintained my mother's sky blue Morris Minor. On his 'watch' a monkey walked away with the car keys and dropped then off at the neighbours' further down the road. It was Ramu, who took us to school, wiped our tears when we fell, and sympathised when things weren't going too well!

My mother was an ambulance driver during the 'war,' and proudly capable of changing a flat in five minutes, however when Abbas arrived she decided she could no longer drive! For the next four and a half decades she sat behind, while Abbas drove her everywhere, to the Legislative Assembly in Bangalore for her two terms as a member, to frequent board meetings and many AGM's, to her School, to the 'Orphanage' to check on the children. He took her to kitty parties, to environmental forums, educational conventions, Girl Guide jamborees and finally, in her later years, he took her to the hospital, for her dialyses three times a week. Well, mannered, quiet, unassuming Abbas drove my mother and her friends' mile after mile, for thousands upon thousands of miles. He was privy to it all, Inner Wheel[20] politics, Knitting Bee gossip[21], the minutes of a recent board meeting, family disagreements and even to Mrs. D's[22] recipe for Chicken Mahiwallah.

20. The Ladies wing of Rotary International.
21. The Knitting Bee was a group of close-knit friends from Mysore, who informally got together, working towards raising funds for the Holdsworth Memorial Mission Hospital.
22. Mrs. D - Nergis Darasha was a very dear family friend.

Wild Mushroom Soup with Pine Nuts

4 mugs of wildly good soup!

In the South, wild mushrooms appear during the wet season. They spring up in fresh open grasslands in solitary splendour, or frequently in colourful crowds jostling for space. Sometimes you will find them nestling in the dark underworld of fallen leaves and rotting wood on the wet forest floor. Monkeys like them, and you have to get there early before the deer, and the bison do. Besides, the mushrooms are of little use once those spirited 'Pleasing Fungus' beetles scurrying around beneath them, have selectively nibbled away their share.

Even after 35 years of picking and eating wild mushrooms on wet and windy monsoon days, we are still very cautious, carefully inspecting the mushrooms to check whether they are edible. While picking wild mushrooms think ecologically, making sure to leave at least half behind to ensure their perpetuity.

You will require the following:

400 grams wild mushrooms

75 grams onions

50 grams pine nuts

3 to 4 cloves garlic

1 teaspoon aniseed

2 tablespoons fresh parsley

20 grams butter

1 tablespoons olive oil

A little milk if required to thin the soup

1/3 cup sour cream to serve [Optional]

Salt and white pepper to taste

Clean the mushrooms removing stray blades of grass, leaves or other twiggy stuff, rinse under cold running water, drain well and chop into pieces. Toss the mushrooms in the butter on medium heat until soft and cooked then set aside to cool. Meanwhile, puree the onions, garlic and pine nuts to a fine paste. Heat the oil in a pot and add the aniseed to it, fry for half a minute. Then add the onion paste and fry well on low heat until the rawness of the onion disappears. Meanwhile, process the mushrooms in a blender and add to the pot along with the parsley, mix well. Season the soup with salt and pepper; thin the soup with a little milk if necessary. When ready to serve reheat the soup but do not bring to the boil, serve with a dollop of sour cream if so desired.

Tomato Soup

Tomato soup is a staple on the menu of every restaurant worth its salt in the mofussil[23] towns of Southern India. I think it's what you could call a 'standard' along with a couple of others, such as a vegetable soup and a sweet corn chicken. One restaurant has in on its menu as 'The Ever Green' Tomato Soup'. Its popularity extends to the Indian Railways, where it makes an appearance on the menus of a number of prestigious trains. The tomato soups look more or less alike, semi-sweet, and well blended and thickened with corn flour. As a sort of reaction to these 'mofussil soups,' I never blend mine entirely, preferring them chunky with bits and pieces of tomato, and other elements bobbing around.

To make a good soup, you need juicy ripe fruit. If available, use traditional heirloom varieties such as the beefsteaks Brandywine or Marmande. Orange tomatoes are especially good in soups, try Orange Verna or Orange Borgoin. Red cherry tomatoes also make an excellent soup. Tomatoes are wonderful to create new and funky soups because they combine wonderfully with other ingredients. Find below two ways of making soup that I regularly serve in our 'mofussil guesthouse.'

23. The term was first used to cover all regions of India outside the purview of the East India Company, later it applied to those parts of the country outside urban centres, in other words, the country or rural areas.

Spicy Tomato with Fenugreek and Cheese Crotons

Enough for 4

You require the following:

1 kg juicy ripe tomatoes
100 grams red onions
1 tablespoon ginger paste
1 sprig mature curry leaves
1/4 cup well packed dried fenugreek leaves [kasuri methi]
1 or 2 teaspoons of brown sugar or palm sugar
2 tablespoons vegetable oil of your choice
Rock Salt to taste
750 ml vegetable or chicken stock[24]
100 grams tomato puree
2 teaspoons sambhar masala[25]

Plunge the tomatoes in hot water for a few minutes, drain and allow to cool, then skin them and cut them up into large pieces. Process the tomatoes in a food processor, but keep the pulp thick and chunky, set aside until required. Meanwhile, thinly slice the onions, heat the oil in a pot, add the onions and brown them lightly. Next, add the curry leaves, the ginger paste and the sambhar powder cook for a few minutes more, adding a little stock as required to prevent the mix from sticking or burning. Now add the tomato pulp and the puree lower the heat and continue to cook until the vegetables change colour. Put in the remaining stock and season to taste, add the sugar and thin the soup with a little water if necessary. Finally, add the fenugreek bring to boil once, and serve with the cheese croutons.

For the cheese croutons:

25 grams butter
1 or 2 tablespoons olive or grape seed oil
200 grams dry stale white or brown bread
1 tablespoon dry fenugreek leaves
150 grams grated cheese

Cube the bread and dry off in the oven if required. Melt the butter in a saucepan, add the oil and the dry fenugreek leaves and cook for one minute on a gentle heat. Add the cubes of bread and fry on all sides until a light golden brown. Sprinkle the cheese onto the bread, stir through and pop under the grill for a couple of minutes until the cheese melts, remove and serve with the soup in one large or 4 individual bowls.

---

24. If stock is unavailable, replace with soup cubes.
25. Replace the sambhar masala with massaman curry paste, sambal olek or Thai shrimp paste. However these can be a lot hotter than sambhar masala, so do keep a check on the amount you use.

Tomato Soup with Sweet Potato leaves

Enough for 6

Serve with a bowlful of Niger seed chutney[26]

You require the following:

1200 grams juicy ripe tomatoes

150 grams red onions

1 tablespoon garlic paste

300 ml strong vegetable or meat stock

150 ml thick tomato puree

3 to 4 pieces Marathi moggu

1 tablespoon hoisin sauce

1 cup well packed sweet potato leaves[27]

2 tablespoons Asian sesame oil

Water as required

Salt and pepper to taste

Place the whole tomatoes into a pot of boiling water for a few minutes, drain and then plunge into cold water. Allow the tomatoes to cool and then skin them and cut into large pieces. Process in a blender but keep the pulp thick and chunky. Lightly crack the Marathi moggu but keep them intact, and finely mince the onions.

On medium heat tip the oil into a pot, add the Marathi moggu and cook for a minute or two, but do not allow to burn. Now put in the onions and garlic paste, let them sweat and turn a light brown adding a little of the stock if necessary. When the onions have softened, add the blended tomato, lower the heat and continue to cook until the tomatoes have changed colour, adding the stock a little at a time as needed. Now add the tomato puree, the hoisin sauce, and the remaining stock and allow the soup to simmer for 10 to 15 minutes. Taste and adjust seasoning. Check consistency thin the soup if you wish. Just before serving tear, the sweet potato leaves into pieces and add to the soup, cook 3 minutes more. Serve the soup with a bowl of Niger seed chutney to sprinkle on top.

---

26. *Recipe for Niger seed chutney on page 284.

27. If sweet potato leaves are unavailable use any greens of your choice, try baby spinach, pigweed or a Chinese green that your family likes.

Dress up Your Soup!

The only way that my grandmother was able to sell us the idea that 'bone soup' was jolly good was by bribing us with a marrow bone; so if 'Bone Soup' was on the menu so were three marrow bones and three marrow spoons. Anglo-Indian bone soup is a delicious full-bodied stock of mutton or beef bones with the addition of a few, mainly root vegetables. Even with an occasional bonus of alphabet macaroni, we saved our marrow bones for the last. Sadly recent years have witnessed the disappearance of the marrow spoon, making a succulent marrowbone lying on your side plate seem somewhat redundant! Serving soup with something on the side is a heart-warming way to complete the dish.

Puffed Fox Nut [makhana] or popped corn can be lightly fried in a little olive oil and then seasoned with garlic or celery salt. A pinch or two of Indian black salt or any other specialty salt will also do nicely. Wasabi is available in powder form. Sprinkle a little on the fox nut as you toss it in the oil.

Serve your soup with freshly popped minor millets such as foxtail, barnyard or proso millet tossed in herb or garlic butter.

Scout around for local family run bakeries; choose any special bread they have to offer. Brush the tops with a little well-beaten egg then roll in black or white sesame seeds, poppy seeds, caraway or sunflower seeds, finely chopped onions or your favourite herb. Place under a grill for a couple of minutes until well heated.

Leftover grilled or fried fish can be flaked and sprinkled on top of the soup. Some added protein in a simple vegetable soup!

Serve your soup with an assortment of unusual papadums. Cut them into quarters rather than keeping them whole.

A swirl of yogurt or sour cream, pesto or a little relish on top will do well. You can also spoon in a little sweet mango chutney.

Apple slices sprinkled with ground cloves, grated nutmeg or freshly ground pepper and quickly fried in a knob of butter can pair up with celery or pumpkin soup.

Lightly butter cheese biscuits dust generously with acacia seed and heat under the grill. Serve with a tomato soup.

4. Salads

Cucumber and Radish Ribbons

Enough for 4 to 5

You require the following:

2 large cucumbers [2 to 2½ cups cucumber ribbons][28]

1 medium long white daikon radish [1 cup radish ribbons][29]

½ cup fresh green whole Bengal gram[30]

2 tablespoon fresh dill leaves or dill microgreens

¼ cup sliced black olives

Salt to taste

Pomegranate Salad Dressing:

1 teaspoon minced Japanese preserved ginger

2 tablespoons rob e - anar

Indian black salt and black pepper to taste

1 or 2 cloves of garlic

Castor sugar a little to taste

4 tablespoons olive or grape seed oil

With the help of a vegetable peeler, peel thin ribbons running the length of the cucumbers. If you are using very young cucumbers then the skin can stay on, do remember to discard the inner core that contains the seeds. Do the same with the radish then mix the cucumber, radish, and green gram together and chill until required, but do not salt the vegetables. Just before serving, add the olives to the salad and mix well, then add the dressing and season to taste. Tip into a salad bowl and decorate with the fresh dill leaves or microgreens.

To prepare the dressing

Beat together the rob e-anar, the oil, and the castor sugar until you get a nice thick emulsion, add the ginger and garlic mix well, finally season with a little Indian black salt and freshly ground pepper.

---

28 As an alternative try the Armenian Cucumber.

29 Replace with a red radish variety such as Long Scarlet or Red Meat, which is white outside and red inside.

30 Just after the monsoons in the months of October and November markets are flooded with bunches of fresh green gram. Strip the green gram off their stalks and shell them and do make a serious attempt not to pop too many into your mouth!

> Japanese preserved ginger or gari is an absolute delight, tender young ginger thinly sliced and pickled in a solution of sugar and rice vinegar. Gari is used to prepare sushi and is essential in its presentation. Nevertheless, nothing should stop you from using it elsewhere, salads, fruity drinks and even in a jug of ice-cold drinking water.

Zucchini Cucumber Salad with Water Chestnuts

Enough for 4 to 5

You require the following:

2 cups zucchini [approximately 3 to 4]

2 cups cucumber [about 2 to 3]

½ a cup moong bean, wheat berry or alfalfa sprouts

½ a cup tinned water chestnuts quartered

1 cup Swiss chard or any other greens of your choice[31] torn up

1 teaspoon black sesame seeds to garnish

For the salad dressing:

1 tablespoon soft brown sugar

2 teaspoon Asian sesame oil

2 tablespoons red pepper relish

Salt to taste

1 tablespoon rice wine vinegar

2 tablespoon mayonnaise

1 teaspoon wasabi paste or more to taste

Choose young zucchini, around 6 to 7 inches long wash well leave on the skin, and with the help of a vegetable peeler, peel thin ribbons running the length of the vegetable. Do the same with the cucumbers, if you are using very young cucumbers, then the skin can stay on, but discard the core. Put the shavings into a salad bowl. Add the sprouts and the water chestnuts and chill until serving time, but don't salt the vegetables just yet.

To make the dressing:

Dissolve the sugar in the vinegar [heat gently if the need arises]. Add the oil, wasabi and the red pepper relish to the mayo and mix well, finish by adding the vinegar and sugar syrup to the dressing, chill until needed. Just before you are ready to serve, toss the salad with the dressing and some salt and finally sprinkle over the sesame seed.

---

31 If you have any Ruby Red or Rainbow Chard [in shades of yellow orange and red] on hand add them to the salad, they look great.

The Auxiliary Group

The auxiliary group, are those that came and went throughout the year, year after year following a routine that seldom changed, faces that rarely changed. Every Sunday morning our Dhobi arrived with his donkeys, bringing in the weekly wash. Marked with indelible 'washerman's ink,' the freshly laundered clothes were checked, counted and marked off in my mother's 'dhobi book. ' The donkeys, loosely tied under the wood apple tree would wait motionless, patiently for the return of their master bringing with him their burden of that week's laundry.

"Long Tong" was my father's barber. The British named him so on account of his height and trade. He was always dressed in white; gold trimmed Mysore turban, and trademark cycle clips. Long Tong took great pride in his occupation, his excellent command of the English Language, and his political analysis, wittily seasoned with a pinch of salacious local gossip. His claim to fame was that he once trimmed Winston Churchill's hair, the one thing he would not forget or ever let you forget.

Perhaps the most tenacious of all was Raju the Painter. Whenever in need of a job or money he simply dropped by; my mother's benevolence never failed him, while my father's lack of enthusiasm was never a deterrent. Paint and paint tins, brushes and turpentine, were a constant in our lives at Krupalaya. My mother simply loved fresh paint! First up were our wooden bathing stools, thickly coated layer upon layer with white enamel paint. Krupalaya's numerous doors and windows of every shape and size were next in line. Some doors were so heavily coated with paint; they wouldn't shut, while the lattice windows in the drawing-room remained eternally jammed!

The one thing that Raju never got to paint were my mother's empty Dalda[32] tins. She collected them from friends near and far, and converted them into lovely waste paper bins, and later sold by the 'Knitting Bee'[33] for charity. The tins received a professional coat of spray paint at my father's factory, and later oven dried, hooked onto the assembly line interspersed with an assortment of motorcycle parts.

---

32 Dalda is a brand of hydrogenated vegetable oil very popular in Indian Kitchens for decades. Available in 5kg tins, empty, they made excellent waste paper bins decorated with contact paper and trim.

33 'The Knitting Bee': In December, the Knitting Bee held an annual fair on the hospital grounds. A white elephant stall, a tea stall, and a stall selling their beautiful craft work, all did brisk business. You could throw rings over a coconut, pin on the donkey's tail and win a grand prize, or for a small fee, judge the weight of Anne Devereux's homemade chocolate cake - Winner eats all!

Vittal Rao was Mysore's leading 'ladies tailor' and in high demand. He did the rounds on his bicycle progressing from one home to the other, while busy telephones helped keep track of his movements. With his two thimbles in place and a needle that flew, 'lightening' tailor' was hardly a misnomer; with ease, he could sew three of my grandmother's frocks in a day.

My parents cherished good company and loved to entertain, and the food served was always home cooked. Natesan was of Burmese Tamilian decent and employed as a cook at the Sports Club down the road. His 'Crumbed Chicken,' guaranteed that when numbers got a little out of hand and extra help was essential, he was the first on call. 'Biriyani' Sattar was Mysore's very own specialist; on special occasions, large family gatherings and at Christmas, he was always there cooking on a wood fire under the Neem tree. Party days were hectic, the bar was bound to be busy, and pre-dinner snacks had to do the rounds, Das and Krishna churning ice cream under the silk cotton tree. My father hired the bearers from Government House to give them a helping hand.

Life at Krupalaya was made much easier by The 'Metropole' Tailor [The Hotel Metropole is where he usually worked] who was intermittently on call to upholster furniture or plump up a cushion or two. There was Murthy, who's 'French polish' was in a master class of its own, while Yacob usually sorted out an electrical problem. The 'Coal Man,' whose clothes must have been a nightmare to wash, paid us a visit once a month. His merchandise was crucial when Nergis Fui was in town; the vibrant glowing embers in the segri[34] slow cooked her dhansak to perfection. The days of the segri are all but over, and all the donkeys left out to pasture, and sadly, the simplicity and spontaneity of those early times too, have more or less been lost forever.

Warm Couscous Salad with Rat Tailed Radish and Other Assorted Vegetables

Enough for 4

You require the following:

200 grams couscous

400 ml chicken or vegetable stock heated

50 grams radish pods [rat tailed or regular]

200 grams zucchini

200 grams red, orange or yellow tomatoes

125 grams fresh homemade panir

34 Segri: A small portable coal-burning stove made of metal or clay.

75 grams red onions

2 to 3 cloves garlic roughly crushed

¼ cup finely chopped dill

1 tablespoon freshly ground pepper

1 tablespoon butter

2 tablespoons vegetable oil of your choice

Sea salt to taste

Thirty minutes before serving time place couscous in a bowl, and pour over the hot stock. Cover the bowl and set aside. Chop the radish pods into pieces, about an inch long. Slice and quarter the zucchini and quarter the onions and tomatoes. Add the vegetable oil to a wok and fry the onions until the rings begin to separate and change colour, then put in the crushed garlic and the zucchini and continue to fry a few minutes more. Season with salt and a generous amount ground pepper. When nearly done toss in the tomatoes and the dill and cook until the tomatoes soften. Fluff up the couscous with a fork and turn into a serving bowl. Pile the cooked vegetables on top. Return the pan to the stove and add the butter, tip in the radish pods and fry until softened. Next, add the panir and fry for a few minutes more, season with a little salt and pepper. Pile the radish pods and panir on top of the vegetables and serve immediately.

The Cecil Hotel

The drudgery of life in boarding school brightened considerably with the prospect of an impending holiday. The school didn't break for the monsoons until late June, but the sweltering heat of the plains was excuse enough for my family to move to the hills for the summer. My father would drive up at the end of each week to join the rest of us; for my brother Raian and me, there were glorious weekend breaks. The family lodged at the Cecil Hotel; wonderfully warm, full of old-world charm and run by Gool Sukidas and her family.

The hotel was a splendid old Colonial building, set in extensive grounds and embraced by a 'Classic' Ooty garden. Dependable herbaceous borders cloaked in colour with delphiniums, lavender, and lupin. Oriental poppies, red hot poker, and lilies of all kinds; painstakingly trimmed boxwood hedges, tea roses and vine bowers of Wisteria and Clematis all proof that a 'legacy' had been left behind. The Cecil had spacious rooms with high ceilings, wooden floors, big bay windows and best of all, outstanding Tamilian cooks.

There were long-term boarders at the Cecil; there was Miss Elfrieda Gay a talented artist whose 'still life's' were showcased in the drawing room, and an old Colonel who had 'Stayed On'. Cosseted in the Cecil and sheltered by the familiar, the changing world outside of an emerging New India could be bewildering. Sometime in the mid-'60's coloured toilet paper entered the Indian consumer market for the very first time. The Colonel bravely bought some of the soft new pink and blue rolls, then rather apprehensively, approached Aunt Gool wanting to know if there were chances that the colours would 'run'!

At the Cecil hotel, the dinner gong went at 7. 00, and a walk to the dining room through draughty corridors was a small price to pay for the meal that lay ahead. There was no loud talk here; the only sound was the movement of the white-gloved bearers on the creaking wooden floorboards, and the elegant 'Made in Sheffield' cutlery gently knocking against the warmed white crockery. Sebastian, the Cecil's 'Jewel in the Crown' did not disappoint. Old fashioned mulligatawny soup, steak and kidney pie, Ooty peas and mashed potato, steamed fruit pudding with custard and cream. Simple, but so full of flavour and substance; simply no place for theatrics here.

The cold crept down the valley at sundown. All the rooms had fires lit, the logs of burning eucalyptus hissing and spitting, with the ensuing warmth and heavy woody smell of the oil so welcoming in those cavernous rooms. My father loathed the cold and no number of blankets or burning logs could curtail his illusion of imminent hypothermia; one unusually frosty morning, we were astonished to find him curled up in bed with the bedroom carpet, bulky and threadbare pulled over him for warmth!

Potato Salad with Curry Leaf Mayonnaise

Good for 3 or 4

You require the following:

350 grams potatoes

100 grams Iranian table dates

75 grams walnuts [halved]

2 or 3 cloves of garlic

1 teaspoon roasted fennel seed

1/3 cup well packed mustard microgreens, watercress or roughly chopped sorrel

Salt and pepper to taste

For the dressing:

1/3 cup mayonnaise

2 or 3 sprigs curry leaves torn up

1 or 1½ tablespoons curry leaf chutney[35]

1 tablespoon olive oil

1 tablespoon pine nuts crushed

Generous pinch of devils dung [asafoetida/hing]

Salt to taste

Mix all the ingredients together and toss into your salad, makes just less than half a cup, store leftovers in the refrigerator for another day.

Peel the potatoes, dice and boil in salted water until just done, drain the potatoes and cool completely. Roughly chop the dates and walnuts, and finely mince the garlic. Add to the potatoes with the roasted fennel seed and set aside until serving time. When ready to serve toss in the mustard microgreens, next add the dressing and season to taste with the salt and pepper. With a squeeze of lemon juice, you are ready to serve, tastes best slightly warm or at room temperature.

Postscript: This salad dressing also tastes good with a chicken or bean salad.

---

35. Recipe for the curry leaf chutney on page 270.

Crisp South Indian Moong Dhal Salad with Wakame

Serves 4

You require the following:

150 grams moong dhal

75 grams tender young zucchini or Armenian cucumber

1 or 2 mild green, red or yellow chillies

50 grams red or white onions

1/3 cup well packed freshly grated coconut

¼ cup fresh green coriander

2 tablespoons dried wakame or any other seaweed

1 tablespoon capers

Juice of half a lime

Salt to taste

Soak the dhal in cold water for about 2 hours or until it swells. Meanwhile, thinly slice and then quarter the zucchini or cucumber. Slice the chillies and roughly chop the capers before adding to the zucchini, then chill altogether in the refrigerator. Soak the wakame in warm water to reconstitute, finely chop the green coriander and the onions. Drain the moong dhal well and tip into a salad bowl, add the zucchini, onions, chillies and the capers. Add the chopped coriander and coconut to the dhal along with the drained wakame. Mix all the ingredients together, and chill until ready to serve. Just before serving, add salt to taste and a generous squeeze of lime or lemon juice.

Lima Beans with Tiger Prawns

Enough for 4 or 5

You require the following:

250 grams lima beans soaked overnight

40 fat tiger prawns or any other in markets near you

250 grams firm tomatoes chopped

1 large yellow capsicum

1 large green or purple capsicum

1 teaspoon dried marjoram

1 teaspoon garlic paste

teaspoon mustard seed

1 teaspoon cumin seed

cup chopped rocket leaves

2 or 3 tablespoons of mayo or horseradish sauce

Squeeze of lime or lemon juice to taste

2 tablespoons vegetable oil

Salt and pepper to taste

Drain the beans and set to boil in fresh water but without any salt. When the beans are soft and velvety, take them off the heat, drain and set aside to cool. Clean and rinse the prawns and marinate for half an hour with the marjoram, the garlic paste and a little salt and pepper. Meanwhile, roast the capsicums on an open flame until they blacken. Cool in a zip lock bag and then peel and slice them into strips.

Heat the oil in a wok or frying pan, and add the mustard and cumin seed and fry half a minute. Next fry the prawns in batches, cook each batch until just done. Squeeze the lemon juice onto the prawns and allow them to cool. Assemble the salad by mixing all the ingredients together, then add the mayo or horseradish sauce toss once again and serve at room temperature.

Post Script: If you attempt to fry all the prawns together, they will stew rather than fry.

Groceries and Home Suppliers

For Granny Ferguson, a visit to Devaraj[36] market three times a week was a necessity, and when home on holiday I loved to accompany her. We always entered the market through the North gate on Dhanvantri Road, most convenient for a visit later on to the Mysore mutton market that flanked Devaraj market to the West. Just outside the arched entrance, we would meet up with our coolie and his baskets, one among many who waited around for shoppers like us. Our progress was slow, cautiously squeezing through the stone bollards, carefully negotiating shaky and irregular flagstones, and finally keeping a hawk's eye out for the odd banana skin or rotten tomato.

Built in 1886 during the reign of Chamaraja Wodeyar IX [1868–1894], Devaraj market has the thoughtful planning that we have come to associate with a bygone era. Sayajirao road flanks the rectangular market on its East side, and its South Gate faces the Dufferin Clock Tower. Dozens of grocery shops line the informal market square selling grain, pulses, sugar and the other essentials of middle-class existence. Located in the heart of Mysore City Devaraj Market pulsed with life, the colours, the sounds, the crowds and the sheer volume of merchandise on sale just took your breath away. In the sixties, many displayed framed photographs of John F. Kennedy garlanded with jasmine and Kankambra [37] alongside those of Nehru and the Mahatma.

Something's haven't changed; the flower stalls still beckon with their marigold and jasmine. The precarious mounds of kumkum in striking colours still catches the eye, and thousands of moist freshly picked beetal leaves stacked in concentric circles are still sold. Nevertheless, the bangles on sale are now mostly plastic, and the fruit could quite easily be from China. The vegetables of my childhood were from open pollinated seed and locally grown. They were wonderfully imperfect; a basket of red tomatoes often had smatterings of green. The shape did not matter, and one size did not fit all, and GM well, that was still far away in the realm of fiction. No longer.

---

36 There are two Maharajas that could have possibly lent their name to this market, Dodda Devaraj Wodeyar [1659-1673] or Chikka Devaraj Wodeyar [1673-1704].

37 Kankambra [Crossandra infundibuliformis]: A delicate peach coloured flower, used for prayer and garland making.

Seaweed or Sea Vegetables: Many cultures around the world have appreciated sea vegetables and included them as a part of their diet for centuries. Sensible too, considering their high dietary fibre and mineral content. Chock full of flavour and simple to cook they will add depth to any dish that needs a bit of a leg up. Some of the best-known sea vegetables include wakame, arame, dulse and Kombu; available in the dry form they require soaking for 10 to 15 minutes before use in soups, stews, stir-fries, and salads.

South Indian Carrot Salad

Enough for 4

You will require the following:

400 grams fresh, firm carrots [single or many colours]

100 grams white onions or shallots

4 to 5 large cloves of garlic roasted[38]

2 tablespoons sunflower or melon seeds

1/4 cup fresh green coriander

1/4 cup fresh green mint

1/3 cup South Indian vattals fried[39]

Drizzle of Asian sesame oil

A generous squeeze of lime or lemon juice

Sea salt to taste

Thinly pare the carrots and then with your vegetable scraper continue to scrape the carrots in thin strips right down to the core. If the carrots are very long, shorten the pieces into more manageable sizes; vary the lengths to add interest. When you have finished, refrigerate a short while. Thinly slice the onions, lightly crush the roasted garlic, finely chop the herbs, add to the carrots and chill for another 15 minutes or so. Just before serving fry the vattals in a little oil and drain, add to the salad along with the melon or sunflower seeds. Season the carrots with sea salt, drizzle with the sesame oil and lemon juice and serve.

> Less Mess: To mix salad greens with the least amount of mess rinse under cold running water and then drain thoroughly. Refrigerate in a plastic bag. When ready to serve, toss the greens with your favourite dressing while still in the bag, and then tip into a salad bowl.

Tomato and Mushroom Salad with 8 Quail Eggs

Serves 4

You will require the following:

8 quail eggs

6 large ripe but firm tomatoes [different colours if possible]

38 To roast garlic see page 146.

39 Buy readymade vattals from any Indian store see page 157.

6 large Portobello mushrooms [or 8 to 10 button mushrooms]

6 to 8 large but tender rocket leaves or mustard greens

1/3 cup purslane or baby spinach

4 pickled gherkins

1 large white onion

4 spring onions

4 tablespoons sweet tomato chutney or sweet mango chutney

4 tablespoons horseradish sauce

Season with rock salt or other specialty salt and freshly ground pepper

Boil the quail eggs, set aside to cool until required. Tear the rocket into bite sized pieces and snip the purslane greens into two with a pair of scissors. Thinly slice the mushrooms, the onion, and the gherkins. Finely chop the spring onions, mix all the ingredients together, and chill for half an hour in the refrigerator. Cut the tomatoes into chunks discarding the seeds if you wish and cool separately.

When ready to serve, add the tomatoes to the rest of the ingredients and mix well, mix the chutney and horseradish sauce together and add to the salad and toss to coat; season with salt and pepper. Tip the mixture into a serving bowl and arrange the quail eggs around it, some in their shells and the others half or fully peeled.

The Art of Salad Making

During my childhood an outing to a smart restaurant in no less than the city of Bangalore usually meant, there was the invariable option of 'Mogalai, Chinese, or Continental' food. Several decades later much has changed, but in the outlying districts, many restaurants still advertise their cuisine this way.

The "Continental" segment includes a variety of salads; a 'Green Salad' is usually a plate of raw onion rings, sliced tomatoes, and cucumber arranged in concentric circles, with oddly cut slices of lime marking the points of a compass. Another perennial is 'The Russian' but of very liberal interpretation. Fruit salad was and still is a staple; in the old days, the one predictable ingredient was the disagreeable 'Bangalore Blue,' a large, juicy but dreadfully sour grape. During the '20's my great grandmother Constance Fergusson grew the Bangalore Blue on her ten-acre farm in Yeshwantpur, on the outskirts of Bangalore city. Its market monopoly meant that she turned an excellent profit, and I am told her homemade wine was a much sought after gift! All through the 60's, the Bangalore Blue was the ruin of many a good fruit salad. Finally with the arrival of the 'Thomson Seedless' came the revelation that not all grapes are necessarily sour!

The popular art of 'Vegetable Sculpture' or 'Vegetable Carving' wasn't just within the purview of the 1960's housewife, but extended well beyond the home and into the domain of the commercial kitchen. There were spectacular displays of vegetable Taj Mahals and Eiffel towers jostling for space on heavily laden buffet tables. Birds and animals were huge favourites, with peacocks perhaps the ultimate challenge. Toothpicks were used as connecting rods, white pumpkin and aubergine, cucumbers, carrots, and beetroots usually made up the larger body parts. Ladies fingers made shapely legs, cabbage leaves were useful kept whole or shredded to look like hair, green peas, and bits of tomato, of course, made excellent eyes and mouth parts! My mother had a set of colourful plastic bits and pieces, which you stuck into large round potatoes, transforming them into a dashing American Cowboy brandishing a handgun, and an attractive Mexican with an outsized moustache wearing a multi-colored sombrero. The 'Wild West' was usually a 'set' at a buffet lunch, the Texan and the Hombre propped up by a pot or two of 'prickly pear' and a potato salad!

5. Salad Dressings

Mayonnaise with Lemon and Ginger Marmalade

Makes a little under half a cup

You require the following:

1/3 cup mayonnaise

1½ tablespoons lemon and ginger marmalade

1 tablespoon apple cider vinegar

1 tablespoon Asian chilli oil

Salt and pepper to taste

Combine these few simple ingredients, and make up a great dressing for your salads. Save any unused salad dressing in your refrigerator to use another day.

Sesame oil: Parsees will tell you pale yellow,refined sesame oil is excellent for frying fish. Richly flavoured Asian style sesame oil on the other hand, has a distinctive aroma and dark amber colour which is great in a stir-fry or salad. The roasted sesame seeds that are cold pressed, add a nutty flavour to salads, especially a bowl or lettuce. Also perfect for marinades, in stir fries drizzle on at the end of the cooking process.

Nasturtium Mayonnaise

Makes a little over a cup

Good with grilled or fried fish

You require the following:

250 ml mayonnaise homemade or store bought

3 to 4 plump cloves of garlic

6 to 8 plump nasturtium seeds

¼ teaspoon grated lemon peel

1 or 2 tablespoons finely chopped nasturtium leaves

A pinch of castor sugar if desired

Sea salt or specialty salt to taste

Finely mince the garlic and crush the nasturtium seeds, add to the mayo along with the other ingredients, chill until needed.

Orange and Basil Dressing

You require the following:

1/3 cup freshly squeezed orange juice

1 teaspoon grated orange peal

¼ teaspoon devils dung [asafoetida/hing]

½ cup fresh basil leaves

2 tablespoons olive oil

Salt to taste

Place all the above ingredients into a food processor and blend well, chill a short while in the refrigerator and use when required. Toss into a mixed green salad or a green salad with fruit such grapes, apples and kiwi.

'Empress of India'

I grew the 'Empress'[40] for the very first time in an old, capacious hollowed out Harda[41] tree trunk. The enchanting vermilion flowers and the sea green leaves spilling down the sides and contrasting beautifully with the dull grey - black of the gnarled and weathered wood. I have loved nasturtiums ever since a child; they grew profusely in the garden at St. Hilda's[42] and I would pluck a leaf and roll a dew drop in it, and watch it pitch around wildly like quicksilver.

Make room for this lovely plant in your garden. Nasturtiums are easy to grow and will bring bountiful colour into your life. They are not only a delightful herb in the kitchen but full of medicinal value to boot. There are two species *Tropaeolum majus* a trailing vine with deep orange flowers vibrantly cascading down trellises and walls like flaming tongues of fire, and *Tropaeolum minus* a semi-trailing vine suitable for window boxes or border plants. A range of colours are now available and include single and multicoloured flowers from a pale buttercup yellow, gold, and burnt orange, to brick red and cherry pink.

Some strategy:

Plant Nasturtiums where you want them to grow. Nasturtium seeds do not have high viability so for better germination use only those that are fresh. Stored seeds are prone to insect attack, seal them well in air tight bags or boxes. Germination can take up to ten to twelve days so keep watering those seeds.

Grow Nasturtiums organically in a loose, friable soil without too much fertilizer. Once established they are virtually free from care, but they do need to be well watered. In the South, they do best in the gentle warming rays of a winter sun. If summers are harsh, they will need semi shade.

---

40 'The Empress' is an old heirloom variety very popular during the Victorian period.

41 Harda *[Chebulic myroblan]*: Is a medium to large tree found mainly in forested areas, and well known for the significant role it plays in Ayurveda as a panacea for any number of diseases. The hard green fruit is pickled or made into a preserve.

42 St. Hilda's School Ooty:Founded in 1892 by Sisters of the Church from Kilburn, in the United Kingdom, to cater to the educational needs of the Protestant European communities living in South India at that time.

From the garden to your kitchen:

Usually described as peppery, the leaves and flowers of the Nasturtium wilt rapidly, so pluck them just when needed, or place stems in a glass of water and refrigerate. Delicious in sandwiches paired with cucumber, tomato or salmon.

- Use the flower petals to decorate a plate of open faced sandwiches. You can also use the chopped flowers and leaves in a sandwich spread.
- Add the chopped leaves, flowers or seeds to butter or cream cheese and serve with warm freshly made bread or toast.
- Add the chopped green leaves or the crushed green seeds to a glass of lassie or buttermilk. Replace the coriander in your raitha with Nasturtium leaves.
- Post Script: Nasturtiums, bursting with vitamin C are a good remedy if you have the sniffles, eat the raw leaves three or four times a day.

Mascarpone and Peanut Butter

Makes just a little over half a cup

You require the following:

1/3 cup mascarpone

2 to 2½ tablespoons hazelnut oil

1 tablespoon peanut butter

1 teaspoon whole grain mustard

½ teaspoon pepper powder

Salt to taste

Bring the mascarpone to room temperature season with the salt, pepper and whole grain mustard. Add the hazelnut oil and the peanut butter and use with your favourite salad.

South Indian Yogurt Dressing

Makes half a cup

You require the following:

½ cup Greek yogurt or thick fresh homemade yogurt

1 teaspoon pepper rasam paste

2 cloves of garlic crushed and then minced

1 tablespoon fresh lemon juice

1 tablespoon fresh dill finely chopped

1 teaspoon liquid jaggery, palm or brown sugar

Salt to taste

Beat the yogurt until smooth and creamy. Add all the above ingredients to the yogurt and chill for a short while before serving. Use on potato salad, with beans or a mixed vegetable salad. Goes well with chicken, replace the pepper rasam paste with any other curry paste or spicy relish you have on hand. I often use Thai or Indonesian condiments to replace the rasam paste.

Our Daily Bread

My beloved father was the head of our household in more ways than one! Not only did he sit at the head of the table but was often served dishes that were off limits to the rest of us! So, while we ate humdrum 'Fish Molee,' he got to eat 'Fish Head Curry,' but there was one 'Das Classic' he was welcome too, a whole sheep's head cooked in a dark, spicy aromatic masala. When he was finished, the bones on his plate confirmed our resolve to let him have it all!

My mother was more conservative in her food habits, other than the fact that she disliked eating anything white; rice was the exception; yoghurt was out as were fried eggs and bacon. Her favourite meal was running dhal and white rice with dollops of mustard oil, liberally spooned out of Nergis Fui's burni of mango achar.

The kitchen at Krupalaya was a bewildering mix of Parsee, Anglo-Indian, and European food, but never beef, forbidden as in most Zoroastrian homes in India. Our Anglo-Indian roots dictated what was served at each meal, rice at lunch you never ate it for dinner! My mother's enormous recipe collection ensured there was ample variety most of it very well received.

Religious festivals were celebrated but mostly without the religion! A feeble attempt was made to acknowledge the spiritual but for the most part, the secular prevailed. The church reclaimed my mother on Christmas Eve, and on Nowroze[43] my father thought it prudent to supervise our prayers. Hindu festivals were also on the calendar, and with the rest of Mysore, we celebrated Dushera, my mother's collection of diya's[44] were on full display during Diwali, and the mali's[45] had a bad day cleaning up after my father's obsession with firecrackers.

My parents loved to entertain and there was a constant stream of visitors, who were always welcome at Krupalaya, there were coffee mornings, luncheon and dinner parties, kitty parties and tea parties. The bar was the axis on which a party revolved with my father in charge. A typical '60's room in purple and cane crammed with colourful bottles, glasses, bottle openers, a prized collection of matchboxes from around the world and other paraphernalia. My mother's collection of 'miniatures' was too much of a temptation for the

---

43 Nowroze celebrated on the 21st of March, the spring equinox it is a festival celebrated by all Iranians, Muslim as well as Zoroastrian.

44 Traditional oil lamps made of clay.

45 Mali: Indian for gardener.

son of a family friend, who helped himself to a dozen on his way back to boarding school! The headmaster subsequently sent back the empty bottles with a sincere note of apology!

The ladies favoured Rum and Coca-Cola until George[46] came along and spoiled the party. A fruit punch, with my father's heavy hand on a bottle of rum, was also a favourite, and occasionally a glass of wine. Cleaning up the next morning, a task that would take Das and Krishna more than half a day, included collecting the empties! [A bottle of Vat 69, a fashionable brand during the sixties, Cognac, and a Red Label or two]. Everybody drank, [mostly in moderation] except on one occasion, when a conservative gentleman, asked instead for a glass of milk. In the years that followed while standing around the bar at 8 in the evening, glass in hand, this was a story often told!

Custard Apple Pulp: Gently scoop out the pulp from the custard apple into a wire sieve leaving the brown gritty bottom layer behind. Hold the sieve over a bowl, and with the help of a potato masher or the back of a large spoon rub the pulp against the wire mesh. Pick out the large black seeds as they surface, they will be easy to remove.

46 George Fernandez was Union Minister of Industries when the Janata Party came to power in 1977. He had a number of 'run-ins' with multinationals such as IBM and Coca-Cola, finally asking them to leave the country.

6. Sauces

Thai Tamarind and Date Sauce

Makes one bottle, requires refrigeration

You require the following:
150 grams sweet Thai tamarind [weighed in after cleaning]
50 grams seedless table dates
1 teaspoon cayenne powder [or to taste]
2 tablespoons liquid jaggery or palm sugar [or to taste] *Salt to taste*

Place the tamarind and the dates in two separate bowls and pour over just enough hot water to cover and set aside to soften. Allow the tamarind and the dates to cool then blend in a food processor until you get a smooth paste, adding the jaggery or palm sugar as you go. If the paste is too thick, add a little warm water and blend again, season to taste with salt and the cayenne powder. Use with a pot roast, grilled fish or chicken, also does very well with pork.

Yogurt and Gorgonzola Sauce

Makes a little over 1 cup

You require the following:
250 grams hung curd or Greek yogurt
75 grams gorgonzola
A little cream to adjust consistency
¼ cup crushed walnuts
Season to taste with salt and pepper

Beat the hung curd or the Greek yogurt well until you get a smooth consistency. Soften the gorgonzola by bringing it to room temperature. Lightly mix the cheese into the yogurt with a fork, then add the cream and adjust the consistency of the sauce. Next, add the roughly crushed walnuts and season to taste with salt and pepper. Chill until required. Serve with grilled or fried fish.

Emerald Cheese Sauce

About one cup

You require the following:

1 cup well packed finely chopped lettuce

¼ cup flat leaf parsley leaves only

½ cup ricotta cheese

1 tablespoon spring onion

1 tablespoon finely chopped preserved Moroccan limes

Chicken or vegetable stock to thin as required

Salt and white pepper to taste

Place the lettuce, the parsley, and the spring onion in a food processor and process to a smooth paste; add the grated cheese, and the limes and process again, using a little chicken or vegetable stock to thin if required. Season to taste with the salt and pepper serve at room temperature or slightly chilled.

Ruby Red Suriname Cherry

Makes just under one cup

You require the following:

450 grams ripe Suriname cherries[47]

1 cup water

1/3 cup castor sugar or to taste

2 or 3 cloves of garlic

½ a teaspoon ground ginger

2 tablespoons Asian lemon sauce

Pinch of salt and pepper

Tip the cherries into a pan with just enough water to cover and bring to a quick boil. Cook the cherries until they are soft, and the juice has reduced by half. Remove from the heat and cool. Hold a wire sieve over a bowl, pour in the fruit, and with the back of a large spoon rubthe pulp against the wire mesh to release the seeds, discard them. Mix the pulp with the juice in the bowl, add the minced garlic and ginger and liquidize in a food processor. Tip the

47 Or any other sour cherry.

pulp into a pan, add the sugar and a pinch of salt and pepper and bring to a boil just once, then lower the heat and simmer until the sauce thickens. Finally, add the lemon sauce and check seasoning. Set aside to cool and then chill in the refrigerator until needed. Serve with fish cutlets or with roast meat.

Custard Apple Dessert Sauce

Makes a little over a cup

You require the following:

1 cup pureed custard apple[48] [Three or four large fruit]

1/4 cup thick cream

1 or 2 tablespoons creamy tahini paste

Castor sugar to taste

1 teaspoon grated nutmeg

Puree the custard apple to a smooth paste. Add the sugar, the cream, tahini paste and the nutmeg and mix in well and chill in the refrigerator until ready to use.

Orange and Yogurt Sauce

Makes over a cup

You require the following:

1 cup Greek yogurt or hung curd

2 tablespoons single cream

1/4 cup homemade orange marmalade

1/4 teaspoon clove powder

1 teaspoon finely shredded orange peel

Castor sugar if required

Lightly beat the cream, add to the yogurt with the other ingredients and mix well. Check the sweetness adding a little castor sugar if required, serve chilled.

48 See page 43.

Bloomfield

42 Sassoon Road

Krupalaya

My cousins Kayandokth and Meherab with their mother Siloo.

My mother and me. Ramu and the mahoot

7. Eggs

Eggs have always been a common thread that links Iranian and Parsee cooking. My father would come home from work between six and half past every evening, and one of his favourite stress busters were - two 'Indian Eggs,' fried, sunny side up, eaten with hot toast and butter. Bacon was a luxury, and when available mostly went into a stuffing for roast chicken.

'Indian eggs,' as opposed to 'English' or farm eggs, are now rarely seen on shop shelves, but you can still get them in rural India. The indigenous Indian village fowl lays no more than 30 to 40 eggs a year and they are comparatively smaller than farm eggs. The brown calcium-rich shells are much harder to crack, and I often have to resist the urge to thump them too hard. A cracked egg will reveal a visual treat, the glorious colour and the abundance of the startling orange yolk. Almost all of them will be fertile evident by the nebulous white spot or streak near the edge of the yolk. A newly laid egg will have a thick white halo surrounding the yolk. When frying an egg, spoon some of the hot oil on top to allow this to cook.

The indigenous Indian village fowl is truly a free bird in every sense of the word! They have the run of the village, the fields, and surrounding areas. They are excellent mothers and live relatively long stress-free lives. Our hen Martha lived for seven years unfailingly laying a few eggs every year, until one inopportune day, like Donald, our duck, was gleefully carried off by an Indian jackal.

Akoori

The Parsee akoori is one of the best ways to cook eggs and a good choice for Sunday brunch. To make it fry the onions well and cook the tomatoes until soft, smooth and sauce like. A heavy hand with the fat is recommended!By using an assortment of ingredients, there are countless ways to make a good akoori. Below are some ideas to help you chart your course ahead, best eaten with freshly baked soft bread or roti.

The 'Standard' Recipe!

Makes a substantial breakfast for 4

You will require the following:

6 large eggs

100 grams red onion

100 grams ripe tomato

1 or 2 long mild green chillies [or to your taste]

3 fat cloves of garlic

½ a teaspoon cumin seed

1 or 2 tablespoons fresh green coriander

2 to 3 tablespoons ghee

Sea salt or rock salt to taste

Finely chop the onions and the tomato, smash the garlic and chop the green chilli into pieces. Break the eggs into a bowl and set aside unbeaten. Choose a heavy-bottomed pan and place on medium heat, add the ghee and allow it to melt; then add the onion, garlic, and cumin seed. Cook until the onions are a beautiful deep yellow but do not crisp or burn them. Next, add the green chilli and cook for a minute more. It is time now to add the tomatoes and to cook them until they are nice and soft, and the oil begins to separate. Season to taste, adding enough salt to include the eggs. Lower the heat, tip in the eggs wait 15 seconds, and then, break them up and mix quickly. Cook the eggs on low to medium heat, but do not let them dry out, remove from the heat while they are still moist. Garnish with the chopped green coriander and serve immediately.

Try the following variations:

Cut down on the onions, and use a little onion leek instead

Add a few blades of finely chopped onion or garlic chives

About 100 grams of fried shrimp

2 tablespoons of cooked sweet corn

2 or 3 tablespoons of tinned crab meat or flaked salmon

Akoori with Herbs in Taco shells

Makes a substantial breakfast for 4

You will require the following:

6 large eggs
1 sprig curry leaves
2 long mild green chillies
2 fat cloves of garlic
½ inch piece ginger
2 tablespoons raisins or dried black currents
100 grams red onion
4 to 6 taco shells
3 or 4 fresh lettuce leaves
2 to 3 tablespoons ghee
1 tablespoon charoli
½ a teaspoon cumin seed
½ a cup mixed fresh herbs [dill/parsley/coriander]

Prepare the taco shells following packet instructions. Tear the lettuce leaves and lightly pack the bottom of the taco shells. Finely chop the onions and green chillies, smash the garlic and mince the ginger. Break the eggs into a bowl but do not beat them. Place a heavy bottomed pan over medium heat and melt the ghee. Now add the garlic, ginger and cumin seeds, and cook one minute. Next, add the curry leaves, chillies, and the onion and cook until the onions are a light golden brown, tip in the raisins, the charoli and the finely chopped herbs. Continue to stir another minute or two. Season to taste and add enough salt to include the eggs. Lower the heat, add the eggs and wait 15 seconds. Then, on medium heat, stir and break them up and mix quickly. Cook the eggs, but do not let them dry out, remove from the heat while they are still moist. Fill the prepared taco shells and serve immediately.

Akooried Hard Boiled eggs with Microgreens

Makes a substantial breakfast for 4

You will require the following:

6 large hard boiled eggs
100 grams red onions
100 grams ripe tomato
2 or 3 cloves garlic
2 long mild green chillies
2 tablespoons charoli or cracked pine nuts/hazelnuts
2 tablespoons sweet mango chutney or Asian lemon sauce

1/3 cup microgreens of your choice

2 tablespoon butter

1 tablespoon vegetable oil

1 teaspoon olive oil

Squeeze of lemon juice

Salt to taste

Shell the eggs and gently remove the yolks, keeping them whole. Roughly chop the white of the eggs. Meanwhile, put the microgreens into a small bowl; add the olive oil with a pinch of salt and a squeeze of lemon juice mix well and set aside. Finely chop the onion and tomato, smash the garlic and chop the green chillies into pieces. In a heavy bottomed pan, heat the oil and the butter then add the onions, garlic, chillies, and nuts and cook on medium heat. Next, add the tomatoes and cook until they are well-done and soft, season to taste now. Add the mango chutney or lemon sauce and mix well into the tomatoes and onions and cook one or two minutes more. Then remove the pan from the heat, add the eggs, stir gently to mix and tip into a serving bowl. Pile the microgreens on top. Serve immediately.

House No 680/1

AMALGAMATED WINERIES
Nazarbad,
Mysore-10
Cable: WHISKERS.

House No. 680/1 or 'Baju Bungalow' as we called it, meaning the house next door was one house away, sharing a common wall with the 'Retreat' and with 'Bloomfield' on the other side. It was a peculiar building; a stranger passing would be compelled to pause and take a second look. Sitting on the rear of a large unkempt compound the building rose upwards but surprisingly wasn't very tall, the low line of wooden shuttered windows in faded green perhaps giving rise to the illusion. It was originally an annexe to the Palace garage,housing spare parts for a stable of dazzling custom-built cars. A reason perhaps, why it had such a large front door, beneficial for unloading steel, metal castings, pipes and rings of natural rubber. Made of wood and glass with peeling green paint, you could see that the front door hadn't been opened in years, adding mystery to the buildings otherwise forlorn, desolate look.

My father rented House No 680/1 from the palace and named it for his father 'Khudamorad' meaning God's Wish, but for the most part, it was just 'Baju Bungalow. 'My father's other business interests laid claim to most of his working life, what claimed his heart and soul was his love for wine making and the manufacture of quirky food products. You guessed right it all happened next door!

Baju Bungalow was our favourite haunt too; at odds with its locale, it was a wild, overgrown space full of insects and birds, squirrels, snakes and whatever else God wished. It is where we could run free without supervision, usually after lunch when the 'powers that be' retired for a well-deserved rest! To get in you had to climb over the wall. The gate was always locked even though there were plenty of people working inside. They also simply climbed over the wall, some with just their lunch tiffin's others hauled their bicycles over as well. Occasionally we took an air gun with us; pot shots at the pigeons that nested in the eaves of the building were often quite fruitful, and Das would always oblige with a grilled snack, plenty of thick brown gravy and tiny roast potatoes.

A gargantuan rain tree shaded the backyard, whose outstretched limbs were home to a colony of crows, nesting birds of prey, coppersmiths, and serenading koels. Below lay bales of paddy straw, wooden crates, outsized green glass bottles secured in metal frames, wooden tubs, and empty wine bottles, all inflicted with the droppings that rained down.

The aroma of maturing wine in huge wooden vats assailed you when you entered the building up stone steps at the rear. Inside, the cavernous room was cool and muted; a maze of stainless steel equipment, measuring cups, bottles and bottle caps, labels is what met the eye. Two small rooms on either side right at the back is where we usually headed, one with test tubes, round-bottomed flasks, crucibles and Bunsen burners the other with heavily laden sacks of sugar, black currants, raisins, and sultanas!

Marketing it as something the doctor order, 'Tonic Wine' was my father's bestseller, Granny Fergusson was a fan and along with Aunt Emma and their good friend Kay would occasionally partake of a glass or two over a game of Lexicon. However, my father's greatest triumph was his Soma Liqueur named for the drink of the Vedic Gods. There was also a Sherry, Tawny, and Ginger wine; no comparison to the sophisticated world of Chardonnays' and Sauvignon's but wines good enough to raise a glass in celebration.

Other products also made their way out of 'Baju Bungalow'; some did very well while others sank without a trace. There was Gingerella a marvellous summer drink delicious with ice and soda. Bovite an off take on Marmite - there was a bottle on every breakfast table at St. Hilda's, and finally even a rat poison rather dubiously named Typhoon!

Baked Eggs on Tomato

Enough for 4

You will require the following:

4 to 5 large eggs
500 grams firm ripe tomatoes any colour
200 grams tiny shrimps
100 grams onion
1 large onion leek
3 or 4 plump cloves garlic
1/4 inch piece fresh ginger root
1/4 teaspoon turmeric powder
2 tablespoons Chinese chilli oil[49]

49 Chilli oil available from Asian stores near you.

2 tablespoon red pepper relish or sweet mango chutney

2 tablespoon finely chopped fresh cilantro or false coriander.

2 or 3 tablespoons ghee [serves 4 after all!]

Sea salt to taste

Skin the tomatoes by first steeping them in hot water for a few minutes and then dropping them into a bowl of cold water. Peel off the skin when cool enough to handle, and chop finely. In a heavy bottomed frying pan heat the ghee and fry the finely sliced onion, then add the finely sliced ginger, crushed garlic and turmeric powder. Next, add the shrimps and fry until just done. Now add the tomato and the finely sliced onion leek and season to taste. Simmer the tomatoes until soft. Now add the coriander, chilly oil, and relish, mix well, and cook for a few minutes more. Let the mixture dry out a bit then empty into a gratin dish and level out the top. With the back of a large spoon make 4 or 5 pockets [deep enough to hold an egg] and gently break an egg into each one. Place in a moderately hot oven and bake until the eggs are set. Serve immediately.

NOOSH –E JAN!

Eggs on New Zealand Spinach with Sumac

Enough for 3 or 4

You will require the following:

500 grams tender New Zealand spinach[50]

4 to 5 large eggs

75 grams onions

1/3 cup single cream

½ cup finely chopped green coriander

1 tablespoon garlic paste

1½ teaspoons sumac

50 grams butter

1 teaspoon olive oil

Salt and pepper to taste

Place a pan over medium heat, add the butter and oil and heat gently. Add the finely chopped onion and fry to a medium brown. Next, add the garlic paste and cook for a minute or two.

50 You can replace the New Zealand spinach with greens of your choice. Try amaranth.

Then add all the greens, the sumac, and season to taste with the salt and pepper. Mix well; cover the pan and cook over a slow fire for about 10 minutes or until the spinach is done and no excess liquid remains. Meanwhile, separate the eggs and beat the whites until soft peaks form, beat the yolks well and then add to the whites. Add the cream to the spinach and mix well. Tip the greens into a buttered gratin dish and level off, pour the eggs over the greens, and bake in a moderate oven until set. Serve immediately.

Noshir's Scrambled Eggs!

Just enough for one

Uncle Noshir, my father's brother taught me how to make the best scrambled eggs ever. I lived in Poona in the late '70's for a few years, attending university there, and I often visited with my uncle and cousins on a weekend. Late Sunday breakfasts were a treat; they started with delicious scrambled eggs with hot buttered toast. A cup of hot lemon grass tea followed, and then freshly baked warm brun pao covered with a thick layer of frozen butter and generous spoonfuls of thick 'buffalo milk' cream. Taken aback? Don't be this was and still is a very popular breakfast order at Irani restaurants, 'Maska Pao with Malai,' usually accompanied by a cup of 'Irani Chai'. I often compare this meal of the past to what I sometimes have to cook for my guests today - an omelette made with two eggs, whites only!

You will require the following:

2 large eggs [or 3 traditional Indian eggs]

1½ tablespoons ghee

1 clove garlic - optional but highly recommended

Sea salt to taste

Break the eggs into a bowl and set aside unbeaten. Chop the garlic fine, or crush with the back of a spoon or the blade of your knife. In a small heavy bottomed pan on medium heat, melt the ghee add the garlic and salt to taste. Turn off heat and let the garlic cook a bit, but do not burn, swirl the dish around so that the ghee coats the bottom of the pan. Turn on the heat to medium, and when the ghee heats up again add the eggs. Wait and watch them beginning to set, and then quickly begin to stir the eggs gently. Remove the pan from the heat and serve immediately with freshly baked bread or hot buttered toast.

Postscript

Don't overcook the eggs; they should be moist with distinctive white and yellow specks.

Use less ghee if you like but the flavour of ghee should come subtly through the eggs.

Cook the eggs on a low to medium heat; a high temperature will result in a dry, rubbery scrambled egg.

Cook just two eggs at a time, wipe the pan clean before your next batch of eggs.

Eggs with Nasturtium Seeds

Good for 4

You will require the following:

4 to 5 large eggs

6 to 7 tender green nasturtium seeds

1 small sprig tender curry leaves

½ a teaspoon aniseed[51]

2 medium nasturtium leaves

1 tablespoon water

2 tablespoons butter with one teaspoon olive oil

Sea salt or rock salt to taste

Break the eggs into a bowl add a tablespoon of water and beat until they combine, season to taste. Chop the nasturtium leaves finely and add to the eggs. Set aside. Crush the nasturtium seeds into pieces. Select a heavy bottomed pan heat the butter and oil on a low flame, add the aniseed, and curry leaves. Add the nasturtium seeds and continue to fry for one minute. Finally, add the eggs. Cook the eggs gently until they set, taking care not to overcook them. Turn out into a serving dish and serve immediately, or serve on toast with a nasturtium flower placed on the side.

Postscript: It is important to remember that the egg continues to cook after removing the pan from the heat.

51 You can replace the aniseed with caraway or cumin seed.

Country Egg Scramble in Nori parcels

Enough for 4

You will require the following:

6 Eggs

50 ml thick cream

50 grams mushrooms

50 grams cheese

1 teaspoon fennel seeds

2 or 3 garlic cloves

1 tablespoon fresh parsley, tarragon, or summer savoury

2 tablespoons butter or ghee with 1 teaspoon oil

2 nori sheets cut in half

Salt and pepper to taste

Lightly beat the cream until smooth. Crack the eggs into a bowl, beat well and add the cream to the eggs. Chop the mushrooms, crush the garlic and grate the cheese. Place a heavy bottomed pan on medium heat and add the fat followed by the garlic, fennel, and mushrooms. Cook until done, now add the chopped herbs and season to taste with salt and pepper. Next, add the eggs and cook until nearly set but still nice and moist. Remove from the heat and add the grated cheese. Lay out the four nori sheets and divide the scrambled egg between them, spread out the egg half way along one side, fold over the sheet and roll up. Alternatively, shape each piece of the nori sheet into a cone, and seal the end with a little water, fill the scrambled egg into the cones and serve at once with sprays of microgreens such as mustard, amaranth or alfalfa.

Scrambled Eggs, Curry Leaves, and Sun-dried Tomatoes

Good for 4 kith and kin

You will require the following:

6 large eggs

6 to 8 young tender curry leaves

¼ cup well packed sun-dried tomatoes in oil

3 to 4 cloves garlic

4 to 6 almonds

1 tablespoon cream [optional but nice]

2 tablespoons ghee or butter

Sea salt pepper to taste

Break the eggs into a bowl, and beat lightly with the cream, season with salt and pepper and set aside until needed. Smash the garlic, lightly crush the almonds, and chop the sun-dried tomatoes into small pieces. Place a heavy bottomed pan on medium heat and melt the ghee or butter. Add the garlic, crushed almonds, and curry leaves, stir well and allow them to colour slightly. Add the tomatoes and cook for a few minutes more. Increase the heat slightly, add the eggs all at once and gently cook until done but still moist. Remove from the heat immediately to prevent the eggs from drying out and serve.

Scrap Books

My mother never formally learnt to cook, and the kitchen was never her domain until her mid-seventies when a rather belated enthusiasm overcame her! With her enormous recipe collection as a reference, she did, however, play an active role in planning the day's menu, while Granny Ferguson looked to its implementation. Nevertheless, one lasting memory is my mother's inherent talent for sandwich making. She would sit at the breakfast table mixing ingredients with wild abandon, with a naturalness and fluidity that took those humble slices of bread to a different level. Setting jelly for the evening's dessert was often a teatime ritual for my mother. None of us was particularly fond of the stuff but never allowed to forget it was 'English' jelly, thoughtfully sent to us by Aunty so and so. 'Jelebee[52] pudding' a rather bizarre Anglo-Indian concoction using stale jelebee's, milk and eggs, or 'Khoa pudding' made with milk solids, bread, and eggs, gave my mother the opportunity to create and innovate. There was a flow in my mother's concoctions; and for her, every leftover scrap in the dooley[53] had possibilities. What went in and how much was random and impulsive, and sometimes accidental! My brothers swear blind that once while multitasking, [painting her nails and baking a cake], she accidentally tipped a bottle of acetone into the mixing bowl. Nevertheless, by the end of it all might I say that the proof of her pudding was in the eating!

While my mother didn't do much cooking, she did collect recipes, with a passion! There are memories of warm summer afternoons with the 'brain fever bird'[54] in a crescendo on the jacaranda outside, my mother sitting on her morrah in the veranda rummaging through cartons full of old magazines and newspapers looking for recipes. Thousands upon thousands of them, multitudes painstakingly cut, snipped, and pasted in dozens of scrapbooks for over five decades.

52 The origins of the jelebee can be traced back to India, a neon orange sweet made with yogurt and flour, deep-fried, and soaked in a sugar syrup. The jelebee also belongs to the cuisines of the Middle East and North Africa.

53 The 'Dooley' or meatsafe [Anglo Indian].

54 Common hawk cuckoo.

The Tamilian Cook

I went off to boarding school in the hills when I was seven, but the food was certainly not one of the reasons I missed home! We witnessed the odd culinary misadventure of course, such as Kannan's hefty brass ring lying at the bottom of the egg curry. In the kitchen, the man in charge was Madurai, Louis, his sous chef, while Mrs. Lobb kept house and the hefty storeroom keys. The result - the food at St. Hilda's was simply first-class.

There is no doubt that all through my life, a Tamilian[55] cook has prepared the best food I have ever eaten, and the most extraordinary among them made The Nilgiris their home. There was often a leisurely meal over the weekend at The Ooty Golf Links on the South Downs, the breathtaking views of the Kunda range helping to settle a belly full of well-made Country Captain. We lunched at The Cecil Hotel run by Gool Sakidas and her family or at The Savoy[56] on Sylkes road that took you back to another time. The Y. W. C. A Eastbourne on Garden Road managed by Mr. and Mrs. Smith was perfect for hot buttered scones, muffins and a cup of Nilgiri tea. My brother Raian favoured the Spaghetti Bolognaise at the Ritz in Coonoor; my brother Kairus the Mulligatawny at the Ooty Club[57]. My favourite was Miss Guthrie's Willingdon House, where every dish put on the table was beyond a success. No Michelin Stars or Red Hats perhaps, but these establishments were blessed with Tamilian cooks that had exemplary culinary skills.

The school going years of so many boarders from the dozens of boarding schools that dotted the hills was chock-full of stripy Bull's Eyes and shocking pink Turkey Eggs, Sticky Lock Jaw and elegant twirls of Barley Sugar. Pocket money was well spent on King Star's homemade chocolates and fudge, or the cakes and pastries from 'Sunnyside' run by the Short family adjacent to that venerable institution the Ooty Library. Crunchy paper dosas from Modern Coffee House opposite the Lawley Institute or a 'rice plate' at Dasaprakash, these were also on the 'to do' list of every captive set free for a day!

55 From the Southern State of Tamil Nadu.

56 The Savoy Hotel: The hotel was originally 'The Mission School' built around 1830 for European boys, the children of those associated with the Church Mission Society. Major Underwood of the Madras Engineers bought the property, and in 1841 set up the Union Hotel. In 1868, Mr. C. Sylk purchased the property and renamed it Sylk's Hotel. Subsequently, the property changed hands through the decades and is now in the portfolio of the Taj Group of Hotels

Source: Ootacamund – A History by Frederick Price published by Rupa & Co. 2002.

57 The Ooty Club sits in a time warp but is a grand old place; with standards and tradition that are never compromised. A formal jacket and tie are mandatory at dinner. Moreover, when you dare talk, it must never be above a whisper!

The Kitchen at Krupalaya was 'Tamilian,' and no one exemplified that better than Das, who cooked the most heart-warming food. When my brothers and I give a verdict on all things culinary Das is our yardstick. When I cook dhansak, the reality that mine is not even half as good as his humbles me. Brain cutlets with their crisp frilly edges, juicy beefsteak tomatoes stuffed with mince and baked, airy sweet and savoury soufflés, ice creams, an unforgettable plateful of culinary memories.

Dhania dhal or Dhana dhal: Here are another one of those innumerable condiments that contribute significantly to taste and flavour but stay buried in an assortment of other ingredients. This time in a bewildering array of intriguing digestive mixtures called Makhwas. Dhania dhal [split coriander seed], are tawny brown, flattened spherical discs. Use them fresh, crisp them on a hot griddle and sprinkle on top of salads, yogurt, soups, and milkshakes.

8. Dips

Beetroot Dip

Serves 5 to 6

Serve with rye or pumpernickel bread

You require the following:

400 grams beetroot

2 to 3 cloves garlic

1 teaspoon Parsee dhanajeera powder

2 tablespoons jambul wine or sweet red wine

½ a cup sour cream

2 tablespoons olive or grape seed oil

Salt and pepper to taste

Pressure cook the beetroot until well done, test by inserting a skewer into the centre of the beetroot it should slide in smoothly. Remove the beetroot cool, then skin and quarter it. Tip into a blender with the oil, garlic and spice powder, and puree until smooth. Empty into a small bowl add the jambul wine and mix well, next add the sour cream and season to taste with the salt and pepper. Chill for a short while before serving.

Pretty Quail Eggs are about one-fourth the size of a hen's egg and beautifully speckled in shades of grey, sea green and black. They are hardly a mouthful but look glorious in a salad or appetizer tray. The best way to cook quail eggs is to hard-boil them. Keep a few shells intact and use them as decorative accents in your salad. Alternatively, you can also carefully crack a boiled egg across the centre discard half the shell, and retain the other half with the egg in it.

Shrimp Dip

Good for 4

You require the following:

1 cup sour cream

1/3 cup mayonnaise

100 grams tinned shrimp

1 or 2 tablespoons Udang Rangup Bercili or a mild shrimp pickle in oil

1 tablespoon finely chopped herbs, coriander, mint or dill

Salt and pepper to taste

Bring the sour cream to room temperature and mix in the mayonnaise. Drain the shrimps thoroughly and add to the sour cream along with the Udang Rangup Bercili, mix well and season to taste. Finally, add the herb of your choice and serve with your favourite crackers or Middle Eastern bread.

Caramelised Butter: Caramelise your butter in a heavy bottomed saucepan for best results. Place the pan on gentle heat and add 25 grams of butter. Watch the butter melt; it will then begin to brown slightly and send out thin liquid foam. Once the foam disappears, and the colour of the butter starts to darken, switch off the heat. Use as required.

Peanut and Yogurt Dip

Serve with bread sticks

You require the following:

400 grams hung curd

3 tablespoons of peanut butter

2 tablespoons roasted peanuts

½ a red or yellow capsicum roasted and peeled

2 tablespoons relish or finely chopped gherkins.

2 tablespoons light cream [optional]

Salt to taste

Lightly pound the roasted peanuts but do not powder them. Finely chop the capsicum, beat the curds then add the cream and mix well. Add all the remaining ingredients, mix in well and season to taste. Chill for a short while before serving.

Cooks tip: The longer the curd is hung, the firmer it becomes, for a creamier dip remove after 20 minutes, if you prefer something more spreadable, for crackers or toast perhaps hang the curd for over an hour.

Sour Cream with Mango Chutney

Makes a little over one cup

Serve this dip with khakra, a Gujarati snack that is ready to eat. It looks similar to a large papadum. Thin and crisp, it comes in different flavours, get hold of some from an Indian store near you.

You require the following:

125 grams cream cheese

100 grams sour cream

1 to 1½ teaspoon sambhar or rasam powder

2 sprigs fresh and mature curry leaves

1/4 cup sweet mango chutney

1/4 cup roasted peanuts

½ teaspoon dhania dhal roasted

Salt to taste

Bring the cream cheese and the sour cream to room temperature and combine. Add the sambhar powder, the mango chutney, and the well-crushed curry leaves, season to taste and chill until needed. Just before serving, add the crushed peanuts and serve with the dhania dhal scattered on top.

Emma Charlotte Kowen

They were seven, like the sisterhood of the Jungle Babbler[58]. Emma third from the bottom and my grandmother Una Maud the youngest, there were also two brothers Charlie and Harry. Emma Charlotte came to live with us at Krupalaya after their sister Ivy passed away. The first wave of feminism was certainly an influence on Emma Charlotte, her life, and disposition. She pursued independence and a career, taught English and spoke fluent Urdu, painted with oils and played tennis. Animated and feisty well into her late nineties she once took a swipe at her bank manager for being too pernickety about paperwork!

The sisters shared a large airy room in the east wing of Krupalaya, the early morning sun spilling in to illuminate the soothing emerald green floor. The rosewood cupboard with its Belgium mirror, the carved wood and rattan seating, the flower-patterned curtains, the scented pomade in its blue glass bottle and the soft green smelling salts on the dressing table all belonged here. We all dearly loved this room and its occupants; my father often spent his evenings here, playing Lexicon.

According to Palace records, Krupalaya had water cisterns installed in 1938[59]. The old porcelain commode with its wooden seat in this east room toilet looked its age. The tank perched high above, gurgled loudly when you pulled its long cast iron chain and ivory handle. Moreover, it leaked! It leaked badly, and its antiquity ensured there were no 'spares' to be had. However, Emma Charlotte was no push over, and so when she needed to perch on that old wooden seat she did so with poise and her large black umbrella!

Emma Charlotte died in 1988 at the age of ninety-nine.

---

58 The Jungle Babbler *[Turdoides striata]* also known as the Seven Sisters, are gregarious birds found in the jungles of the Indian Subcontinent foraging in groups of seven to ten.

59 Source: Palace Maramath, Karnataka State Divisional Archives, Mysore.

9. Yogurt

Lightly spiced yogurt and vegetables are a pleasing combination, and the perfect medium to try out specialty salts. Serve as an accompaniment to a meal or as an appetizer with any crusty or flat bread such as brun pao, naan or lavash. Use only a fork to beat the yogurt lightly to retain its thick and creamy consistency. To enhance its flavour Middle Eastern cooking often marries yogurt with caramelized butter. Just before you are ready to serve to family and friends, add a generous dollop of salted butter to a pan and caramelize it, pour over any of the following dishes.

NOOSH –E JAN!

Smoked Yogurt with Winter Squash or Pumpkin

Enough for 3 to 4 kith and kin

You can add anything you like to smoked yogurt, but winter squash tastes particularly good. You also have a whole spectrum of spices to choose from to smoke the yogurt; it's great fun!

You will require the following:

400 grams thick well-set yogurt
30 ml cold water
400 grams winter squash or pumpkin
1½ teaspoon minced ginger
2 tablespoon green peppercorns
75 grams minced red onion
2 mild deseeded green chillies [optional]
1/3 cup black bibiya seeds[60]
1 tablespoon dried wakame
Sea salt or another specialty salt to taste.

Chop the winter squash or pumpkin into bite sized pieces, sprinkle with a little salt and toss to coat well, then steam until done, cool. Reconstitute the wakame in a little warm water

60 See details on page 286.

and keep aside until needed. Beat the yogurt well with a fork, adding a little water if it is very thick. Smoke the yogurt [see directions below]. Next, add the finely chopped ginger, chillies if using, and the peppercorns. Finely chop the onion and add to the yogurt with the bibiya seeds. Add the cooled pumpkin and chill in the refrigerator for 15 to 20 minutes. Just before serving add the wakame, and you are ready to go!

To smoke the yogurt:

You require the following

3 to 4 pieces of red hot charcoal

A small steel container to hold the coal

A larger steel container to keep the yogurt

A large wok with a flat base or a large vessel with a well fitting lid

Smoking ingredients:

3 to 4 fresh lime leaves, [or try curry or cassia leaves]

1 tablespoon black peppercorns

1 tablespoon coriander seed

1 teaspoon cumin seed

Just outside my kitchen door is a wood fire that heats our bath water. The smoldering coals also smoke my yogurt. You can get yours easily enough, by heating pieces of coal on an open flame on your stovetop. While the coals are heating, put the beaten curd into the larger of the stainless steel vessels, and place to one side of the wok. Make sure that there is enough room for the smaller vessel. Keep all the smoking ingredients handy. When the coals are hot transfer them into the smaller container with a pair of tongs and place next to the curds. Immediately sprinkle the smoking ingredients onto the coals, and cover the wok or vessel with the tight fitting lid. Smoke for 8 to 10 minutes, depending on how strong a flavour you want.

Postscript: Ditch the coals for a modern smoker

Cucumber in Yogurt

Enough for 3 to 4 kith and kin

You will require:

400 grams thick well-set yogurt

50 ml cold water

1 medium cucumber

50 grams white onion

½ to 1 teaspoon ground garlic or 2 to 3 garlic cloves smashed

1 or 2 mild green chillies, deseeded [optional]

4 to 6 plump green Nasturtium seeds

2 large Nasturtium leaves without the stems

3 or 4 Nasturtium flowers in different colours

1 teaspoon black sesame seeds to garnish

Sea salt or rock salt to taste

Peel the cucumber and slice thinly into rounds. If the slices are too large, quarter them. Finely chop the green chilli and add to the cucumber, mix well and refrigerate. Don't salt the cucumber slices at this stage; it makes them limp and tasteless. Beat the yogurt with a fork adding the tablespoon of water if it is very thick. Chop the onion finely and add to the curds along with the salt and garlic. Crush the nasturtium seeds and add to the curd, stir well and chill. Just before serving tear the Nasturtium leaves into small pieces and add to the curd along with the cucumber. Sprinkle the black sesame seeds on top and garnish with the jewel-like flowers. Serve with lavash[61] or freshly made naan.

Cooks tip: Choose a young firm cucumber that does not yield under pressure, a very mature cucumber has too many seeds. Poinsett is a good variety to use; you can also use long melon or the Armenian cucumber, no need to peel it.

61 Lavash is thin, crisp bread, round or oval from Iran and the Middle East.

Christmas at Krupalaya

My mother's sister Verna and my cousin Paul lived in England. They paid us an extended visit one Christmas in the 1970's and their presence at Krupalaya that year made it a very special one. Paul is a geologist and while on holiday collected rock specimens with a passion. He was all over Mysore district and up in the Nilgiris, collecting stones and rocks, which he would eventually crate and send back to the U. K. He had a whole heap of them stored at the back of the house under the neem tree. He checked on his pile now and then and continued to add to it as the days went by oblivious to the fact that the servants thought him very eccentric.

My mother's buffet lunch for family and friends on Christmas day always included a rich mutton biriyani, served with an onion kachumber and a tomato raitha. Biriyani Sattar and his assistants arrived early on Christmas morning to start the day's cooking, and this particular year was no different. Work began with the initial preparations of marinating the meat, cleaning and soaking the rice and preparing the vegetables. Meanwhile, Team Sattar also discovered Paul's pile of precious rocks; and then helped themselves to the limestone, quartzite, and granite to build the stoves for the wood fires that cooked the biriyani. Paul was also a keen photographer, and trooped along mid-morning to photograph the chefs at work; it didn't take him long to recognize the blackened rocks supporting the huge cook pots as his very own precious samples of Karnataka's geological history!

Christmas morning was hectic; my mother bleary eyed after midnight mass putting the final additions to the Christmas table, my grandmother timing the puddings she had set to boil, Das and Natesan in the kitchen trussing the turkey. Breakfast was a family affair brought to a conclusion with a large helping of 'Sev,' always prettily decorated with pink rose petals. There was constant chatter around the breakfast table usually about overflowing stockings and an outrageously generous Santa Claus. We wrote our letters in the first week of December with assurances from my father that he would post them. Fears that the old man would not be able to find his way in, [there were no chimneys in Krupalaya], were laid to rest when our father promised to leave the back door open. Many Christmas's and Christmas stockings later, when the Santa hoax was finally revealed we lapsed into a state of shock that lasted for days!

Carrots in Yogurt

Enough for 3 to 4 kith and kin

You will require the following:

400 grams thick well-set yogurt

30 ml cold water

100 grams carrots

75 grams white onion

1 mild green chilli

1 teaspoon ground garlic paste

1 teaspoon nigella seeds

1 sprig curry leaves

1 tablespoon dry Persian barberries [zereshk]

1 tablespoons charoli

1½ tablespoons olive oil or grape seed oil

Fresh coriander leaves for garnish

Sea salt or rock salt to taste

Beat the yogurt with a fork adding a little water if necessary. Pare the carrot and grate a medium grade. Chop the onion and the chilly finely. Add the carrot, green chilli, onion and garlic to the yogurt, season with salt and chill until needed. Just before serving, heat the oil in a frying pan, and add the nigella seeds, curry leaves, barberries and charoli and cook for 30 seconds to a minute but do not burn. Remove from the heat and cool a little, then add it to the curds. Mix gently, garnish with the chopped coriander leaves and serve.

Roasted Beetroot in Yogurt

Enough for 3 to 4 kith and kin

You will require the following:

400 grams thick well-set yogurt

30 ml cold water

250 grams beetroot

75 grams red onion

2 green chillies deseeded [optional]

½ inch piece ginger

1/3 cup stuffed green or black olives

1/3 cup crisp salted or unsalted pistachio nuts

2 teaspoon dhania dhal[62] to sprinkle on top

Olive or grapeseed oil to drizzle

1 or 2 tablespoons fresh herbs

Sea salt to taste

Peel the beetroot, slice thickly and tip into a roasting tin, season to taste with salt and pepper and drizzle with the oil. Pop into the oven and bake until the beetroot cooks through. Cool, the beetroot and then cut into bite-sized pieces and chill. Chop the onion and chillies and mince the ginger. In a large bowl beat the yogurt, thinning with a little of the water if necessary. Add salt, the onion, ginger, and chillies, mix well and chill separately. When ready to serve, tip in the beetroot, the pistachios, and the stuffed olives. Lightly dry roast the dhania dhal and sprinkle on the yogurt along with the finely chopped herbs.

Postscript: If you are using salted pistachios, reduce the quantity of salt that you add.

Tomatoes in Yogurt

Enough for 3 to 4 kith and kin

You will require the following:

600 grams thick well-set yogurt

30 ml cold water

150 grams tomatoes in different colours

1 ripe kiwi fruit

4 or 5 blades garlic or onion chives

1 teaspoon garlic paste

2 teaspoons green peppercorns

75 grams red onion

½ tablespoon black tukmaria seeds

Sea salt to taste.

Lightly beat the yogurt add a little water to thin if needed. Mix in the salt, the garlic paste, and the peppercorns. Chop the tomatoes into small chunks and finely chop the onion, peel

62 Dhania dhal is roasted split coriander seeds.

the kiwi fruit and cut into pieces, soak the tablespoon of tukmaria seeds in water until swollen, then drain well. Add all the ingredients to the yogurt, and chill until serving time.

Cooks tip: Green peppercorns are available bottled or use a teaspoon of capers instead. If the chives are unavailable use spring onions

Ladies Fingers with Carambola [Okra with Star Fruit]

Enough for 3 to 4 kith and kin

You will require the following:
400 grams thick well-set yogurt
30 ml cold water
275 grams okra[63], weighed in after cleaning
100 grams just ripe carambola[64]
2 or 3 tablespoons vegetable oil
75 grams red onion
1 teaspoon Persian lime powder or sumac
1 teaspoon fennel seeds
A little brown or palm sugar to taste
Sea salt to taste.

Beat the yogurt with a fork, adding a little water if required. Season to taste and refrigerate until needed. Wash the okra, dry with a towel and sun for 5 minutes before slicing very finely. Next, finely mince the onion. Then with the help of a vegetable scraper remove the rind on the edges of the star fruit, slice thinly and set aside. Heat the oil in a pan, add the fennel seeds, fry for one minute, then add the finely chopped okra, and fry until crisp. Remove and drain the oil and season lightly. In the same pan fry the minced onions until lightly browned, sprinkle in the sugar toss well, remove and drain excess oil. Add the okra, onions and carambola to the yogurt, sprinkle the sumac or lime powder on top and serve.

Coconut milk: The liquid squeezed out of freshly grated coconut, is now available in cans and tetra packs, and very convenient to use. Do not confuse it with coconut cream, a similar but thicker product. Coconut water is the clear and flavoursome liquid found within the hard shell, a cool and refreshing drink, and not usually used in cooking.

63 Heirloom varieties of okra such as the Star of David are good choices.

64 If carambola is out of season, replace with kiwi fruit. Half a red dragon fruit will look quite dramatic, but won't contribute much to the flavour.

Making the Perfect Yogurt

It is seven in the morning; Katrina and I are waiting for Dhakliya to turn up with our can full of warm creamy buffalo milk, straight from the village dairy. He finally arrives, grumbling that the lid has come loose causing some of the milk to spill. I accept the can, and while Katrina holds a piece of muslin in place, I pour out the milk; plenty of grass seeds are trapped in the cloth. The cows are milked by hand and dairymen have to bribe their wards by feeding them. I believe it cannot get better than this! Full cream buffalo milk makes excellent yogurt, and if you are lucky to live where it's available, it should be your first option. Alternatively, select the best fresh whole milk available to you.

You require the following:

4 cups milk

½ cup plain natural yogurt [the starter]

Before you begin, it is important to make sure that the utensils and other equipment you are likely to use are clean, as contaminated yogurt sours very quickly. Put the milk on low heat and gently bring to the boil, then lower the heat and simmer for ten minutes, remove from the heat and allow the milk to cool. In curd making, the temperature at this stage is important, and the milk should be just warm to the touch. If you are using a thermometer, the temperature should read 115°F or 45°C. Add the curd culture to the milk and stir gently, be careful not to incorporate too much air because this delays setting. Pour the mixture into a bowl, cover with a lid and wrap a towel around to keep it warm. A terracotta/clay pot is an ideal container to use because it absorbs the excess liquid but wash first with hot water. Leave the curd to set in a warm place and do not disturb during the setting period that should last 6 to 8 hours. After the curd has set, refrigerate and use as required. Warm weather will accelerate the process; during winter, the setting time will be longer.

The quality of the natural yogurt that you use as a starter is relevant. It will determine how good your yogurt is and whether it will set at all. For well-set,delicious tasting yogurt, use a starter that is fresh and sweet. You will need to replace your starter if you notice a decline in the quality of your yogurt. Borrow new starter from a kindly neighbour[65] or buy some yogurt from your local store. Store bought yogurt is often 'treated,' you will need to check the label for natural yogurt that contains live culture for it to be of any use.

65 In South India, loaning curds to friends and neighbours during and after sundown is considered inauspicious. If you are likely to run out of the starter and need to borrow, do get your timing right!

Yogurt is an incredibly versatile food, and there is always a bowlful on hand in my kitchen, as is the case in most South Indian homes where it usually makes an appearance at every meal. The possibilities range from uncomplicated combinations of fruit and yogurt to more demanding yogurt curries. To optimize its potential I keep a few things in mind:

Extend the short shelf life of yogurt through refrigeration, and by making sure that there is no contamination by using clean spoons and storage containers.

Long term freezing of foods made with yogurt, such as vegetable and meat curries is not advisable. Frozen desserts that use yogurt should also be eaten within a day or two.

Vigorous beating breaks down the yogurt, so beat gently with a fork or wire whisk to retain a thick creamy texture. Use a blender only when making a smoothie or lassie.

The acid content of Yogurt makes it a good marinade to tenderise meat. Mix in a little ground garlic, cumin, and coriander powder and then add to the meat. Allow the meat to rest for at least an hour or two.

When using yogurt in a curry, be weary of its tendency to curdle. To avoid this culinary disaster reflect on the following:

Using high-fat yogurt for cooking is a better option. Bring the yogurt to room temperature and beat it gently before adding to the pan.

Once you have added the yogurt, cook on low heat and don't let it come to the boil. Ideally, add the yogurt towards the end of the cooking process.

A foolproof way to stabilize yogurt for cooking is to blend two teaspoons of cornflour with water and add it to the yogurt.

Home Made Panir

You will require the following:

1 litre full cream milk [preferably buffalo milk]

250 ml fresh, natural yogurt

Sea salt to taste.

Put the milk to boil and watch it carefully. When it begins to rise, lower the heat and tip in the well-beaten curds. You can salt the milk here if you so wish. With a spoon give the milk just one quick stir to mix in the curds. Then allow the milk to simmer until it breaks, the whey will separate from the solids. Continue to simmer the milk until the whey is no longer milky and begins to run clear. Then, take off the heat and cool. As soon as the curd is cool enough to handle, pour into a muslin bag and hang up to drain. [You might need some help with this.] Allow the curd to hang for an hour, then remove and place the bag in a large flat dish and weigh down heavily. Leave for a further hour or two. Finally, gently remove the panir from the bag and cut into pieces, use immediately or store in the refrigerator in a bowl of cold salted water.

Homemade Yogurt Cream Cheese

You don't require much more than a spot of enthusiasm, a little spare time, and a few basic ingredients to produce a sumptuous homemade yogurt cream cheese. Easy to make, the outcome is a spreadable cream cheese that goes admirably with warm toast and butter or a freshly baked baguette. Serve with a bowl of fresh fruit or combine with chocolate, castor sugar and walnuts and use as a cake filling.

500 grams thick freshly made plain yogurt

100 grams thick fresh cream

Pinch of salt

Herbs, spices and seasonings of your choice

Line a strainer with cheesecloth, or use a coffee filter, place over a pot and tip in the yogurt. Cover with a plastic wrap and refrigerate for about 12 hours or until the moisture drains out and the yogurt firms up. Tip into a bowl, add the cream and with the help of a fork beat until well mixed. You can flavour your cream cheese with herbs and spices of your choosing; season to taste with a speciality salt. A few ideas:

Finely chopped capers combined with your favourite herb or herbs preferably fresh.

Sun dried tomatoes in oil finely chopped, and combined with crushed hazelnuts or roasted Niger seeds.

Green or black olives finely sliced with a little olive oil and a squeeze of wasabi or horseradish sauce.

Black sesame seeds or crushed pine nuts

Minced red onions or spring onions

Onion or garlic chives with finely chopped with ham or salami

Crushed nasturtium seeds and garlic

Finely chopped Japanese preserved ginger with mint or coriander

10. What is your Pulse Rate?

In Krupalaya, they put in an appearance at every meal sometimes in a supporting role and at other times as the protagonist. At lunch, the lentils appeared in an antiquated yellow ceramic bowl. The odd, conical shaped dish with its surface covered with a fine web of hairline fractures could easily have been replaced. Nevertheless,whatever the day and whatever the occasion, whether tur, mung or masoor it never failed to appear on our dining table, eventually becoming one among many such familiar objects that made Krupalaya the warm, wonderful home it was.

Black Eyed Peas with Roasted Veggies

Serves 4

Try it with that wonderful Tibetan bread called Ting Mo.

The very first seeds that we sowed as greenhorn farmers were a monsoon crop of Black Eyed Peas. I just cannot describe the excitement and exhilaration that David and I felt when those seeds sprouted, metamorphosed into magnificent greenery and then burst into bloom. In time, the young tender pods emerged and with them a break in the weather, a weak sun valiantly pushing through thick layers of cloud. Apparently, we were not the only one's rejoicing; a humungous army of black blister bugs wearing red helmets arrived and pretty much agreed that our field of black-eyed peas was an incredible sight to behold!

You require the following:

150 grams dried black eyed peas

75 grams red onion

200g sweet potato

100g carrots

100 grams winter squash or pumpkin

100g broccoli

275 grams tomatoes

2 tablespoons tomato puree

50 ml sweet red wine

2 teaspoons fresh or 1 teaspoon dried thyme

1 teaspoon caraway seeds

3 bay leaves

1 to 2 tablespoons pomegranate molasses [rob- e anar]

3 tablespoon vegetable oil

Salt and black pepper to taste

Soak the black eyed peas in plenty of water overnight. Drain the next morning, and cook in fresh water until nearly but not quite done. Use a pressure cooker to save time. Retain the cooking water. Meanwhile, cube the carrot, winter squash, and sweet potato, tip into a roasting pan sprinkle with salt and pepper, a little of the thyme and a tablespoon of oil, mix well. Place in a moderately hot oven and roast until nearly done. Break the broccoli into small pieces; finely chop the onion and tomato.

Add the remaining oil to a pot, and heat. Then add the bay leaves and the caraway seed. Now add the onion and cook until it changes colour to a nice warm brown. Next, add the tomatoes and continue to cook on a medium heat until the vegetables soften, add the puree and some of the cooking water. Tip in the broccoli, season to taste and cook until the broccoli is a little more than half done. Then add the red wine, the pomegranate molasses, and the remaining thyme. Next, add the black eyed peas and the roasted vegetables, adding a little more of the cooking water if need be, check seasoning and finish cooking.

NOOSH –E JAN!

Getting High on Neera

Neera or toddy was an integral part of our childhood. Our introduction to it from a very young age was probably because toddy has always been a much-loved beverage of the Parsee and Irani communities, so much so, that they often start the day with a glassful before breakfast. Toddy finds its way into their food; meat and chicken dishes sizzle in it. Tea time snacks such as bhakras [similar to a doughnut], sadhnas - steamed rice flour cakes, and poppatjis, fascinating dried fruit fritters all have toddy as a star ingredient.

In Poona my Grandfather Khudamorad owned a toddy shop just behind Poona's Sassoon General hospital in the area known as Maal Dakka; a grand Uncle Aspandia Khansaheb Irani had his toddy shop at Quarter Gate. Not far behind was Nergis Fui, who won her toddy shop at auction and set up her business in Khondwa. The work, however, was more than she bargained for, predawn negotiations with toddy tappers for the day's supply, transporting the toddy to her shop, filling the bottles for sale, boiling eggs to sell as a snack!

While growing up in the South during the sixties and seventies, toddy shops had high visibility everywhere, especially in the rural areas where you also saw the toddy palm growing in abundance. Uncle Sanath was a very close family friend and well aware of our family addiction to Neera. He would, on many occasions very graciously surprise us with a pot full. The Neera would arrive just after sunrise and left on our doorstep, the black earthen pot loosely covered with a banana leaf and crawling with gigantic black ants.

Neera is the sap procured from the inflorescence of various species of palm, in Kerala, it is the coconut palm, but also tapped are the date palm and the palmyra. Toddy tapping takes place late evening and the sweet, frothy, white liquid collected at dawn. This is when it is at its nutritional best, full of vitamins and trace elements, and when it commands the status of a health drink! Many hours past sunrise, the Neera, which is predisposed to the process of natural fermentation, begins its transformation into toddy. With an alcohol content of about 4%, it is the time; many would say it's at its very best!

Running Dhal with Devils Dung - With plenty of Lime to serve

Enough for 4 or 5 as a side dish

The consistency of this dhal, as the name suggests should be runny, just so that it flows freely but not thin or watery. You can replace the moong dhal with tur dhal for some interesting variation.

You require the following:

200 grams moong dhal

150 grams red onions

2 to 3 mild green chillies

800 ml water [approximately]

2 sprigs curry leaves

6 to 8 cloves garlic

½ to 1 teaspoon devils dung[66] [love it!]

1 teaspoon cumin seed

½ teaspoon turmeric

2 tablespoons parsley or coriander

2½ tablespoons ghee

Salt to taste

Cook the dhal, the turmeric, garlic, devils dung and green chillies with 600 ml of water until done, the dhal should be nice and soft. Remove from the heat, and with a slotted spoon carefully remove the green chillies onto a plate and set aside. Blend the dhal until smooth adding a little water if necessary. Put the dhal back on the heat, add the chillies and gently heat through, season to taste, adding more water to thin the dhal if required. Just before serving, thinly slice the onions and chop the parsley or coriander, then heat the ghee in a small pot on medium heat, and add the curry leaves and cumin seed. Fry and let them brown lightly, then add the onions and continue to fry on low heat until the onions are a nice golden brown. Heat the dhal, and then pour into a serving dish, sprinkle the chopped green coriander on top and then pour over the onion and ghee mixture that should be sizzling hot. Serve immediately. Devil worshipers may lightly sprinkle some more powdered dung on the top!

Very nice served with white rice, prawn patio or mutton pepper fry and an assortment of papadums.

---

66 Hing/asafoetida.

Sprouted Horse Gram in Spicy Black Bean Sauce

Good for 4 or 5 as a side dish

Soak horse gram [kulith] a flat, oval red-brown seed 8 to 10 hours, or overnight. Cooking it is best done in a pressure cooker. However, horse gram sprouts in no time, and is ready to eat in just 36 hours. A staple in all our village homes, make it a 'regular' in yours!

You require the following:

3½ cups sprouted horse gram [about 150 dry grams soaked and sprouted]

100 grams red onions

1 cup chopped onion leeks

1 cup well packed roughly chopped oyster mushrooms

2 bay leaves

½ tablespoon garlic paste

1 teaspoon pepper powder

2 teaspoons Asian spicy black pepper sauce

1 tablespoon grated palm jaggery or brown sugar

3 tablespoons vegetable oil

¼ cup finely chopped green coriander or parsley

Salt to taste

Finely chop the onions and fry to a light brown with the bay leaves. Add the garlic paste and the pepper powder and cook for a few minutes more. Then add the mushrooms and the onion leeks and cook until they soften but retain their shape. Next, add the sprouted horse gram and mix well, stir in the spicy black bean sauce and the sugar and check seasoning. Cook for a further minute or two, before mixing in the green coriander. Serve filled in pita bread if available.

Post Script: Similar to pita bread, is a local Goan bread called 'poee,' soft, spongy and hollow inside. Traditionally leavened with toddy but now mostly with yeast, the bread, butterfly-shaped has a slash down the centre. Made by small family-run bakeries, and available all over Goa, if you have ever visited the state, the early morning call of the man on his bicycle, tooting his noisy horn will be very familiar.

Street Food

Street food was strictly off limits; there was no question of sampling the sugar cane juice sold from handcarts just outside the gates of Krishna Rajendra Government Hospital. 'Give you enteric' my grandmother declared. Rules were rules, and I had to wait until I was 24 before my husband David introduced me to a delicious glass of sugarcane juice laced with ginger and chilled with crushed ice.

When I was around 13 years of age and home for the holidays, Nergis Fui paid us a visit. Her arrival meant delicious Parsee cooking, fun and games, and often the breaking of usually well-kept rules! And so it was, with my father's blessings, my aunt, my grandmother, and we three set off on a picnic to the backwaters of the River Cauvery, with Singh the driver responsible for safely getting us there and back. With our well packed 'picnic basket,' it was very clear we were unlikely to starve.

It wasn't long before the familiar and beloved sights and sounds of the countryside replaced the chaos of the city. Like any good Irani, my aunt soon spotted a toddy shop on the outskirts of a little village. With plenty of encouragement from us, but with grave misgivings from my grandmother that's where we headed. With community life as a moving backdrop, the unobtrusive toddy shop was a small roughly built structure like many of the others around it. At the back of the shop stacked high in wooden crates, were the bottles of neera. Right in front was an enormous built up wood burning stove keeping a dozen or more dishes warm, their aroma and colour a stark contrast to the drab mud and cow dung caked walls of the oven. Boiled eggs and egg curries, fried fish and fish curries, mutton chops and claret coloured mutton curries, all blisteringly hot. Nevertheless, there was plenty of neera to help offset the heat, but it was well past 11 O'clock and the neera had surreptitiously changed its character to toddy its other heady avatar. But for a mere two bucks a bottle, no one bothered to give this much thought!

Eventually, my grandmother thought it expedient to move on. Fully sated with all that food and drink and now deliriously happy, we decided to head over to the other side of the river. Though I was just 13, and my brothers considerably younger, for us it was the mother of all picnics and remains the benchmark to measure all the others!

Masoor Dhal with Wakame [Sea Weed]

Good for 4 as a side dish

You require the following:

200 grams masoor dhal

750ml water [approximately]

1/3 cup dried wakame or any other seaweed on hand[67]

1/3 cup green peas

2 or 3 mild dry red chillies

1 good sprig curry leaves

80 grams onion

1 small vegetable or chicken soup cube

A small knob of fresh ginger

3 to 4 cloves garlic

½ teaspoon fenugreek seeds

½ teaspoon cumin seed

¼ teaspoon turmeric powder

2 tablespoons vegetable oil of your choice

Set the dhal to boil in 500 ml of water with the green peas, the turmeric, curry leaves, soup cube and the red chillies. Meanwhile, rehydrate the wakame in a little warm water, and finely slice the onions, mince the ginger and garlic. Heat the oil in a pan and add the cumin seed, fenugreek seeds and fry half a minute on low heat, then add the ginger and garlic and fry half a minute more. Next, add the onion and cook until a medium brown. Tip in the dhal and green peas and mix well adding a little more water to thin it if needed, finally add the drained seaweed and season to taste. Ready to eat!

---

67 All seaweeds expand when rehydrated, sea veggies such as arame, hijiki or wakame are all varieties that you can use, just remember that they have different characters, wakame expands to seven times its original size hijiki roughly quadruples.

Masoor Dhal, Sundried Tomatoes, and Fitweed

Serves 5 or 6 as a side dish

You require the following:

200 grams masoor dhal

1 cup false coriander [fitweed]

750 ml vegetable or meat stock

100 grams onion

1/3 cup sundried tomatoes in oil

2 sprigs curry leaves

2 or 3 green chillies

½ tablespoon ginger garlic paste

1 teaspoon coriander powder

1 teaspoon mustard seed

1 tablespoons oil

1 tablespoon ghee

Boil the dhal in 500ml of stock until soft. Finely chop the onions; roughly chop the false coriander into pieces, and keep the chillies whole. Heat the oil and ghee in a pot add the mustard seed and get them to crackle but don't allow them to burn. Next, add the curry leaves, green chillies, and the onions and cook over medium heat until the onions brown lightly. Then, add the ginger - garlic paste and the coriander powder, followed by the false coriander. Cook the greens until they are soft. Now add the sun-dried tomatoes, stir for two minutes more, then add the dhal and mix well. Finally add the remaining stock. Cook for five minutes more and you are ready to serve.

Gram Dhal with Breast Meat

Serves 4

The lime gives this dish an edge. You can replace the Persian limes with one large preserved Moroccan lime quartered, or the juice of a lime or lemon, but add these towards the end of the cooking process.

You require the following:

500 grams breast meat

200 grams channa dhal [gram dhal]

3 dried Persian limes

175 grams onions

½ teaspoon turmeric

2 or 3 Kashmir chillies, Chilli Guajillo or Chilli Ancho[68]

¼ cup vegetable oil of your choice

¼ cup green coriander leaves

Salt to taste

For the masala:

1 teaspoon cumin seeds

1 teaspoon coriander seeds

1 tablespoon ginger garlic paste

½ "piece of cassia bark

6 to 8 black peppercorns

Grind to a fine paste with a little water

Soak the gram dhal for 2 hours in just enough water to cover. Pierce the Persian limes with a fork and finely slice the onions. Heat the oil in a pressure cooker, add the onions and on medium heat cook until brown. Remove half the browned onions with a slotted spoon and set aside. Now add the turmeric powder, the red chillies, and the ground masala to the remaining onions. Cook the masala until done, adding a little water now and then to prevent it from drying out. Next, add the mutton and cook for a further five minutes then add the dhal and the Persian limes, and season to taste. Add water and pressure cook the meat and dhal until the mutton is soft and tender. Just before serving reheat and turn into a serving dish, sprinkle over the finely chopped green coriander and the fried onions. Serve with white rice, yogurt, and a salad.

68 Use any dried red chilli such as the Goa [Mapsa] red chillies. They only seem to be available in the Mapsa market in North Goa, so if you are in the area you might like to pick some up. Judge quantity according to heat of the chilly you plan to use. Mexican chillies are great to use.

Oose Mir

For 6 to 7

In this Old Iranian dish that Nergis Fui often made, the beetroot is an essential ingredient turning the dish to a translucent light pink. Use a pressure cooker if you are in a hurry otherwise slow cook for 2 hours on a gentle flame. Oose Mir is similar to Ash-e Reshteh of modern Iranian cooking and is a meal in itself.

You require the following:

1 cup red kidney beans

1 cup white lima beans

1 cup large white chick peas

½ cup whole moong

2 large beetroots

250 grams winter squash or pumpkin

2 cups spinach

1 cup dill

1 cup coriander

6 spring onions

½ to ¾ cup flat rice or egg noodles

1250 ml water or stock

To finish:

3 onions

6 to 8 cloves garlic

1 teaspoon turmeric

1 tablespoon black pepper powder

3 tablespoons olive oil

Soak the first four ingredients in cold water overnight. The next morning drain and rinse the beans. Discard any beans that have refused to swell. Put the red kidney beans in a pot and cook until tender. Cook the white lima beans and the white chickpeas together in a pan until soft, when a little over half done add the whole moong and finish cooking. Use a pressure cooker to save time. Meanwhile pare the beetroot and the squash and cube them, place in a roasting pan drizzle with a little oil and a sprinkling of salt and roast until just a little underdone. Roughly chop the spinach, dill, spring onions and coriander, thinly slice the onions, and crush the garlic.

In a large pot gently heat the oil and tip in the garlic and cook half a minute, next add the turmeric and cook for half a minute more, then add the onions and fry until they change colour. Add the pepper powder to the onions, then add all the beans and stir-fry two minutes. Tip in the beetroot, squash, and the stock and simmer until the beans are like velvet. Finally, add the noodles and greens and cook until soft. The consistency of the soup should be thick like a stew, but thin with more stock if that's what you prefer.

Cooks tip: If you are not a pepper fan reduce to half a tablespoon.

Limas with Sumac and Harbora Greens

Enough for 4 or 5 as a side dish

You require the following:

200 grams large white lima beans
1 cup harbora greens[69]
100 grams shallots or sambhar onions
3 to 4 rashers of lean bacon [optional]
1 green chilly
1 fresh red or yellow chilly
3 to 4 cloves garlic
1 tablespoon vegetable oil
1 tablespoon butter
A sprinkling of sumac, dried mango or pomegranate powder

Soak the beans overnight, drain the next morning and discard those that have refused to swell. Cook the beans in fresh water until soft and velvety adding salt to taste towards the end of the cooking process. Drain and set aside. Meanwhile, roughly chop the greens, crush the garlic and clean the shallots keeping them whole.

Gently heat the oil and butter in a frying pan add the chopped rashers of bacon, cook until crisp then remove and set aside. In the same pan add the whole chillies and the garlic and fry for half a minute. Next, add the onions and cook until they change colour, followed by the harbora greens. Stir fry on medium heat until lightly crisped. Add the beans and the bacon and season to taste with salt and a little freshly ground black pepper. Finally, sprinkle with the sumac, mix well and serve immediately.

---

69 *Harbora Greens see page 261.

The Betel Leaf [Piper Betle]

An afternoon spent at the 'The Three Aces' necessarily meant a substantial indulgence in all things 'Mogalai.' At the end of the meal, the need of the hour was a digestive, in the form of a refreshing 'Sweet Paan' available just outside the door of the restaurant. Rookies are surprised with its wacky 'nothing quite like it' taste. Paan is a fusion of numerous elements; areca nut, sugary confectionery, coconut, spices of all kinds and sometimes tobacco, all parcelled together in a betel leaf first smeared with lime, and then pinned with a clove. The ingredients, the folding and even the presentation of paan are regional idiosyncrasies, as are the names. Growing up in the late sixties during those tumultuous adolescent years, giggling school girls [and boys] went into hysterics over an inspired new pan called 'Palang Thod'[70] An indigenous and early frontrunner to the blue pill!

The lime green, heart-shaped betel leaf with its protruding petiole neatly stacked in concentric circles was, and still is a familiar sight in local markets. Intrinsically tied to Indian social and cultural life and the ceremonies and rituals governing them, the betel leaf and the areca nut are like the twins from Siam. The small paan shops outside restaurant doors are still visible, perhaps not where the food is 'plated,' but elsewhere along the highways and by lanes, and in the burgeoning cities of provincial India. Some of the ingredients may have changed and the presentation a little different, but the Paan quintessentially remains the same.

70 Break the Bed.

11. Pepper Water

A dreary wet monsoon evening, pitch dark because the power lines are down is an excellent excuse to make a jug full! There are many variations of this South Indian staple, with pepper, tamarind, and lentils the common ingredients. The Anglo-Indian kitchen took it further using a good meat stock as the base. Purists will probably disapprove of some of the elements I use and question the 'Rasam' tag, but the experiments have been fun!

Pepper Water Flavoured with Lemon Grass

Enough for 4 to 5 Kith and Kin

You require the following:

1000ml vegetable/meat stock or 3 small stock cubes and water

120 grams red onions

120 grams ripe red tomatoes

2 sprigs curry leaves

2 tablespoons lemon grass stalks finely minced

1 stalk lemon grass

½ teaspoon turmeric powder

2 tablespoons pepper rasam paste or rasam powder

2 tablespoons vegetable oil of your choice

2 tablespoon green coriander

1 tablespoon ghee [optional]

Sea salt to taste

Remove the hard outer layers of the lemongrass, before mincing the stalks, white part only. Cut the other stalk into two or three lengths and set aside. Finely chop the onions, tomatoes, and the green coriander. Add the oil and ghee to a pot and place on medium heat add the onions and curry leaves and cook until the onions turn a pale yellow, then add the turmeric powder and the minced lemon grass and cook for five minutes more. Next, add the tomatoes with a little stock and cook until they are soft. Add the pepper rasam paste or rasam powder and cook for a few minutes more. Then add the remaining stock and the stalks of lemon grass bring to the boil just once, and then lower heat and simmer for 8 minutes, season to taste and simmer for a further 5 minutes. Just before serving reheat the rasam and add the green coriander, remove the grass stalks and serve hot.

Postscript: You may need a little more water depending on the strength you like your rasam. Use any rasam powder of your choice. I often experiment with Southeast Asian curry pastes in place of rasam powder. A lot of them have their ingredients in Chinese, which I don't understand so the results can be very interesting, to say the least!

Weighing Scales

The family's blue and white weighing scale remained permanently lodged under the old-fashioned ironing board in the large bathroom upstairs. It's existence was perceptible to all, but no one paid much attention and even the servants while cleaning, conveniently swept around it. This lack of interest was probably due to the negative conclusions those weighing scales always seemed to display!

Certainly, none of us belonged to pharaoh's lean kind. Just after my daughter Katrina was born, the vegetable sellers in Belgaum's City Market had a moniker for me – Tusker, the name of a popular Ashok Leyland 14 tonner! However, I don't remember my mother ever on a diet, and my grandmother didn't quite understand the need. However, my father did on occasion announce he had plans to lose weight, a decision based not on the weighing scales but solely on the 'fit' of his impeccable white drill trousers. The announcement became official when Das was brought in for a discussion. My father's diet usually lasted no more than three weeks. He would lay off his whiskey at sundown, which, we all acknowledged a tremendous sacrifice, and he stuck to his two toasts at breakfast. His rather remarkable diet centred on the afternoon meal. While the rest of us tucked into our deliciously cooked food and indulged in routine mealtime chatter, Das would walk in with my father's lunch; three large skewers of grilled meat darkened and scarred, and infused with the smoky aroma of the charcoal on which they were cooked. Salted, peppered and grilled to perfection, all through my childhood, I linked weight loss to a three-week stint of cholesterol-rich kidney and liver.

A 'Betel' in Your Rasam

Enough for 5 to 6 Kith and Kin

The betel leaf used here is *Piper betle* [paan leaf] and not the Asian species known as wild beetle or wild pepper leaf [*Piper sarmentosum*] commonly used in Thai cooking.

You require the following:

1250 ml stock

120 grams red onions

120 grams tomatoes

3 fresh paan leaves

2 sprigs of mature curry leaves

1 or 2 tablespoon tamarind pulp

1/4 teaspoon turmeric powder

1 teaspoon cumin powder

1 teaspoon coriander powder

1 tablespoon garlic paste

2 teaspoons mustard seeds

2 generous pinches of devils dung [hing]

2 tablespoons vegetable oil of your choice

1 tablespoons ghee [optional]

Sea salt to taste

Finely chop the onions and tomatoes. Heat the oil in a pot and add the mustard seeds. When they begin to crackle sprinkle in the turmeric, coriander and cumin powders and heat through for 20 seconds. Add the chopped onions and the curry leaves and fry until the onions turn a medium yellow. Next, add the garlic paste and cook for a few minutes more. Then add the tomatoes and some stock, and cook until the tomatoes are soft and mushy. Add the remaining stock, tamarind pulp, the hing and season to taste, simmer for 8 minutes. Just before serving, snip off the petiole of the paan leaves and cut into strips. Reheat the rasam, add the tablespoon of ghee, the paan leaves and simmer a further 2 or 3 minutes. Serve immediately in a jug or individual mugs.

Caramelized Onions: Delicious sprinkled on top of rice, dhal, a spicy tomato soup, or even on scrambled eggs! Finely slice a generous quantity of red onions and deep fry briskly in oil or ghee on medium heat. If the heat is too low, they will absorb too much fat, and if too high they will turn rubbery and may turn bitter. So brown the onions but also take care not to burn them. Remove the onions from the oil with a slotted spoon and spread out on kitchen paper to drain. Leave the onion slices whole, or while still warm and crisp crush them lightly.

Rasam with Shrimps and Wakame

Enough for 4 to 5 Kith and Kin

You require the following:

1200 ml water

120 grams red onions

250 grams cleaned shrimps

1/3 cup garlic chives [onion chives or spring onions as an alternative]

2 sprigs curry leaves

2 tablespoons tamarind paste

1 tablespoon brown sugar

2 tablespoons rasam powder

1 tablespoon Udang Rangup Bercili

1 teaspoon garlic paste

¼ cup dried wakame

2 soup cubes

2 tablespoons vegetable oil of your choice

Sea salt to taste

Finely mince the onions; roughly chop the garlic chives. Heat the oil in a pot, add the onions and cook until they just begin to change colour. Next, add the garlic paste, udang rangup bercili, curry leaves and chives, and continue to cook on medium heat. If the onions begin to stick to the pan, add a tablespoon or two of the water. Add the shrimps and crumble the soup cubes into the pot, stir well and continue to cook for a further 3 to 4 minutes adding more of the water as the mixture thickens. Pour in the rest of the water and bring to the boil, add the sugar, tamarind paste, and rasam powder, season with salt. Finally, add the dried wakame and simmer for 8 to 10 minutes. Serve piping hot.

First Aid: Your mouth is on fire, too much chilly! Instead of reaching for that glass of cold water, head to your refrigerator and pour yourself a cup of ice-cold milk. Sweeten with sugar and sip slowly, swirling the milk around in your mouth before you swallow!

12. Fish

Fish and Okra Curry

Makes enough for 2 or 3

You require the following:
250 grams of your favourite fish sliced
100 grams okra chopped into 1-inch pieces[71]
¼ cup cashew nuts
1 cup thick curds
4 whole cardamoms
1 teaspoon sugar
1 tablespoon oil of your choice
1 tablespoon ghee
Salt to taste

For the Masala:
100 grams onions
2dry, mild red chillies [deseeded if you wish]
1 tablespoon ginger garlic paste
Grind with a little water to a smooth paste

Heat the ghee in a pan and fry the cashew nuts on low heat until lightly browned, then remove the cashews and set aside. Gently pound the cardamoms and fry for 2 minutes in the same pan. Next, add the oil and tip in the ground masala. Cook until the rawness of the masala disappears, adding a little water from time to time if the mixture begins to stick or burn. Next, add the okra, mix well and cook a few minutes more, then add a little water and cook the okra until half done. Season with salt and add the teaspoon of sugar. Using a wire whisk lightly whip up the yoghurt until smooth. Then lower the heat, add the cashew nuts, the yoghurt, and the fish to the pan. Allow the fish to cook until just done, check seasoning once again and serve immediately.

71 Try Burgundy, a red okra variety that holds some colour after cooking.

No. 42 Sassoon Road

My father's family home in Poona no longer exists it was pulled down a few years ago to make way for beehives of glass and steel the familiar face of contemporary urban living. It had no name, just a number 42 Sassoon Road. The fine old bungalow with its stately rooms had outlived its usefulness; disowned and abandoned the extensive garden; mango and chikko orchards are now routine parking lots. The city of Poona is where our father grew up and where our mother spent much of her young adult life, it is where my parents met and married. Our extended family lives here; it's the place where I met David and where I went to university.

For those four eventful years, I lived with my father's sister, Nergis Fui at No. 42 Sassoon Road, and though its halcyon days were well and truly over, it was nonetheless still a magnificent home. My suite of 4 rooms was just a cameo in the fifteen thousand square feet of living space, set in a bountiful two acres of garden. The family wholesale liquor business, conducted from godowns set right at the back, ensured an endless stream of buyers, cycles, rickshaws, and trucks providing a constant but unobtrusive hum in the background.

My aunt was a fun loving, but also a formidable, fearless, and deeply religious woman. She was frequently called upon to do a man's job in a man's world, often travelling alone past midnight with large sums of money to release the liquor trucks at the Octroi Naka's[72] on the outskirts of Poona city. She dedicated her life to her ailing parents, tilled the land, owned a liquor store and dabbled in politics. She loved dogs and always had one by her side, alternatively naming them either Lancer or Bingo. When I moved to Poona in the late '70's, a Lancer had just passed on, and there was now a Bingo in residence.

My aunt was a remarkable cook, her talent so natural it made her cookery look effortless. There were no recipe books, measuring cups or weighing scales in Nergis Fui's Kitchen, a room so straightforward and uncomplicated, that only the presence of a gas stove and the kitchen sink gave its function away.

Nergis Fui's mango achar was sublime. During the hot weather when the mango flies swarmed, and her orchard burdened with fruit she would set to work. Many months later, after the spices had softened and mellowed, and the pieces of fruit gleamed in their bath of mustard oil, she would apportion burnis full to family favourites. Ours would arrive by truck, tucked in among various motorcycle parts for the factory. In the autumn of her life

72 Naka - check post, Octroi a tax collected by local authorities.

and with the onset of blindness, my brother Kairus made one final request for a burni of Nergis Fui's mango achar and was obliged with not just one but many, enough achar to last us over five years!

I seldom opened the refrigerator at No 42; it was old and decrepit and occasionally gave you a nasty shock. It stood just outside my bedroom door its noisy rattling compressor desperately trying to make it through another day. There was never very much in it anyway, the butter dish, a jug of milk, a bottle maybe two of cold water, and a dozen eggs.

I went off to university each morning with a tiffin box. It sometimes contained the left over's from the previous night's dinner, but usually, my lunch was freshly made. Time was a constraint, so Nergis Fui would frequently cook up a dish of vegetables and then break a couple of eggs on top. The easier Bheeda per eeda [eggs on okra], the more demanding Papeta per eeda [Eggs on potatoes][73] and the string of other variations, meant we were forever running out of eggs. As luck would have it, a deliveryman who frequented No. 42 in connection with the family business, was also a wholesale egg dealer, so it wasn't much of a surprise when my aunt announced where our next supply of eggs were coming from. Later, back home from university, I opened the refrigerator for a bottle of cold water and to my utter disbelief found it crammed with eggs, over four hundred of them!

Fish in Buttermilk

Enough for 4

You require the following:

500 to 600 grams fish thickly sliced and filleted if you like

100 grams finely chopped onions

3 long mild green chillies, deseeded if you wish

3 to 5 red birds eye chillies [Optional]

2 sprigs curry leaves

½ teaspoon mustard seeds

3 to 4 tablespoons oil

200 ml buttermilk

1 tablespoons lime juice

2 tablespoon chopped green coriander

Salt to taste

73 Parsee classics.

For the masala:

½ cup firmly packed fresh grated coconut

1 teaspoon cumin powder

1 teaspoon coriander powder

1 teaspoon pepper powder

½ teaspoon turmeric

Grind to a fine paste with a little water

Sprinkle the fish with a little salt and the lime juice and set aside for no longer than 15 minutes. Heat half the quantity of oil and quickly fry the pieces of fish until brown and crisp on the outside, then remove from the pan and set aside. Add the remaining oil to the pan, add the mustard seeds and allow them to crackle, then tip in the onions, the chillies, and the curry leaves, and cook until the onions turn a light brown. Next, add the ground masala, season to taste and fry well adding a little water as it begins to dry. When done add the buttermilk and the fish, and cook a few minutes more. Then sprinkle on the green coriander, heat through and turn into a serving dish.

Ready to eat when you are!

Cook's note: Use mullet, seer, or pieces of sliced pomfret. Try whole butterfish, fillets of kokar or rockfish done this way.

River Fish with East Indian Bottle Masala

Enough for 3

You require the following:

400 grams river fish such as walaga or carp filleted or sliced

100 grams tomato

100 grams onions

1 tablespoon ginger garlic paste

3 tablespoon tomato puree

2 sprigs curry leaves

1 teaspoon cumin seed

2 teaspoon bottle masala [3 if you like it spicy]

2 tablespoons fresh coriander chopped

2 tablespoons vegetable oil

A little lemon juice

Salt to taste

Sprinkle the fish, with a little salt, lime juice, and set aside until needed. Finely mince the onion and tomato. Heat the oil in a pan then add the curry leaves and cumin seed and cook one minute, then tip in the onion. Fry until the onions turn colour to a medium brown, and then add the tomato, the ginger garlic paste, and the tomato puree. Cook for a further 8 minutes adding a little water now and then. Next, add the East Indian bottle masala, a little more water and cook for a further 5 to 8 minutes. The curry should now be thick and smooth, check seasoning. Finally, add the pieces of fish and cook until just done. Before serving, gently reheat the curry, turn into a serving dish and sprinkle over the chopped coriander leaves. Serve with rice or roti.

It was in the early eighties that my Mother-in-law Marie introduced me to The East Indian Bottle Masala, that marvellous stuff that I have never stopped using ever since. Unbelievably versatile, delicate but also with an awesome punch,it is a masala blend belonging to the cuisine of the East Indian community of Bombay. The masala is usually prepared in the hot season when markets are flooded with crisp red chillies and aromatic spices, pounded into a fine powder and tightly packed into recycled brandy bottles.

Green Crab Curry

Enough for 6 people

You won't find a better finger food than this! To enjoy the dish, I suggest that you make it a close-knit family affair because there is going to be a lot of crunching, finger licking, and other indications of bad table manners! A nutcracker is a handy tool!

You require the following:

10 medium land or saltwater crabs

100 grams red onions

2 sprigs curry mature leaves

200 ml thick coconut milk

1 teaspoon turmeric powder

3 tablespoons vegetable oil of your choice

1 or 2 tablespoon rob- e anar [pomegranate molasses]

Salt to taste

For the masala:

3 to 4 green chillies

200 grams onions

1-inch piece fresh ginger

8 fat cloves of garlic

½ cup well-packed fitweed [or fresh green coriander]

¼ cup fresh green mint

1 teaspoon cumin seeds

1 teaspoon mustard seeds

6 to 8 peppercorns

4 cloves

1 "cinnamon

Grind to a paste with a little water

Clean and joint the crabs, and lightly crack the larger pieces, then set aside until needed. Heat the oil in a large pan or pressure cooker and brown the thinly sliced onions. Next, add the curry leaves and the turmeric powder, cook a minute more, and then tip in the ground masala. Cook the masala on a low flame until done, adding a little water now and then to prevent the masala from drying out. Then add seasoning, the crab and about 2 cups of water and pressure-cook the crab until nearly done. Next, add the coconut milk, a little more water if required, and cook the crab without the lid on for another 10 minutes. Finally, add the pomegranate molasses simmer a few moments more and serve hot. Serve the curry with plain boiled rice, sweet mango pickle, and papadums.

Prawn Patio

Enough for 4

You require the following:

500 grams cleaned medium prawns [weigh in after cleaning]

200 grams red onions

150 grams juicy red tomatoes

¼ cup tomato puree

1 or 2 teaspoons Parsee sambhar masala

1 teaspoon garam masala

1 teaspoon coriander powder

½ teaspoon turmeric powder

1 teaspoon brown sugar, jaggery or palm sugar

¼ cup fresh green coriander

3 tablespoons oil

Salt to taste

For the masala:

1 tablespoon garlic paste

1 long mild green chilly

1 teaspoon cumin powder

Grind into a fine paste with a little water

Thoroughly drain the cleaned prawns, add a little salt and the turmeric powder mix well, and set aside for 15 minutes. Mince the onions and tomatoes and chop the green coriander. Heat the oil in a pot, and fry the onions to a medium brown. Next, add the tomatoes and cook until the tomatoes are soft and mushy, adding a little water now and then to prevent them sticking, [about 15 to 18 minutes]. Next, add the ground masala and the masala powders and cook a further 5 minutes. Next, add the tomato puree and season to taste. Finally, add the prawns, and on medium heat cook until just done. Check seasoning and finish with a teaspoon of sugar. Just before serving, reheat the prawns and add the green coriander. Best served with coconut rice, tomato and onion salsa, and a steaming mug of rasam!

NOOSH –E JAN!

Mackerel with Stir Fried Onion Flowers

Makes 4 servings

Serve with a small bowlful of sour cream sauce!

You require the following:

4 large mackerel

1 tablespoon finely crushed garlic

1 tablespoon fitweed or green coriander

4 long fresh yellow or green chillies [optional]

1 teaspoon freshly ground pepper powder

1 tablespoon lime juice

1 tablespoon Asian chilli oil

Vegetable oil of your choice for shallow frying

Salt to taste

For the onion flowers:

400 grams tender onion flowers

200 young zucchini

100 grams oyster mushrooms

1 medium red capsicum

4 medium Hungarian Wax chillies

6 cloves garlic

1/4 cup basil

2 tablespoons oyster sauce

2 or 3 tablespoons vegetable oil

Salt and pepper

Clean the fish leaving them whole with the head intact. Pat dry and with a sharp knife make 2 or 3 long incisions diagonally down the sides of the fish on both sides. Roughly pound together - the tablespoon of oil, the garlic, the fitweed or fresh green coriander and the freshly ground pepper. Season with salt and rub the mixture into the incisions on the fish and inside the body cavity. Place one chilly in the cavity of each fish, drizzle over the lime juice, and set aside for 20 minutes to half an hour.

Clean the onion flowers removing any hard or dry bits and chop roughly. Slice and quarter the zucchini, chop the mushrooms, and lightly crush the garlic. Keep the chillies whole, but make a long slit down one side. Cut the capsicum into medium pieces. Heat a little of the vegetable oil in a wok, add the capsicum and the chillies and cook 3 or 4 minutes or until a little soft. Then add the garlic and the onion flowers cook a further few minutes. Next, add the mushrooms and zucchini, and season to taste with a little pepper and salt. Cook a further few minutes until the zucchini is soft and the mushroom lightly cooked through. Then add the oyster sauce and roughly chopped basil and stir-fry a few minutes then turn off the heat. In the remaining oil, fry the fish on both sides. Divide the onion flowers between 4 individual plates, and place the fried mackerel on top and serve with sour cream sauce on the side.

Rustom Mama and Other Uncles

Though Rustom Mama was my father's uncle, they were both the same age and the best of friends. They were shooting partners and business partners, and he was an important and influential member of the family and highly respected. Gentle and soft-spoken, we nevertheless rudely nicknamed him 'Tank' because of his size. In his younger days, Rustom Mama was a 'pehlwan' or wrestler, and like others of his ilk performed remarkable feats to demonstrate his phenomenal strength.

Rustom Mama and his family lived on a farm on the periphery of Bombay city with dozens of pedigreed dogs and other farm animals. The sprawling farmhouse sparkled with priceless Bohemian cut glass, and the drawing room had interesting peg tables made of cannibalized motorcycle parts, and rexine chairs and sofas to accommodate the steady flow of guests. The house was once the set for a famous Bollywood movie. Porichay Mami was very proud and protective of her collection of Bohemian crystal, so in 1979 there was a crisis of sorts with the news of Skylab's[74] premature demise, and it's impending decent. There was panic that it would make landfall at Borivali.

Many enjoyed the bountiful hospitality of my grandaunt and uncle; their home was thrown open to all. We visited on occasion, one such being a family wedding in the late sixties. An occasion well remembered on two accounts, the food that overwhelmed with its richness and flavour, particularly the fantastic kebabs and delicious homemade panir. We also remember it well because it is the day my brother Kairus all spruced up in a grey 'safari suit,' decided to inspect the piggery. He attended the wedding of course, but in borrowed clothes and not before a thorough cleaning in the capable hands of Nergis Fui!

Another uncle, Aspandia Khan Sahib Irani was also a pehlwan of magnificent stature. When he wasn't exercising with his hefty wooden dumbbells, or overdosing on dozens of eggs, gallons of milk and copious amounts of animal protein as was customary among pehlwans, Grand Uncle Aspandia was busy recruiting 'natives' for the British army in India. He was so accomplished at his job he rewarded him with 400 acres of land and the title of Khan Sahib. A title bestowed on Parsee, Muslim and Jewish subjects of the British Indian Government and awarded by the Viceroy and the Governor General of India for services rendered.

74 Skylab was America's first space station and orbited the earth from 1973 to 1979. In early 1979, Skylab's malfunctioning and ultimate demise became a worldwide media event, with tremendous speculation as to where it would land on re-entry. Finally, on the 11th of July Skylab broke up over Western Australia near a small township called Esperance.

Boman Mama was Rustom's younger brother, kind, caring and generous to a fault. Severely asthmatic, he was never without his handkerchief and nose drops but managed a brisk walk to work each morning. Boman Mama and his family, which included by dear cousin Sheroy, lived in a large spacious old-fashioned apartment, and with them lived Suzie a disgruntled Pomeranian, Mesta their inebriated cook, and Ritchie general dogsbody and Man Friday. If on a visit to Bombay, everyone stayed with Boman Mama for his warmth and hospitality, and of course for the food, for despite the bottle Mesta would deliver. This home cook was a genius with fish, fresh Bombay duck dipped in a delicate batter and lightly fried, slices of Pomfret cooked in sesame oil with a twist of lime, or a fish molee served with basmati rice and mori dhal. At the dining table, we would wait with our fingers crossed, for a teetering Mesta to bring in the food, hoping against hope that tragedy wouldn't strike!

12 Fish Cakes with Zereshk Sauce [Persian Barberries]

Enough for 4

Serve with grilled tomatoes and a rocket salad

You require the following:

1½ cups cooked flaked fish

300 grams boiled mashed potatoes

100 grams red onions

1 or 2 long mild green chillies

2 tender young spring onions

2 tablespoons minced parsley

½ tablespoon of ginger garlic paste

50 grams butter at room temperature

2 or 3 tablespoons milk or cream

1 well-beaten egg

Panko or breadcrumbs as required [About half a cup or less]

Oil of your choice to shallow fry

Salt and pepper to taste

For the Sauce:

1/3 cup well packed zereshk

2 tablespoons sugar

2 tablespoons of butter

2 large cloves garlic

3 tablespoons red wine

Dash of cayenne pepper powder

Pinch of salt

Mix the flaked fish, the mashed potato, and half the butter. Finely mince the spring onions, onions, and the green chillies. Add the spring onion to the fish and potato. Heat the remaining butter in a small pan and fry the onions and green chillies until soft, add the ginger garlic paste and mix well. Cook for a minute more then remove the pan from the heat and cool. Then add to the fish and potato along with the finely chopped parsley. Using your hands, knead the mixture well adding a little milk or cream to moisten, season to taste with salt and pepper. Make 12 cakes in any shape you like, and chill in the refrigerator for 2 or 3 hours. When ready to serve, heat the oil in a large pan, coat the cakes with beaten egg and roll in the crumbs, fry until brown on all sides and serve hot with the sauce.

To make the sauce tip the barberries, the sugar, the finely minced garlic and butter into a small saucepan, and cook on gentle heat until the sugar melts and the berries take on a glaze. Remove from the heat add a dash of cayenne pepper and a pinch of salt. Stir in the wine, mix well and serve with the fish.

Postscript: You will need approximately 500 grams of raw fish cooked in just enough water to cover with a pinch of salt and two sprigs of fresh green mint.

NOOSH –E JAN!

Jaggery or Gur: Sugarcane juice boiled down to a thick concentrate, which is then poured into moulds and allowed to dry. A pale milder yellow variety is less flavorsome than the dark brown almost black variety that is allowed to mature and develop for much longer, resulting in an intense and very distinct flavour. Jaggery stores well, though the wet weather can cause some stickiness. Liquid Jaggery an intermediate product is a thick sweet golden brown syrup.

Baked Fillets of Sole with Tarragon Butter

Enough for 6

You require the following:

1 kg fillets of sole, or two large fish kept whole

50 grams butter at room temperature

1 tablespoon fresh tarragon

1 tablespoon fresh chives

½ a tablespoon fresh parsley

1 tablespoon coriander powder

A squeeze of lemon juice

Salt and pepper to taste

Rinse the fish fillets and pat dry, season with salt, pepper, and the coriander powder. Drizzle with lemon juice and set aside for 15 to 20 minutes. Gently heat half the quantity of butter and pour over the fish, place in a lightly greased ovenproof dish, cover with kitchen foil and bake in a moderate oven until done. Meanwhile, heat the remaining butter, add all the herbs, fry until they crisp and darken, but taking care not to burn them. Remove from the heat and set aside. When the fish is ready, reheat the herb butter gently, and pour over the fish and serve immediately.

Hook Line and Sinker

When the mood got to her, my mother would spring clean the family medicine cabinet. Rather than flinging out unused and surplus drugs, they were collected, boxed and sent off to The Holdsworth Memorial hospital[75], with the chore of checking expiry dates often assigned to me. Going through one lot ready for dispatch, I noticed a glass container full of rather bizarre looking round red pills. On closer inspection the bottle of 'red pills' turned out to be 'Balls of Fire,' my father's prized imported fish bait.

It was in the early 70's that Colonel Rue a close family friend persuaded my father to try his hand at fishing. A great fervour of enthusiasm rubbed off onto all of us, soon replacing an earlier lack of interest. It wasn't long before an extended fishing trip followed our morning shoot for geese. Not only did the Colonel teach our family to fish but also introduced us to the fascinating world of streams, rivers, and lakes. Soon a holiday also included a spot of fishing, and the stories proliferated, about accidents and incidents and about the big ones that got away. There was trout fishing in Kashmir, the backwaters of Kerala, or hooking reef fish from a trawler off the Goa coast.

The Nilgiris, a majestic stretch of mountains just across the border in the state of Tamil Nadu, with its bewitching sweep of wilderness is where we pursued much of this hobby. Here amid the undulating hills of Avalanche, Emerald, or Upper Bhavani, you could spot sambhar, guar and the Nilgiri thar running free. We spent many days of our childhood here tentatively dipping our toes into the still, chilly but pristine waters, while intermittingly doing a spot of trout fishing.

Dr. Francis Day introduced sport fish into the Nilgiris when he experimented with the Brown trout in 1863. While W. McIvor Superintendent of the Ooty Botanical Gardens and H. C. Wilson Conservator of Fisheries get the credit for introducing Rainbow trout imported from Sri Lanka and New Zealand. The Nilgiri trout of today best caught on a fly rod is a

75 The Holdsworth Memorial Hospital: The Holdsworth Memorial hospital was the brain child of Reverend George Sawday; a missionary of the Wesleyan Mission. This good man lived and worked tirelessly in Mysore for over fifty years. The hospital is named for Mary Calvert Holdsworth the wife of Reverend W. W Holdsworth also of the Wesleyan Mission. The foundation stone was laid on the 3rd of June 1904 by Mrs. Holdsworth, and the hospital declared open on the 21st of August 1906 by His Highness Krishnaraja Wadiyar. Our family has had a very close association with the Mission hospital as it is often called; my brothers and I were born there, as were our children. First my parents and later my brother Raian served on the hospital board for many years.

fine-looking rainbow coloured fish and a descendant of the strains brought in by the early pioneers of sport fishing[76].

The tranquil countryside of Mysore and Mandya districts offered the fishing enthusiast a fantastic day out. Fishing for walaga is best attempted during the early morning or late evening, while the best time for murrel is mid afternoon when the fish come up to the surface to feed. For my brothers and me, setting up the rods, agonizing over what to choose, the gold or silver Mepps, or picking the right place to cast off, was just as exciting as landing a fish.

After casting off at the falls in Chunchanakatte a visit to the temple nearby usually followed; all of us salivating at the teeming masheer fed and looked after by the temple priests, and strictly out of bounds for the angler! A picnic lunch at the 'dak' bungalow usually followed a visit to Nugu dam[77] and a great day of fishing in the dam's backwaters. Sometimes we chose Balmuri on the River Cauvery, where the day ended with a spectacular sunset. It was not so long ago, that our waters ran clear, an abundance of fish swam in our rivers, and when gelatine wasn't so routinely used as a weapon of mass destruction.

Postscript: The masheer *[Tor khudree]* highly prized as India's best game fish with numbers now in decline due to habitat loss and overfishing.

The walaga *[Wallago attu]* is a freshwater fish largely found in the sub-continent and South East Asia. It is a species of catfish found in rivers and large lakes and a bottom feeder, preferring the mud and silt of slow moving waters. An aggressive and fast swimmer it can weigh in at 50 kgs. Fillets of walaga dipped in a beer batter and shallow fried are delicious.

Murrel *[Channa striata]* also known as the snakehead murrel is a native species of South and Southeast Asia. A freshwater fish found in rivers and streams and often migrating to flooded rice fields during the monsoons. The famous Bathini Goud brothers of Hyderabad use the fingerlings of the snakehead murrel for their treatment of asthma. You are asked to swallow a live fish. I prefer mine cooked in a spicy curry!

---

76 Source: Ootacamund- A History by Frederick Price published by Rupa & Co. 2002.

77 NuguDam: This earth and gravity dam across the Nugu River built under the supervision of Sir M. Visveshwariah, Mysore's great Statesman, is a part of the Cauvery river basin.

My Grandmother
Motibai

My Grandfather
Khudamorad Irani

Emma Charlotte Kouwen
In her late nineties

My mother as an ambulance driver
during the war

My Grandfather George Fergusson

My Great Grandparents James Fergusson and Jane Constance Gager with their 6 sons

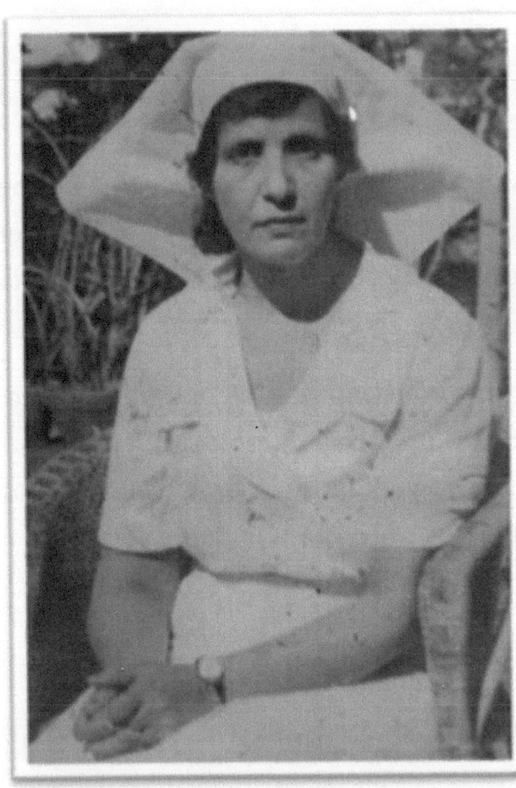

My Grandmother Una Maud

My Great Grandmother Shirine- e anok

13. Chicken

Baked Chicken with Figs and an Apple

Enough for 4 or 5

You require the following:

500 grams chicken

1 firm red apple

200 grams onions

6 to 8 dried figs

2 or 3 red dry Kashmiri chillies or any other mild chilly

¼ cup fresh sage leaves

3 tablespoons olive oil

¼ cup fruity red wine, [I use homemade fig wine]

2 teaspoons Parsee dhanajeera powder

Salt and pepper to taste

Cut the chicken into large pieces, season with salt and a generous amount of pepper and the dhanajeera powder, and set aside for 30 to 40 minutes. Soak the figs in warm water until they swell. Soak the dry red chillies in hot water until they soften, cut the onions in quarters and the apples into eighths.

Lay out the chicken, onions, chillies and figs in a roasting pan or baking dish, add two tablespoons of oil and toss to coat all the ingredients. Pop into a moderate oven and bake for about 20 minutes. Then turn the chicken over, add the apple, the sage leaves, the wine and the remaining oil. Bake for another 10 to 15 minutes or until the chicken's cooked.

Sojourn at Bangalore

A visit to Bangalore had to be justified; in the early days, it was frequently the need to see the dentist. Unhappily, none of us inherited my father's perfect set of teeth that he confidently put down to the toothpaste he used, an uninspiring gritty brown paste called Forhans[78]. The disconcerting prospect of a visit to the dentist was cushioned by the anticipation of a good lunch. There were three options to choose from 'The Continental' that served Chinese food, unpretentious but good value for money, 'Kwality' restaurant with their selection of ice creams a big draw, or the Three Aces, a typical eating place of the '60's and '70's with heavy upholstered furniture, dim lighting, and a long winded menu. Here, patrons could enjoy a late night dinner with a cabaret show; photographs of the voluptuous women who shimmied the night away were pinned up on a noticeboard at the entrance of the restaurant. We looked more than once at these before we sniggered away to our table.

Fitting in a tight schedule necessitated an early departure. The first step was procuring a window seat in the car; usually, there was a negotiated compromise with a switch over at Channapatna, a small town on Highway 17 famous for its wooden toys. We often stopped here for a short break and a steaming hot cup of South Indian filter coffee. The second step required getting into the car without sneezing. My superstitious father believed that a single sneeze at the start of a journey very inauspicious and must be followed by a second, barring which there was a delay of 5 minutes.

A trip to Bangalore wasn't just about dentists and lunch at Three Aces. Every winter holiday during the sixties, my grandmother and I spent a weekend with her sisters at Rose Cottage, in Fraser Town, Ivy in her late eighties and Emma in her seventies. Rose Cottage was an enduring old colonial home where 'Thunder Boxes' still ruled in the toilets. The aunts, whose lifestyle could best be described as late Victorian, introduced me to a different world. I spent most of my time mooching around their shoe rack, trying on their antediluvian collection of black lace up boots and buckled shoes.

78 Forhans, a popular brand of toothpaste during the 50's, 60's and 70's, and created by a dentist.

Yellow Chicken Curry with Eggs

Serves 4 or 5

You require the following:

600 grams chicken cut up in pieces

4 hardboiled eggs

2 or 3 bay leaves [*Laurus nobilis*]

1 teaspoon fennel seeds

1 teaspoon turmeric powder

50 ml thick coconut milk

1 cup spinach torn up

2 tablespoons vegetable oil of your choice

Salt to taste

For the masala:

50 grams ripe red tomato

1/3 cup cashew nuts

75 grams red or white onions

1½ tablespoons ginger garlic paste

1 large green chilly

1 teaspoon coriander powder

Grind all the above masala ingredients into a fine paste using two to three tablespoons of water.

Heat the oil in a heavy bottomed pan on low heat, then add the bay leaves and the fennel seeds and cook gently for 30 seconds. Next, add the turmeric powder, followed up by the ground masala and fry gently adding a little water if necessary, to prevent the masala from burning. [The cashew nut in the ground masala is likely to stick.]Add the chicken and mix well, season with salt and fry another 5 to 8 minutes. Then add just enough water to cover the chicken and cook until nearly, but not quite done. Then add the coconut milk and finish cooking. To serve, slice the hardboiled eggs in half add to the chicken curry along with the spinach, reheat and simmer until the spinach wilts. Serve hot.

Cook's note: Try Asian morning glory, New Zealand Spinach or Komatsuna

Chicken and Wild Mushroom Casserole

Enough for 5 or 6 hearty folk

600 grams chicken cut up

500 grams wild mushrooms

100 grams any fresh pork sausage

175 grams red onions

75 grams bacon

250 ml strong chicken stock

5 cloves garlic

½ teaspoon pepper powder

¼ cup red wine or sherry

½ teaspoon dried rosemary

2 tablespoons fresh parsley

2 tablespoons oil

Sea salt to taste

Marinate the chicken with the crushed garlic, pepper and sea salt for an hour or two. Halve or quarter the mushrooms depending on their size, dice the onions and snip the bacon into pieces. Place a heavy bottomed pan on medium heat, add the oil and when hot tip in the chicken and brown on all sides. When done remove the chicken with a slotted spoon and set aside. In the same oil add the diced onions, sausage meat, and the bacon and fry until lightly browned, then add the mushrooms and the herbs and cook for a few minutes more.

Tip the chicken into a casserole along with the garlic marinade, the onions, sausages, bacon, and mushrooms. Then add the chicken stock and the sherry, and cook in a moderately hot oven until done. Check seasoning and serve with crusty bread or white rice.

Grilled Honeyed Chicken

Enough for 5 or 6

You will require the following:

800 grams chicken [leg and thigh portions]

400 grams zucchini

200 grams red and orange tomatoes

1 tablespoon ginger paste

1 teaspoon freshly ground cumin powder

3 tablespoons store bought honey soy sauce

1 cup chopped bok choy

¼ cup oil as required

Sea salt and pepper to taste

Season the chicken with salt and pepper. Then add the cumin powder, the ginger paste and two tablespoons of the honey soy sauce. Add a tablespoon of oil, mix well, and set the chicken aside for two hours. Quarter the tomatoes, cut the zucchini into large chunks and add to the bok choy. Next, add the remaining soy sauce to the vegetables with a tablespoon of oil. Set the grill on medium heat and grill the chicken, first on one side for about 8 minutes then turn over, basting all the time with the marinade and oil. Test the chicken, remove and set aside when done. Grill the vegetables for 4 to 5 minutes or until done, place the chicken on a platter with the grilled veggies on the side and serve.

Spiced Chicken in Yogurt

Enough for 6 or 7

You require the following:

1 kg chicken

200 grams potatoes

150 grams onions

100 grams tomatoes

1 teaspoon saffron strands

3 cardamoms

3 cloves

1 piece cinnamon, about 2″ long

¼ teaspoon turmeric powder

250 grams thick well-set yogurt

2 tablespoons ghee

1 tablespoons oil

Salt to taste

Grind to a fine paste with a little water

2 tablespoons ginger garlic paste

½ teaspoon cumin

1" stick cinnamon

3 cloves

3 cardamoms

3 dry red chillies

¼ teaspoon turmeric powder

To garnish

200 grams onions thinly sliced and deep fried a nutty brown

Cut up the chicken, finely chop the onions, and mince the tomatoes. Lightly beat the curds and season to taste. Next, add the saffron to the curd along with the ground masala, mix well and marinate the chicken in the yogurt for three hours. Peel and quarter the potatoes sprinkle with a little salt and fry the potatoes in a little oil on all sides until a crispy light brown. Remove with a slotted spoon and set aside. Add the ghee to the remaining oil in the pan, then add the cardamom, cloves, and cinnamon, add the turmeric powder and the onions and fry until they change colour. Next, add the marinated chicken and the chopped tomato. Check seasoning and cook the chicken on a gentle heat until nearly done. Add the potatoes and finish cooking. Just before serving fry the onions until crisp and golden, heat the chicken and pile into a serving dish, sprinkle the onions on top. Super!

> During our childhood, when there was roast on the table, my father would strictly monitor the amount of mustard we helped ourselves too; making sure that it was just enough and no more. He maintained that Mr. Coleman was a wealthy man because most of us take far more mustard than is needed, it's true! Check the evidence on dinner plates after the party.

Baked Rosemary Chicken with Butternut Squash

Enough for 5 or 6

750 grams chicken thigh and drumsticks with skin

350 grams butternut squash

8 to 10 cherry tomatoes

A few sprigs of fresh rosemary

A generous splash of sherry

The juice of one large lemon

The zest of one medium lemon

1 tablespoon butter

1 tablespoon olive oil

3 tablespoons hazelnut oil

Salt and freshly ground pepper

Rub the chicken with salt and pepper and drizzle with the lemon juice, and set aside for an hour. Cut the butternut squash into wedges roll in a little salt and pepper and fry in the butter and olive oil until nicely browned on all sides. In an ovenproof dish tip in the chicken, the rosemary and the squash, add the lemon zest and the hazelnut oil and mix well. Pop into a medium hot oven for 20 minutes. Then turn over the chicken, add the cherry tomatoes and the sherry and return to the oven to finish cooking. Serve immediately.

Pintails and Spot Bills

To a stranger staring at the unfamiliar countryside, the recently harvested paddy fields might have looked lifeless under the November sun. However, to the insider, this was just an illusion. For it was on brisk winter mornings, that we snuggled deep down into the warm toasty haystacks of paddy straw, our heads gently nodding waiting for sunrise, and the arrival of the Bar- headed Goose.

In the millions they came, the slow flapping of wings and the typical honking or 'clanging' note when on the wing, each squadron in a 'V' formation one limb longer than the other one. Temporarily darkening the sky, they would descend onto the freshly cut paddy fields, and feast on the fallen grain strewn through the dry stubble on the hard, cracked earth. Several species of geese visit India, but the Bar-headed Goose, *[Anser indicus]* is the only Southern visitor.

Our day started even earlier, my father woke us at three in the morning, and we had to be up and about and ready to leave by four. It was never the best part of the day, and we promptly fell asleep in the car. Our shooting party was always a small one, a maximum of 4 or 5 guns. Nevertheless, by the end of the day it was not the sport that ruled, but the overwhelming enchantment of the countryside and the affable company of family and friends. Among them, Colonel Jerry Rue, close family friend - our idol. Sanath Kumar, a schoolmaster and always full of good humour, Rustom Mama on a sabbatical from Bombay, Ivan Royal and family, his son Cedric one of our best shots, and Roman, who once preferred pursuing wild duck to his pregnant wife who had just commenced labour!

I was the Colonel's gun bearer with the privilege of carrying his Perdi, a leather cartridge belt secured firmly around my waist, the two's, four's and six's neatly arranged in groups for easy access. The deliberations were endless; the weight of my father's cumbersome but dependable old Greener, the lightness of Rustom Mama's Holland and Holland. There were questions and answers on birds and their habitat, the natural world around us, war stories from Burma and the tenets of good sportsmanship - never shoot a sitting duck, never shoot to injure always to kill, and take only what you need, no more.

Duck habitat is usually fresh water lakes, marshland, reedy ponds, and streams, both big and small. Scattered across the Indian rural landscape are village tanks or ponds, shallow basins holding rainwater often all year round. The resident and migratory ducks both love these community tanks, sharing them with self-indulgent water buffaloes, women washing clothes, and the odd angler or two. The muddy margins are throttled with weeds and brimming with life, fat tadpoles, water striders and dragonflies, the perfect environment for snipe.

Most Indian ducks are migratory, winter visitors arriving post monsoon and staying on until the arrival of spring. The resident ducks include the Spot-bill, usually seen in pairs or small groups, an excellent table bird and recognizable by their slow take off from the water. Other residents include, The Common or Lesser Whistling Teal, large flocks flying in sweeping circles just skimming the surface of the water and The Cotton Teal usually in smaller groups of 10 or 12, inhabiting the smaller lakes and reedy village ponds. They are fast fliers but not good divers unless shadowed by a raptor.

The Pochard and the Gadwall are among the winter visitors venturing south – but very rarely seen. The Ruddy Sheldrake or Brahminy duck also ventures south, a duck strong on the wing and a very good swimmer, but not considered a good bird for the table. You can also spot The Common Teal and the Garganey Teal, usually in large numbers, flying over village tanks. For Christmas lunch, though, only the handsome Pintail would do. The finest and fastest of swimmers its elegant form is easily distinguishable both on the water and on the wing. Cleaving the air with such effortlessness, beauty, and speed, there is also no doubt that as a table bird, the Pintail is truly without equal.

Puttamadiya was the family shikari. With a rock solid rural background, he was indispensable on a duck shoot - responsible for retrieving birds that fell in the water. Stripped down to his green and white striped cotton underpants he would step into the cold water with trepidation. Then treading carefully and working his way through the reeds, he would swim purposefully in the direction of the ducks, with plenty of enthusiastic encouragement from the embankment. Collecting each duck, usually a bag of three or four, he would stick their heads into the top of his underpants so that he could have his hands free to swim back to shore.

14. The Iranian Khoresh

The Iranian khoresh is one of the most delightful dishes to prepare; it's actually a stew with meat and vegetables slowly cooked in a flavourful broth. The many ingredients such as beans and lentils, pumpkin and potatoes, or tart fruit such as plums, quinces or barberries all contribute to making it a great comfort food on a cold winter's day. Though usually served with rice, it is also excellent eaten with fresh crusty bread, brun pao or ting mo. The cooking process cannot be hurried; the khoresh tastes best when allowed to cook slowly in a heavy pot over low heat allowing all the many flavours to meld, an ideal dish for an informal get together of close family or friends.

NOOSH –E JAN!

Apple and Chicken Khoresh [Khoresh-e sib]

Enough for 4 or 5

Brown your meat and onions well!

You require the following:

600 grams chicken [cut up]

100 grams onions

5 medium tart cooking apples

1/3 cup pitted dried cranberries or cherries

3 tablespoons brown sugar

3 tablespoons apple cider vinegar

25 grams butter

1 teaspoon freshly ground pepper

1 teaspoon ground cinnamon

½ teaspoon saffron, dissolved in 2 tablespoons hot water

3 tablespoons vegetable oil of your choice

Sea Salt to taste

Place a heavy bottomed pan on medium heat, add two tablespoons of oil and fry the onions a light yellow. Next, add the chicken, pepper, salt to taste and ground cinnamon and fry the chicken until nicely browned on all sides. Next, add the vinegar, brown sugar and the saffron water to the chicken, and stir a few minutes more. Finally, simmer the chicken with 2 cups of hot water on very low heat until half done.

Meanwhile, core the apples, peel them if you wish, then cut into wedges. In a frying pan add the remaining oil and butter, heat gently and add the apples. Fry the apples until all the sides are a nice rich brown. Transfer the chicken to a deep casserole, along with the cranberries or cherries. Place the apples on top, and pour over any remaining juices from the frying pan, cover and bake in a moderate oven until the chicken is tender.

Aubergine Khoresh [Khoresh-e bademjan]

Enough for 4 people

This is a great favourite of mine because you can recreate the dish each time by varying your selection of eggplant. Baby eggplant, medium, large, long or squat, purple, green, red or white the choices are endless! Try heirloom varieties such as Black Beauty dating from 1901, the lovely Rosita or the Korean Red, some modern hybrids are nearly seedless and are an enjoyable option. Use a non-stick Dutch oven if you have one to make this khoresh.

You require the following:

600 grams mutton or beef cut up

400 grams eggplant

200 grams onions

1 teaspoon garlic paste

1 teaspoon advieh[79]

3 tablespoons tomato puree

½ teaspoon saffron dissolved in a little hot water

½ teaspoon turmeric

1 teaspoon freshly ground pepper

1 or 2 tablespoons lemon juice

1/3 cup vegetable oil of your choice

Salt to taste

79 Advieh is a spice mix used in Iranian cooking, the number of ingredients used can vary, from 8 to 16 elements, buy from a store near you or online.

Place a heavy bottomed cook pot on medium heat, add a little of the oil and brown the onions and meat. Now add the garlic paste, pepper powder, and saffron water, coat the meat and fry a few minutes more. Add two cups of hot water, salt to taste and allow the khoresh to simmer gently on very low heat. Halfway through the cooking, add the tomato puree, lime juice, and the advieh. Add a little hot water now and then if required.

Cut the eggplant into large pieces and sprinkle both sides with salt and the turmeric powder. Rub in gently and set aside for 10 minutes. In a frying pan add the rest of the oil, quickly fry the eggplant on both sides until they crisp and change colour. When the meat is nearly done, add the slices of eggplant and finish cooking on very low heat until done.

Cook's note: If you are using baby eggplant keep them whole, cut off the stem and calyx, then at the other end make two cross cuts half way up. Traditionally the eggplants are peeled, I prefer to retain their skin; it helps the eggplant to hold their shape and adds some colour to the dish.

Crab Hunting at the Hermitage

Recurrently heard at the Hermitage, is the long eerie wail of the Indian jackal *[Canis aurles].* The jackal sometimes prowls around near our homestead, waiting to pounce on a gullible hen. A sturdy bright little fella full of character the jackal is an accomplished poultry thief. The jackal also loves to hunt crabs and is just as accomplished at it. His main hunting grounds are the streams and rivulets of which the jungle abounds. Local lore has it that the jackal dips the tip of his bushy tail into the crabs burrow, mostly found along stream embankments. After the credulous crab grabs hold of it, the jackal yanks him out of his burrow, whacks him hard on the ground, and then proceeds to eat the spoils of his ingenuity.

Throughout the '80's, when the South West monsoons arrived, torrential rains cut us off from the outside world sometimes for a good three months. Low bridges went under water and roads disappeared. During this time, crabs formed an essential part of our diet. Despite the lack of a bushy tail, we did manage to catch quite a few using the following technique described below. With some very simple equipment, enjoy a day out with family and friends. Who knows you might even catch your dinner!

To try this 'at home' you will require the following:

Two bamboo canes of equal length, approximately 3¾ to 4 feet long and around 3/8th of an inch in diameter

24" length of heavy gauge plastic coated all-purpose garden wire

Frog meat for bait but a piece of offal will work just as well

Twine to tie the bait

Sharp penknife

Bucket

Patience [quite a bit]

The canes should feel light and flexible so choose a length that makes you comfortable. Select one of the canes and firmly tie the frog meat directly onto the tip; you don't want it dangling like a fishing rod.

At one end of the second cane, pare off the last 3" of the cane with the penknife, thin it down until it is flexible enough to bend but not break. Using the flexible garden wire form a ring of 3 to 4 inches and attach it just below this point, and secure it firmly by twisting the wire around the cane. Finally, pass the 3" of thinned, [pared]cane through the ring bend it over and secure with the balance of the wire. You are now all set to hunt crabs.

The time of day does not really matter. Pick a shallow stream or brook so that you can more or less walk in it, a pair of reef shoes comes in handy. Look out for crab burrows they are usually at, or just below water level. Burrows under rocks are prime real estate, so poke around.

Hold the cane with the loop in your left hand, slip the cane with the bait through the loop and hold it in your right hand. Insert the cane with the bait into a crab burrow and keep still, it may take a while to interest a mistrustful crab so be patient. The instant you feel a tug lower the loop towards the bait, the crab will grab the bait with its claw, gently but firmly try to draw it out. The moment a sizeable section of the claw emerges, slip the loop over it and twist it tight by turning the cane in an anti-clockwise direction. Gently draw the crab out of its burrow using both the canes, if you jerk or pull too hard the crab will drop his pincer and scuttle back into his burrow. Once you have your crab, tip it into the bucket, release the loop, reload the bait and move on!

Postscript: Plastic coated all-purpose garden wire is an alternative to what we use out here, thin strips of the inner bark taken from the young branches of either the Kemani or Kumbai tree. Choose a material that is stiff but still flexible enough to twist.

Khoresh with Beans [Khoresh-e lubia sabzi]

Good for 4 to 5 hungry people

You require the following:

750 grams meat [choose your favourite]

3 cups runner beans, winged beans or Chinese red snake beans

200 grams red or white onions

1/3 cup tomato puree

100 grams tomato quartered

1 tablespoon freshly ground pepper

½ teaspoon turmeric powder

4 tablespoons vegetable oil of your choice

Juice of one lime

Sea Salt to taste

In a heavy bottomed pot heat two tablespoons of oil, add the meat and brown on all sides. Add the onions and fry until golden brown. Then add the turmeric and pepper powder, and stir until well blended. Add the tomato puree and a little water if necessary and allow the mixture to cook for a few minutes, season to taste with the salt. Add 2 cups of hot water and bring to boil. Then let the Khoresh simmer for about 45 minutes, adding more hot water during the cooking process if needed. Meanwhile, cut the beans into pieces, heat the remaining oil and fry the beans until they begin to glisten, and then add to the meat. Cook the meat on a low heat until done. Towards the end, add the lime juice and quartered tomatoes, adjust seasoning and allow the khoresh to cook a few minutes more until the tomatoes soften. Partners very well with yellow coconut rice serve nice and hot.

Khoresh with Herbs [Khoresh-e ghormeh sabzi]

Enough for 4 to 5

This dish needs some long slow cooking; make it for Sunday lunch or on bank holidays. Patience is well rewarded!

You require the following:

600 grams mutton or beef

100 grams dried red kidney beans or black beans

100 grams red or white onions

100 grams onion leeks or spring onions

1 tablespoon freshly ground pepper

1 teaspoon garlic paste

1 tablespoon lime juice

1 teaspoon turmeric

4 cups mixed herbs[80]

4 whole Persian limes[81]

1 or 2 tablespoons dried Persian lime powder

1/3 cup olive oil or any vegetable oil of your choice

Sea salt to taste

Soak the kidney beans for several hours or preferably overnight. Drain the beans and rinse with fresh water. In a heavy bottomed pot, add a little oil, and on medium heat fry the

80 Use your favourite herbs, which can include parsley, coriander, dill, fenugreek, and garlic or onion chives.

81 Persian limes See page 274.

onions. When they start to change colour, add the chopped meat, black pepper, turmeric powder and garlic paste and brown the meat well, about 10 to 12 minutes. Add a little water now and then if the meat begins to stick. Next, add the onion leeks or spring onions and fry until they start to wilt. Next, add the beans, salt to taste and the pricked Persian limes. Next, enough water to cover and simmer on low heat for 30 to 40 minutes.

Finely chop the herbs. Heat a heavy bottomed frying pan, add the herbs and dry them off as much as you can without burning them. Remove from the heat and cool. Add the remaining oil to the pan, heat again and add the herbs. Fry until they begin to crisp and darken about 15 to 18 minutes. Finally, add the herbs to the cook pot along with the lime juice and Persian lime powder. Add a little more hot water if required. Cover the pan and cook for a further 20 minutes or until the meat and beans are soft. Check seasoning. Serve with white Basmati or Jasmine rice

NOOSH -E JAN!

Ghee: An early memory that lingers is the guilt free usage of ghee or clarified butter in South Indian cuisine. At the Woodlands, they poured the stuff onto your steaming rice and sambhar. You cooked with it and swallowed your unpleasant Ayurvedic medication with a spoonful. The Vaidya* still endorses it. I agree, ghee gives a curry that distinctive flavour that no other cooking medium can. Scrambled eggs taste much better cooked up in ghee and be generous!

*Ayurvedic physician

15. Meat

Anglo-Indian Pepper Fry

Plenty for 4

Traditionally eaten with pepper water and white rice but just as delicious mopped up with warm crusty bread, lavash or Tibetan 'Ting Mo'!

You require the following:

500 grams mutton or beef

150 grams red onions

2 tablespoons freshly ground pepper

1 teaspoon cumin powder

1 tablespoon ginger garlic paste

½ cup fresh or frozen green peas

100 grams potatoes diced

3 tablespoons vegetable oil

Salt to taste

Place the cubed meat in a pressure cooker with a little salt and just enough water to cover and cook until nearly, but not quite done, set aside to cool. Fry the finely chopped onions in hot oil until golden, but do not burn. Add the pepper and cumin powders and the ginger garlic paste to onions, and cook until the oil separates from the masala. Next, add the potatoes and green peas and fry both for a few minutes, until the potatoes brown on all sides. Next, add the meat and fry for further two or three minutes. Add a little of the meat stock cover the pan and allow the potatoes, peas and meat to cook. Keep adding a little stock now and then as required until the meat is tender and the vegetables are cooked. Uncover and dry off some of the liquid, leaving you with thick brown gravy clinging gently to the meat.

Railway Mutton Curry

4 helpings

In the sixties and early seventies, long distance travel entitled first class passengers to an entire bogie to themselves. In the days of the steam locomotive, a journey to Poona took a good two days. Daylight hours revolved around 'snakes and ladders,' 'happy families,' a large red thermos and biscuit tins full of surprises. At sundown, our attention turned to bulging canvas bedrolls. At country stations, we watched the signalman's cane hoop with its leather pouch and precious key being handed over, the subsequent waving of green flags, running feet, and a flash of red as a harried coolie rushed past. Doors banged, and a quick sharp whistle followed. A sudden jerk and then slow movement, and more whistles, thin and piercing as we picked up momentum. There are memories of shunting engines, switching from narrow to medium gauge, and above all a fulfilling evening meal of Railway Mutton Curry!

You will require the following:

500 grams plump mutton chops

100 grams potatoes

150 grams onions

100 ml thick coconut milk

1 tablespoon ginger garlic paste

2 sprigs curry leaves

2 tablespoons tamarind paste

2 or 3 tablespoons ghee

Salt to taste

For the ground masala:

4 mild red chillies

1 teaspoon cumin seed

2 tablespoons coriander seed

½ a freshly grated coconut

Grind to a fine paste with a little water retain the masala water.

Prepare the meat and marinate it with the ginger garlic paste and a little salt, set aside for two hours. Finely slice the onions, heat the ghee and fry along with the curry leaves for 3 to 4 minutes. Add the meat and brown on all sides, and then add the ground masala.

Continue to cook until the raw smell of the masala disappears, adding a little of the masala water if required to prevent the masala from drying out. Then add just enough water to cover the meat, lower the heat and cook until nearly but not quite done. Next, add the potatoes and the coconut milk, and simmer until done and the meat is soft and tender. Finally, add the tamarind paste and cook for a further 5 to 6 minutes. Serve hot with rice, naan or paratha.

Tomato Glassie with Plain White Rice

Good for 4 or 5 people

Made of succulent Bannur mutton, it is delicious eaten with fluffy white rice. One of the ingredients in the glassie is a generous amount of sweet pickle. My grandmother used a 'Bolts' specialty called 'Major Grays Sweet Mango Pickle.' If the pieces of mango in your pickle are large, chop them up.

You will require the following:

750 grams mutton chops
400 grams fully ripe red tomatoes
100 grams tomato puree
200 grams onions
1 teaspoon paprika powder
½ teaspoon turmeric powder
2 teaspoons coriander powder
1 teaspoon cumin powder
1 tablespoon garlic paste
300ml strong meat stock or one or two stock cube's dissolved in water
1/3 cup homemade or store-bought sweet mango chutney
2 teaspoons red wine vinegar
¼ cup vegetable oil of your choice
Sea salt to taste

Blanch the tomatoes, skin them, and chop them as fine as you can. Finely mince the onions. In a large pot or pressure cooker heat the oil, add the onions and fry to a nice light brown. Next, add all the spice powders, and fry for a minute more, then add the garlic paste and stir well, adding a little stock if the onions begin to stick. Next, add the tomatoes and fry for a few minutes, as the mixture starts to thicken pour in the stock a little at a time to keep the mixture moist, continue until the tomatoes are soft and a nice thick gravy forms, takes about 20 to 30 minutes. Add the tomato puree and season to taste. Next, add the meat, any remaining stock, a cup of water and cook until the meat is tender. Finally, add the vinegar and chutney and cook a further 10 minutes. Save leftovers, scrumptious the next day!

Cooks note: You can add a potato and half a cup of green peas to the dish if you like.

Lemon Grass: a tropical grass with a swollen leaf base used to flavour Asian food. Peel off the tough outer layers to uncover a white under layer. It is best to use only about 12 cms of the leaf base, crushed lightly to release more flavour. For a continuous supply, slice and sundry the lemongrass and store in an airtight container. Soak in warm water for 1 hour to reconstitute the quantity you require, before using it to cook.

Anglo-Indian Brown Stew

Makes 4 to 5 servings

Stews are the epitome of home cooked food, and so it was, that brown stew was the first thing we asked for when home from boarding school, simple, down to earth but also an affirmation that we were home at last!

You require the following:

750 grams mutton chops

200 grams onions

1 tablespoon ginger garlic paste

2 teaspoons brown sugar

100 grams potato

100 grams carrot

1/4 cup green peas

3 rashers of bacon

6 to 8 small button onions

6 to 8 black peppercorns

3 tablespoons tomato puree

3 tablespoons vegetable oil of your choice

Salt to taste

Dice the carrots and potatoes and finely mince the onions. Peel the button onions and keep them whole. Place a pot on medium heat, add the oil, and throw in the peppercorns and the brown sugar and heat gently for a couple of minutes. Then add the minced onions and cook them until they turn a nice golden brown. Next, add the bacon and fry a few moments more, then add the chops and the ginger garlic paste. Cook the meat until it browns lightly adding a little water now and then to prevent the meat from sticking, season to taste. When done, add enough water to cover the meat and cook until nearly done. Finally, add all the vegetables, the button onions, and the tomato puree and check seasoning again. Finish cooking the meat and vegetables. Serve the brown stew with fluffy basmati or jasmine rice!

Curry of Breast Meat

Enough for 5 people

Best served with slices of lime, tomato and onion salsa and rice

You require the following:

800 grams breast meat

200 grams red onions

3 sprigs of mature curry leaves

100ml thick coconut milk

2 tablespoons ghee or vegetable oil of your choice

Salt to taste

Grind to a fine paste with a little water:

1 tablespoon ginger garlic paste

2 teaspoon cumin seed

1 teaspoon mustard seed

2 tablespoon coriander seed

½ teaspoon turmeric powder

Cook the breast meat with a little salt and just enough water to cover cook until nearly done. Place a pot on medium heat, add the oil and sauté the finely chopped onions. Add one sprig curry leaf to the onions. Add a little of the meat stock from time to time if the pot starts to run dry. Continue until the onions turn a golden brown. Then add the ground masala and continue to fry the masala for at least 5 to 8 minutes, adding more stock if required. Add the breast meat to the cook pot, and let the meat simmer until done. Check seasoning, add the remaining curry leaves and the coconut milk and simmer for 5 to 8 minutes more. Serve hot with rice, and if you like, a small bowl of melted ghee on the side.

NOOSH –E JAN!

The Irani Restaurant

My grandfather, Khudamorad Jamshed Irani, owned a piece of land in Golibaar Maidan, an area once on the outskirts of Poona city but now, of course, a part and parcel of it. It was a stretch of grassland and being a thrifty man; he rented it to local shepherds to graze their sheep albeit for a pittance. Nevertheless, three times a week he would cycle to the Maidan to collect his rent, and on his return, like clockwork, drop in at 'The Kohinoor,' an Irani restaurant on Main Street. He looked forward to his visits and his cup of hot Irani tea. But most of all, my grandfather went to rekindle memories of the 'old country,' to bond with his fellow compatriots who congregated there, to muse and to reminisce in a patois that only they could understand.

The arrival of Iranian immigrants, both Muslim and Zoroastrian into India in the mid to late 19th century saw the burgeoning of these niche restaurants mainly in the cities of Bombay and Poona. Found everywhere, on lively high streets, bustling markets, at the junction of busy crossroads they were the first eating houses that catered to the common man irrespective of caste or class. Moreover, the common person approved, unequivocally, and so the quintessential Indian 'Irani Restaurant' became an icon of social equality, enterprise, and integration.

The décor of the Irani Restaurant was, and still is, distinctive, nothing ostentatious but certainly with subtle colonial overtones. Spacious high ceilings, round marble-topped tables on ornate wooden stands, bentwood chairs and a plethora of Belgium mirrors; simple even basic but genteel nevertheless. The food, like the décor, was unpretentious and straightforward, cheap but wholesome. Profits were sustained because of the sheer number of patrons that streamed in throughout the day, and on the 'Chai,' that cup of ubiquitous 'Irani Chai'. The menu bordered on the eccentric, a confluence of disparate food traditions, which meant that you weren't too far away from a spicy mutton samosa, vegetable palau or roast chicken with potatoes.

Numbers have dwindled, and the ethos may have changed. My grandfather and his fellow compatriots are long gone, and with them the sweet, gentle notes of their foreign tongue, but to a large extent, the Irani restaurant is still an oasis in today's urban sprawl, providing succour and a cheap, wholesome meal no matter what your caste or creed.

OoseBrenj - Meat and Lentil Stew

Enough for 6 hearty appetites

The origins of Oos are lost in time but believe it has its roots in the old Zoroastrian communities of Iran. Though similar, it is not in the repertoire of modern Iranian cooking.

You require the following:

1 kg mutton[82] on the bone

1¼ litre water

1 litre additional meat stock

¼ cup black eyed peas

¼ cup whole black masoor [whole masoor]

¼ cup whole green moong [whole moong]

2 tablespoons gram dhal

1½ cups boiled rice [leftovers will do nicely]

250 grams onions

1 tablespoon ginger garlic paste

¼ teaspoon turmeric

2 teaspoons pepper powder

¼ cup fresh coriander leaves

¼ cup fresh dill leaves

¼ cup fresh parsley

2 tablespoons ghee

Salt to taste

Serve with slices of limes or lemons

Soak the dhals in water overnight, drain, and pressure cook until just done. Cook the gram dhal separately. Cube the meat and marinate with the ginger garlic paste and a little salt for 3 hours or overnight. Finely chop the onions and herbs. In a heavy bottomed pan, add the ghee and fry the onions until they change colour, then add the mutton and brown on all sides. Add the pepper and turmeric and fry a minute more. Add the water, season to taste and cook covered on a slow fire until the meat is just over half done. Then, drain the dhals and add to the pot along with the stock. Cook the meat until nearly done, check seasoning

82 Beef is taboo in Zoroastrian homes in India, but if you should prefer to use it instead of mutton, I am sure it will work just as well.

again. Next, add the rice,the herbs, and simmer until cooked, the meat should be tender and the lentils soft and creamy. Remove from the heat, rest ten minutes then serve with slices of lime.

Meat and Peas

Enough for 3 or 4

This thick dry curry is delicious eaten with fresh hot parathas, chapatis or freshly made dosas. Dry out the curry until you get to the consistency you like. Eat with your fingers.

You require the following:

500 grams meat

1 cup fresh or frozen green peas

75 grams onions

2" piece of cinnamon

¼ cup tomato puree

½ cup green coriander

1½ tablespoons of ghee

Salt to taste

For the masala:

1/3 cup freshly grated coconut

100 grams onions

3 dried red chillies

¼ teaspoon turmeric powder

½ teaspoon ground cloves

1 teaspoon coriander seeds

1 teaspoon cumin seeds

3 cloves of garlic

Grind the above ingredients to a fine paste with a little water. Rinse out the grinder and retain this water.

Place a pot on medium heat, add the ghee, the finely sliced onions, and cinnamon, and cook until the onions turn colour. Then add the ground masala, mix well and allow it to cook slowly adding the masala water a little at a time to keep it moist. Once the masala has cooked, add the meat and brown for about 3 to 4 minutes. Add the tomato puree, season to taste and just enough hot water to cover the meat, and cook until nearly done. Add the green peas and finish cooking. Just before serving reheat and add the finely chopped fresh green coriander.

Meat in Beans

Makes 4 generous servings

You require the following:

500 grams meat cubed

100 grams dried beans

150 grams onions thinly sliced

4 tablespoons pomegranate paste

1 or 2 teaspoons brown sugar

3 tablespoons ghee

Salt to taste

For the curry paste:

3 to 4 dry Kashmiri chillies

2 tablespoons coriander seeds

2 teaspoons cumin seeds

½ teaspoon turmeric

2 tablespoons ginger garlic paste

2 teaspoons peppercorns

1 teaspoon mustard seeds

3 cardamoms

Grind the masala ingredients above to a fine paste using a little water.

Soak the beans overnight or for at least 6 hours, drain and pressure cook in fresh water. Cool and drain the beans. Next in a heavy bottomed pan or pressure cooker, heat two tablespoons of ghee and nicely brown the meat on all sides, then remove the pieces of meat with a slotted spoon and set aside. Add the remaining ghee to the pan, tip in the onions and fry until they turn a light brown. Next, add the curry paste and continue to cook a few minutes more, adding a little water if necessary to prevent the mixture from sticking. Put the pieces of meat back into the pan, and season to taste. Then add just enough hot water to cover the meat and cook until nearly done. Then add the beans and check seasoning once again. Cook until the meat and beans are soft and tender. Towards the end, add the pomegranate paste, and a teaspoon or two of sugar cook two minutes more. You're done!

Cook's tip: Use any dry beans of your choosing; Lima, kidney or garbanzo beans are all good. Do not add salt or acidic ingredients such as lemon, vinegar, wine, or tomatoes to the beans as they cook. These ingredients cause the beans to toughen and to split.

Wasabi Paste: Treat this 'Pistachio' green, pungent paste with respect, too much of it and your nose will catch fire! Made from the green roots of the Japanese Wasabi plant it is similar to horseradish or hot mustard. Usually sold in tubes or as a powder, wasabi paste is great in a pasta sauce, mayonnaise or mixed into a sandwich spread.

Bannur

I have not visited Bannur in years, but like so many places elsewhere in the provinces, this small moussafil town just an hour's drive from Mysore must be quite changed. Bannur was highlighted on our childhood map of the world, for we often passed through on our way to the temple town of Somanathpur while officiating as guides to visiting relatives, or distinguished guests from overseas.

The region's other claim to fame is its sheep. Indian sheep breeds are classified rather loosely; there are neither breeding societies nor any formal agency to register breeds, maintain breeding records or to ensure the purity of a line. Certain distinctive characteristics and location are what give a breed its name. The Bannur Sheep is small in stature; white but sometimes with a pale brown face, and long droopy ears. It is without a doubt, the best meat breed of the country.

The Mysore mutton market always had 'Bannur' on sale. The hanging carcasses all sporting white woolly tails to guarantee potential customers that what they were buying was authentic. Our butcher had his stall near the entrance. A leg of mutton and breast meat were favourite cuts, and available for a princely sum of six rupees a kilo.

Bannur mutton is simply outstanding, and every Mysorean will agree that nothing else compares! Rustom Mama thought so too, and on his frequent visits to Mysore, meals at Krupalaya were adjusted to accommodate an extra meat dish or two! A day before he left for home Granny Fergusson would make a special trip to the Mysore mutton market and purchase a good 5 to 6 kilos of prime Bannur. Chilled for 24 hours and then well packed, Rustom Mama would board his Indian Airlines flight back to Bombay, his five kgs of prime Bannur mutton and his signature black briefcase taken on board as hand luggage!

'Dhan Sakh, French Beans and Tongue of Goat'

My father wrote this letter to his parents in 1957. Dhan Sakh is a Parsee classic made with breast mutton, lentils, vegetables, and spices. It is prepared and eaten during a wake after the completion of the four-day prayers; hence, it is a dish that is never served on auspicious occasions such as a birthday celebration. At Krupalaya, it was a Sunday lunch regular. The Tongue of Goat recipe that my father asked for is an Irani speciality; often cooked by Nergis Fui for my father on her visits to Mysore. All 'Irani's' eat French Beans!

"Bloomfield"

Vasantha Mahal Road,

Mysore

9/11/57

My dear mother and dad,

This is to inform you that I have arrived safely in Mysore. I am giving you herewith the recipe how to make mulberry wine, so please do exactly as I tell you. Please write to me clearly in Gujarati and let me know how you make "Dhan sakh" French Beans and Tongue of goat. The whole family is most welcome to come to our house in Mysore, and if you want to come down for a holiday, you are most welcome. Try and come in this month as the weather is very good. Give my salaams to all.

The recipe is. . .

Take 4 lbs of mulberries in sound condition, i.e., they must not be very soft or very hard and pour on top of them 2 gallons about 12 bottles of boiling water. Then crush the mulberries with a spoon and make them into a pulp and cover it up with a cloth.

Next day strain it through a Sadra and put 2 lbs of sugar to every gallon of the juice and 2 cloves [lavang]. Boil all this very slowly for about an hour removing the dirt all the time from the top by a spoon. Then take it down. When the liquor has cooled down add to it a very small quantity of yeast [which you can buy from Drug Stores] and pour it in a big jar. Leave the jar open** for 20 days. After 20 days add 2 Pegs of Brandy, and then close the jar. It will take about 6 months for the wine to be ready.

**Because fermentation is taking place

Your loving son

Farrokh

The Sadra that my father mentions is a cotton vest worn by the followers of Zarathustra along with the Kasti, the sacred thread that is tied as a girdle around the waist, both are of great religious significance. The kasti that symbolizes the tenets of the faith is made up of 72 strands of the purest lamb's wool, corresponding to the seventy-two chapters of the Yasna, the Book of Worship. The Sadra is made of white cotton or muslin and must be worn next to the skin. It has a 'V' shaped neck at the bottom of which, is a 1" square pocket the gireban, or pocket of good thoughts, the most important symbol of the Sadra. A young Zoroastrian is given his or her first Sadra and Kasti at an initiation ceremony called the Navjote.

Nobody throws away their old Sadra's, in the old days, every household had a cupboard set aside to store them. They are required for a person's last journey to the Towers of Silence; the gehan or iron bier is covered with strips of cloth made from them. Shrinking living spaces may have hastened the extinction of this serviceable old cupboard, but we still don't throw away our old Sadras. My cousin Kayandokth first cuts out the gireban and uses her old Sadra's to polish the family silver. At Krupalaya, strips were handed over to Murthy to brighten the sheen of his French polish.

In Poona, the family's wholesale liquor business was located in the backyard of No. 42 Sassoon Road. Trucks bringing in stocks from all over the country often travelled long distances on potholed roads, and as a result, there were many breakages. Nergis Fui who was a firm believer in 'Waste not Want not' strained the liquor from the broken bottles through her old Sudras. Not only did she and I enjoy many a glass of good malt whiskey, the truck drivers, cleaners, and the 'hamals' who loaded and unloaded the trucks were also beneficiaries of her largesse, thanks to the Sadra!

Here are some things we do with our old Sadras:
Used as a strainer for Mulberry wine!
Perfect for making homemade panir and cottage cheese
Covering burnis of mango or gajer nu achar [mango and carrot pickle]
Cleaning computer screens
Sprouting moong beans
Polishing spectacles
Wrapping up jewellery
Storing a precious heirloom sari

16. Pork

Farrokh's Pork Curry

Enough for 5 or 6

Pork has always been a family favourite, and wild boar with it's incomparable and unique gamey flavour often graced our table. Farm reared, free range is probably the contemporary option, if available near you.

You require the following:

1 kg boneless pork with some fat

200 grams red onions

120 grams carrots

100 grams sweet potatoes

1 teaspoon black pepper powder

½ teaspoon turmeric powder

½ cup tomato puree

2 teaspoon sugar

¼ cup pomegranate [paste rob-e- anar][83]

2 or 3 tablespoons vegetable oil of your choice

Salt to taste

For the masala paste:

3 Goa chillies [Mapsa] [84]

2 tablespoons ginger garlic paste

6 peppercorns

6 cloves

6 cardamoms

---

83 If Kashmiri or the Goa chillies from Mapsa not available near you, use a mild Mexican variety.

84 Replace with any other acidifying agent such as tamarind or kudampuli syrup, but adjust quantity accordingly.

2 "piece cinnamon

1 teaspoon cumin seeds

1 teaspoon coriander seeds

Grind all the above ingredients to a fine paste using a little water.

Cube the pork, finely slice the onions and dice the carrots and the sweet potato. Heat a tablespoon of oil in a pan; add the carrots and the sweet potato, a little salt to taste and the black pepper powder and fry on all sides until crisp. Remove from the heat and set aside untill needed.

In a pressure cooker heat, the remaining oil and add the onions and the meat and fry until browned on all sides. Add the turmeric powder and fry a minute more, next add the curry paste and cook until done, adding a little water if required to stop the masala from sticking. Add the tomato puree and season to taste. Then add just enough water to cover the meat and pressure cook until just done. Then tip in the vegetables and cook a few minutes more without the lid until the veggies are cooked. Add the sugar and the pomegranate paste mix well and serve piping hot.

Ginger Garlic Paste: My companion for life! To make the paste at home, grind two large, plump pods of garlic and a plump piece of ginger 4 to 5 inches long with a little water to a fine consistency. Store in the refrigerator for up to two or three weeks, but if you can't be bothered with the extra work, there are plenty of commercial brands to choose from in the stores.

Goan Chorizo with Adzuki Beans

Enough for 4

Excellent with a traditional heirloom rice and green chutney on the side

You require the following:

300 grams Goan Chorizo

100 grams dry adzuki beans

175 grams white onions

150 grams tomatoes

1/4 cup tomato puree

50 grams green peas

1 teaspoon sugar or palm sugar

¼ cup coarsely chopped green coriander.

¼ cup parsley

¼ cup chives

Salt to taste

Soak the adzuki beans overnight, then rinse the beans and pressure cook without any salt in approximately two cups of water until just done. Drain and set aside until needed. Meanwhile, place the chorizo in the pressure cooker with about 1½ cups of water and cook until done, remove from the heat and cool. Quarter the onions and roughly chop the tomatoes and the herbs. Tip the chorizo, the beans, green peas, tomato puree, and onions into a heavy bottomed pan and season to taste. Top up with a little water if necessary, cover the pot and cook on a low heat for 30 minutes, or until the beans are soft, and the chorizo is cooked. Halfway through, add the chopped tomatoes, and towards the end add the coriander and other herbs. Cook a few minutes more, remove from the heat and serve hot with rice, fresh Goan poee, brun pao or pita bread.

Cook's note: There is a broad range of homemade Goan Chorizo available on store shelves varying in heat from mild to blistering. Choose something mild. If Goan chorizo is unavailable near you, use any other chorizo that has a mild but spicy flavour.

If adzuki beans aren't available near you, substitute with any other beans of your choice, such as black-eyed peas, baby kidney beans, navy beans and so on.

In hot weather kitchens, refrigerate beans while they soak to prevent fermentation.

Pork in Yogurt and Black Pepper Sauce

Enough for 4

You will require the following:

500 grams pork with some fat

250ml thick well set yoghurt

100 grams red onions

1 teaspoon turmeric powder

3 sprigs curry leaves

1 tablespoon Asian black pepper sauce

2 tablespoons vegetable oil of your choice

Salt to taste

For the Masala
6 black peppercorns
3 green cardamoms
1" piece cinnamon
1 tablespoon ginger garlic paste
Grind together to a fine paste with a little water

Cube the pork and finely slice the onions. Heat the oil in a pressure cook, and on medium heat add the onions and fry until a light brown. Next, add the turmeric and stir a minute more, then add the ground curry paste and cook until the rawness of the masala disappears. Then add the pieces of pork and fry in the masala for about 8 minutes, adding a little water now and then to prevent the meat from sticking. Season with salt, and then add just hot water to cover the meat and pressure cook until done, remove from the heat and cool.

About 15 minutes before serving beat the yoghurt well with a fork. Place the pork back on the heat, and add the yoghurt along with the curry leaves and the tablespoon of pepper sauce. Mix well and cook through on low heat, do not bring to boil, serve immediately with white rice and a vegetable on the side.

17. On the Side

Green Peas and Carrots in Asian Lemon Sauce

Enough for 6 as a side dish

You require the following:

400 grams tender yellow or orange carrots

300 grams fresh or frozen green peas

1 teaspoon caraway seed

1/4 teaspoon turmeric powder

1 teaspoon coriander powder

1 tablespoon butter

1 tablespoon olive oil

The zest of half a lemon

1 or 2 tablespoons Asian lemon sauce

A few microgreens to scatter on top

Salt to taste

Heat the oil and the butter together in a heavy bottomed pan. Add the caraway seeds, turmeric and coriander powder and fry gently for half a minute. Then add the green peas, finely sliced carrots, lemon zest and coat well with the oil and spices. Add just enough water to cover the vegetables, season to taste, and cook on medium heat until done. Dry off the water and add the lemon sauce. Serve with the microgreens peppered on top.

Glazed Carrots and Prunes with Orange and Coriander

Good for two or three

You require the following:

350 grams bright orange or yellow carrots

1 medium red capsicum

1/3 cup ready to eat prunes [roughly chopped]

1 cup freshly squeezed orange juice

1 tablespoon orange zest

1 tablespoon brown sugar

25 grams butter

½ a teaspoon coriander seeds

1 teaspoon dhania dhal

1 or 2 tablespoons fresh parsley

A few grains of salt

Dice the carrots and cut the capsicum into strips, removing the inner pith. Lightly roast then grind the coriander seed. Place a heavy bottomed pan over medium heat add the butter and brown sugar. When the sugar has melted, and the butter caramelized, add the carrots and toss well. Then add the orange zest and continue to fry the carrots until they begin to glisten. Add the salt, the coriander powder, and the orange juice and cook on medium heat. When the carrots start to soften, add the capsicum and continue to simmer the vegetables until done. When the liquid begins to dry up, tip in the dhania dhal and the prunes and cook through. Sprinkle with the chopped parsley and serve warm.

The Cheese Board

Krupalaya was home to serious cheese aficionados! We were a family that was constantly nosing around for that rare slice of well-made cheese. Imports made up for the scarcity of any cheese in our local markets. A great favourite was Dutch ball cheese with its coating of thick red wax, which we loved to peel off and squish. A ball didn't last very long at Krupalaya.

A good family friend lived in Madras and was an assiduous purveyor of an assortment of imported cheese to satisfy our insatiable appetites. The news came in one morning that the arrival of a courier was imminent bringing us a parcel of our favourite Dutch ball cheese. Much to our delight, the package turned out to be a well-secured large wooden crate. The family gathered around while Krishna with a pry bar and claw hammer broke into it. The peculiar and unpleasant smell that emanated was ominous, and with expectations running high, picture our utter dismay, when we discovered a dozen delicious balls of cheese rendered inedible by six-inch nails piercing through them like needles in a pincushion.

The Humble Mashed Potato

Basics!

The perfect mash requires a variety of potato with high starch content; Lasoda, Pink eye, Yukon gold and the Russets are good varieties to choose. The potatoes should have a fresh looking taut skin, and do reject any tinged with green or what looks suspiciously like rot.

You can pressure cook the potatoes as long as they are not overcooked. Or else peel, roughly chop and steam, boil or microwave them. The age of the potatoes, the variety you use, and the cooking method all determine how much liquid the potatoes absorb. For the perfect mash, the quantity of milk required therefore varies, and must be determined as you go along.

Remember to mash the potatoes while still hot, and any liquid added to the mash must also be hot, this is best done by using a potato masher, or push the potatoes through a fine sieve. Avoid using a food processor as the result will be a gluey mess and you don't want that. Serve the mashed potato at room temperature or heat gently under the grill for a few minutes.

Repurpose leftover mashed potato by filling buttered individual ramekins; top with a mixture of roughly minced nuts, Parmesan or Cheddar cheese your favourite herb and buttered breadcrumbs. Bake in a medium oven until warmed through and the cheese has melted. Use leftover mash to form cakes with a vegetable or meat filling, dip in beaten egg roll in breadcrumbs and shallow fry.

Roasted Garlic: I roast my garlic in the dying embers of the wood fire that heats our daily bath water. Choose two large plump garlic bulbs; gently pull off any loose papery skin and with a sharp knife knock off the 'head' and a little bit more, about a ¼ of an inch. Place the bulbs on a piece of heavy-duty aluminum foil to protect against charring, sprinkle with salt and freshly ground black pepper and a tablespoon of olive oil, mix well. Fold the aluminum foil into a secure parcel, using another piece or two to protect the garlic. Roast in the embers of a wood fire for 20 minutes or under a grill for 15 to 20 minutes. Gently squeeze the soft cloves out of their skins when done.

Mashed Turnips and Potatoes with Turnip Greens

Makes 4 to 5 servings

You require the following:

300 grams potatoes

400 grams turnips

50 grams red or white onions

2 or 3 cloves of garlic

½ cup turnip or radish greens or any other greens of your choice

¼ cup cream or milk or as required

Knob of butter

1 tablespoon olive oil

Salt and pepper to taste

Wash, peel and dice the potatoes and turnips, then steam until done and set aside to cool slightly. With a knob of butter, mash the vegetables until nice and smooth, do this while still hot. Meanwhile, mince the onions, crush the garlic and chop the greens. Heat the olive oil in a pan, add the onions and garlic, and fry until the onions turn a nice medium brown. Now add the greens and continue to fry until cooked but still a little crisp. Remove from the heat, cool slightly then add to the potato and turnip mash. Add cream or milk as required to reach a smooth, creamy consistency, season to taste with salt and pepper and serve warm.

Mashed Potato with Red Amaranth

4 servings

You require the following:

600 grams potato

150 grams onions

1/4 cup milk or cream or as required

1½ cup well packed ruby red amaranth greens

3 to 5 cloves garlic

Small knob of ginger

1 small green chilly [optional but gives a satisfying bite]

1 teaspoon Parsee dhanajeera powder

30 grams of butter

1 tablespoon oil

Salt and pepper to taste

Pressure cook the potatoes and set aside to cool slightly, and then peel them. While still hot, add half the butter and mash them until nice and smooth. Finely chop the amaranth and the onions, and mince the garlic, chilli, and ginger. Place a pan over medium heat, add the remaining butter and oil and fry the onions, ginger, garlic and green chilli for a few minutes. Add the dhanajeera powder, and season to taste with a little salt and pepper. When the onions have turned a light brown, add the amaranth and cook until well done. Dry out the amaranth, remove from the heat and cool. Add the amaranth to the mashed potato with the milk or cream, making sure that the amaranth is well distributed. Check seasoning again. Best served warm, heated under the grill at serving time.

Sweet Potato Mash with Zereshk

5 to 6 servings

You require the following:

500 grams sweet potato

300 grams potato

50 grams butter

100 ml light cream

¼ cup zereshk

2 tablespoons sugar

1 or 2 tablespoons finely chopped parsley

1 tablespoon garlic chives

Season to taste with salt and pepper

Pressure cook both the potatoes and the sweet potatoes but do them separately. Set aside to cool slightly then peel them. While still hot, add half the butter and mash them until nice and smooth. Add the parsley and chives to the mash and mix the ingredients together, making sure that the sweet potato is evenly distributed. In a small saucepan add the zereshk, sugar and remaining butter and place over low heat, cook until the zereshk has a glossy sheen and thick syrup forms. Add a tablespoon of water if required to prevent the berries from burning. Remove from the heat cool slightly, add to the mash and mix well. Finally, add the lightly beaten cream and season to taste with the salt and pepper. Serve warm.

Butternut Squash with Bok Choy

Good for 6 people

You require the following:

700 grams butternut squash

300 grams bok choy

150 grams chicken or pork sausages

2 teaspoon crushed acacia seed

4 cloves of garlic

1 tablespoon minced fresh ginger

1 teaspoon black pepper powder

3 tablespoons vegetable oil

Sea salt to taste

Rinse the bok choy and drain completely. Crush the garlic, chop the butternut squash and the bok choy into bite size pieces. Then cut the sausages into large pieces, heat half the oil in a pan, and fry the sausages until done. Remove from the pan with a slotted spoon and set aside until needed. In the same pan, add the remaining oil, the ginger, garlic and the butternut squash, season to taste with a little salt and all the pepper. Cook until nearly done, then add the bok choy and cook together until the vegetables soften. When done, sprinkle in the acacia seed powder, mix in well and check seasoning again. Add the fried sausage, stir once again and cook for another two minutes, remove from the heat and serve.

Quick Fried Guavas with Devils Dung

Enough for 4

Without a doubt, guava seeds are full of flavour, but a dish full of them can be very tiresome. For this recipe choose a variety that is seedless[85] or has fewer seeds. If you are unable to find one, scoop out and discard the seeds. The guavas should be just ripe, but firm.

You require the following:

600 grams seedless white or pink guavas
2 or 3 tender spring onions with a small section of green
1 teaspoon mustard seed
1 teaspoon *bunium persicum* seed [shahjeera]
1 teaspoon fennel seed
1 teaspoon powdered devil's dung [asafoetida]
1 sprig curry leaves
1 teaspoon coriander powder
3 mild fresh chillies [red/yellow/red]
1 or 2 tablespoons fresh pomegranate pearls
2 tablespoons oil
Lime juice and green coriander to sprinkle
Salt to taste

Remove all the surface spots and blemishes, and cube the guavas. Slice the spring onions and chillies. Heat the oil in a pan, add the mustard, bunium and fennel seeds and allow them to crackle. Add the curry leaves and the chillies and fry another two minutes. Sprinkle in the asafoetida and tip in the guava. Cook for 4 minutes on medium heat. Now sprinkle in the coriander powder, add the spring onions and season to taste. Squeeze on some lemon juice, and stir once more before removing from the heat. Tip into a serving dish and sprinkle with some fresh green coriander and the pomegranate pearls.

85 Some seedless varieties include the Nagpur seedless from Maharashtra, the seedless Chittidar from Madhya Pradesh, and the Mirzapuri Seedless from Uttar Pradesh.

Chayote with Green Olive Tapenade

Enough for 4 as a side dish

You require the following:

400 grams chayote weighed in after cleaning

150 grams shallots, sambhar onions, or regular onions quartered

2 or 3 mild green/ red/yellow chillies

½ teaspoon aniseed

2 vegetable or chicken soup cubes

½ cup mixed sprouts

2 or 3 fresh tender spring onions

2 tablespoons oil of your choosing

Salt and pepper to taste

For the Green Olive Tapenade[86]

75 grams pitted green olives

2 or 3 plump cloves of garlic

½ tablespoon capers

2 tablespoons olive oil

Grind all the above ingredients to a paste and season to taste.

Steam the chayote for 8 minutes or until half done. Clean and keep the shallots whole. Chop the chillies and the spring onions into large pieces. Thoroughly rinse the sprouts and then drain well. Heat the oil in a pan; add the onions, aniseed, and fry for a few minutes until the onions turn translucent. Next, add the chillies and cook for one minute more. Then add the chayote and sprouts. Crush the soup cubes over the vegetables and mix well, season to taste with a little pepper. Cover and cook the vegetables until they are done, adding a spoonful of water if needed. Finally, add the spring onions and heat through until they soften and begin to wilt. Then stir in the Green Olive Tapenade, mix well and serve.

Scented Sweet Potatoes with Golpar

Enough for 4 as a side dish

The golpar gives the potatoes a unique flavour and aroma

You require the following:

750 grams sweet potato such as 'All Gold'

86 Or use shop bought tapenade.

1 tablespoon golpar [Persian hogweed]

2 tablespoons raisins

2 tablespoon charoli seeds

2 or 3 tablespoons hazelnut oil

Sea salt to taste

Scrub the sweet potato, peel and cut into wedges. Line a shallow roasting pan with aluminium foil and tip in the sweet potato wedges, the raisins, and charoli. Sprinkle the golpar, season with a little salt and drizzle with the oil. Pop into a medium oven for 30 minutes, or until the sweet potato is soft but still crunchy, and brown around the edges. Serve immediately

Cook's tip: Orange sweet potato is a better choice than the cream coloured varieties – looks better.

Humus with Asian Flavours

Makes one large bowl full

You require the following:

3 cups cooked chickpeas [approximately 240 grams dried]

5 to 6 plump cloves of garlic minced

1/3 cup olive oil

2 tablespoons udang rangup bercili [Crispy prawn chilly]

2 tablespoons Asian plum sauce

1 large mild green chilli minced

½ tablespoon kaffir lime leaves shredded [See Cook's tip below]

1 tablespoon fresh green coriander

1 tablespoon Asian sesame oil to drizzle

Sea salt to taste

Soak the chickpeas overnight. Drain, rinse and pressure cook without salt until soft and velvety. Drain the chickpeas retaining 1/3 cup of the liquid. Process the chickpeas along with the cooking liquid, crushed garlic, and olive oil. When nice and smooth add the Udang Rangup Bercili, Asian plum sauce, chilly and salt to taste. Process again. Turn into a wide shallow serving dish. To serve, drizzle with the tablespoon of sesame oil, and scatter the finely chopped green coriander and kaffir lime leaves on top.

Cook's Tip: The kaffir lime leaves that I have used here are preserved in brine, and most likely available in an Asian store near you.

18. Stir Fry a Quick Meal

Broccoli Stir Fried with Black Bean Sauce

Serve as a side dish for 4

You require the following:

500 grams broccoli [weighed in after cleaning]

3 to 4 fat cloves of garlic

100 grams oyster mushrooms

½ a cup pistachios

1 tablespoon fresh ginger

2 tablespoons spicy black bean sauce

1 teaspoon freshly ground black pepper

1 teaspoon liquid jaggery or brown sugar

1 tablespoon black or white sesame seeds

2 tablespoons peanut or sunflower oil

Rock salt to taste or any speciality salt

Lightly steam the broccoli until nearly done, the florets should remain crisp and firm. Finely mince the ginger and garlic. In a pan or wok, stir fry the pistachios in a little oil with a pinch of rock salt. Remove from the heat and set aside. In the same pan add and heat the remaining oil, then add the ginger, garlic, and sauté until fragrant but do not brown. Next, add the mushrooms and cook until done. Then, add the broccoli stir fry for two or three minutes. Push the broccoli and the mushrooms to one side of the pan and add the nuts, black pepper, black bean sauce and the jaggery or sugar. Fry for half a minute and then mix well into the vegetables. Check for seasoning, tip into a serving dish and sprinkle with the sesame seed before serving.

Carrots Stir Fried with Preserved Moroccan Limes

Enough for 3 to 4 as a side dish

I have mixed feelings about growing carrots because the seeds are so tiny and so loved by ants that I often wonder how I could get any harvest at all. However, the plant is so pretty and graceful and the roots so delicious it is always worth the effort to try!

You require the following:

300 grams carrots

100 grams onions

2 or three bay leaves

1/2 to 3/4 of a preserved Moroccan lime

1 teaspoon caraway seeds

1 teaspoon ginger paste

1 tablespoon flat leaf parsley

3 tablespoons dried black currents

1/4 teaspoon turmeric [optional]

2 tablespoons vegetable oil of your choice

Salt to taste

Wash, peel and grate the carrots to a medium grade and finely cut the onions. Heat the oil in a heavy bottomed pan and add the caraway seed and bay leaves. Allow them to colour but do not burn. Next, add the onions and cook until golden yellow. Then add the ginger paste and the currents and stir well, adding salt to taste. If your carrots do not have a good rich colour, add a sprinkling of turmeric powder then stir fry the carrots. Add a tablespoon or two of water if the dish dries out but allow the carrots to cook through. Then add the chopped parsley and stir well. Roughly chop the preserved Moroccan lime and add too the carrots. Mix and take off the heat. Rest the dish for about 10 minutes and reheat gently if required, before serving.

Cook's note: Grating the carrots too fine makes it difficult to blend in the other ingredients. A coarse texture also gives the carrots body.

Both caraway seed and the bay leaves need gentle handling because they burn quickly.

Colonel Rue's Prawns and Ladies Fingers [Okra]

Enough for 4 to 5

You require the following:

500 grams medium size prawns [weighed in after cleaning]

400 grams whole baby okra [an heirloom variety if available][87]

200 grams red onions

2 large mild green chillies [optional]

Juice of 1 lemon

1 tablespoon brown sugar

¼ cup dried fenugreek leaves [kasuri methi]

3 tablespoons vegetable oil of your choice

2 tablespoons red wine vinegar

Salt to taste

For the masala paste:

2 to 3 dried red chillies

2 teaspoon cumin seeds

2 tablespoons garlic paste

Grind the above ingredients to a fine paste using a little vinegar

Niger seed chutney to sprinkle on top [optional]

Soak the fenugreek leaves in a little warm water for 10 minutes then drain. Soak the red chillies in the vinegar until soft. Marinate the cleaned and deveined prawns in a little salt and some of the lemon juice for half an hour. Wash and dry the ladies fingers thoroughly and fry in a little of the oil in a wok until just done. Remove from the pan with a slotted spoon and set aside. Chop the onions roughly, and in the same wok and on a medium heat, add the remaining oil and brown the onions for a couple of minutes. Next, add the prawns and the green chillies fry for 2 minutes then add the masala paste and season to taste. Stir-fry for another 2 minutes and then add the sugar and the fenugreek leaves. Cook until the prawns are done, then add the ladies fingers and check for seasoning again. Serve immediately with a squeeze of lemon and a sprinkling of Niger seed chutney if so desired.

87 No more than 2 or 3 inches long, 'Star of David' is ideal.

Daphne's Stir Fried Mince with Lemon Juice

Enough for 3 to 4

You require the following:

500 grams tender minced beef or pork

1/3 cup sweet green peas

2 or 3 stalks celery finely chopped

4 plump spring onions thickly sliced

¼ cup freshly chopped parsley

1 teaspoon garam masala powder

1 teaspoon pepper powder

1 teaspoon Parsee dhanajeera

3 tablespoons olive or grape seed oil

2 tablespoons lemon juice or to taste

Salt to taste

Season the minced beef or pork with a little salt, the pepper powder, and the Parsee dhanajeera powder and set aside to rest for two hours, or overnight in the refrigerator. Heat a tablespoon of oil in a wok, add the green peas and stir-fry lightly for a few minutes. Remove the peas with a slotted spoon and set aside. Reheat the wok, add a little more of oil and add the beef or pork in batches, and cook until nicely browned, removing each batch before adding a new one. Add the remaining oil to the wok with the celery and parsley, and quickly stir until crisp but do not burn. Then add the spring onions and cook, season to taste. Put the meat back into the wok along with the green peas, add the garam masala powder and mix well. Check for seasoning once again and cook through. Drizzle with the lemon juice and serve with a green salad and flatbread, such as a freshly made naan or paratha.

Peppered Panir Stir Fried with Capsicum

Serves 4 as a side dish

You require the following:

400 grams fresh firm preferably homemade panir

3 large capsicums, [1 each of yellow, red, and purple]

3 medium white or red onions

1 onion leek

1 teaspoon cumin seed

1 tablespoon garlic paste

½ a tablespoon freshly ground pepper or more to taste

1 tablespoon sunflower seeds

1 teaspoon powdered Szechuan pepper

2 tablespoons vegetable oil of your choice

1 tablespoon Asian sesame oil or Niger seed oil

Sea salt to taste

Cut the Panir into cubes, deseed the capsicum and chop into pieces a little bigger than the panir. Cut the onions into quarters and roughly chop the onion-leek. Heat the wok, add the oil and swirl it around before adding the cumin and sunflower seeds. Next, add the garlic paste, quartered onions, capsicum, and stir-fry until the onions are translucent, and the capsicum has softened. Now add the panir, salt to taste and a generous amount of pepper. Let the panir heat through for a couple of minutes, and then add the sesame or Niger oil. Remove the wok from the heat and sprinkle the Szechuan pepper on the panir, toss and serve immediately.

Stir Fried Calamari with Greens

Just right for 4 to 5

There is a wide choice of greens, masala's and other ingredients that you can use for this dish. At first, Komatsuna was my favoured green, but I eventually substituted this with bok choy, portulaca, radish leaves and Chinese mustard greens. You can use just one variety or a mixture of two or three. Garam masala is a reliable ingredient to use and never fails to please, but there are other options, including dhansak masala, goda masala, or East Indian bottle masala.

You require the following:

600 grams calamari [weighed in after cleaning]

100g red or yellow peppers [or a mixture of the two]

350 to 400 grams komatsuna, bok choy or your favourite greens

2 teaspoons garam masala

75ml chicken stock

1 teaspoon corn flour

2 teaspoons rice wine vinegar

1½ tablespoons oyster sauce

3 tablespoons vegetable oil of your choice

Salt to taste

Clean the squid including the tentacles and rinse well. Cut open the tubes lengthways and score the inner surface, and then cut into squares, chop the tentacles. Marinate the calamari with the garam masala and a little salt to taste for 15 minutes. Mix the corn flour with the stock. In a wok heat some of the oil and stir-fry the calamari in batches on high heat. Remove when just tender and set aside. Add a little more oil and stir fry the capsicum, and then add the greens. Return the calamari to the wok, and add the vinegar and oyster sauce. Stir to mix, now add the blended cornflour and stock, cook until it thickens slightly, remove from the stove and serve immediately with fried rice or noodles.

The South Indian Vattal: Vattals are sun-dried vegetables that are usually deep-fried and served as accompaniments to rice and curry, just like papadums. Cook in a curry in place of or with other fresh vegetables. Most popular among the different varieties are vattals from the Turkey Berry [Solanum torvum] locally known as Sundaikkai, and Manathakkali [Solanum nigrum or Black Nightshade]. Another favourite, Okra is very popular in the Southern states of Tamil Nadu and Karnataka, where there is a flourishing home based industry with women producing the most delectable vattals for sale. Vattals are available in small grocery stores and supermarkets across the region. Your local Asian store is sure to stock some.

My Mother
In her early
Twenties

Little Women
My mother and her sisters
Verna, Lorna and Thelma

Dad in the late 1950's

Adershir Irani with his Favourite Piece of Equipment

Grand Uncle Aspandia Khansaheb Irani

Rustom Mama And Other Uncles

Rustom Mama - Greatly Missed

Noshir Uncle

19. Other Vegetables

Baked Kohlrabi

Enough for 4

You require the following:

400 grams tender green or purple kohlrabi[88]

150 grams of onion

1/4 cup fresh herbs of your choice

1/4 cup finely diced celery

2 tablespoons butter

1 tablespoon oil

1 cup of single cream

1/3 cup panko or as required about

Salt and pepper to taste

Peel off the thin outer skin of the kohlrabi, then grate it, sprinkle with a little salt and set aside for an hour. Then squeeze out all the water that collects and set aside. Finely mince the onions and finely chop the herbs. Heat half the butter and oil in a pan, tip in the onions and fry a light brown. Then remove from the pan and add to the kohlrabi. In the same pan add the remaining butter, oil, and sauté the celery and herbs for about 8 to 10 minutes until crisp. Then add to the kohlrabi and mix well. Lightly grease a gratin dish with butter and tip in the vegetable mixture, level it out. Season the lightly beaten cream with salt and pepper and pour over the kohlrabi. Set aside until the cream settles then, evenly dust on the panko and bake in a moderate oven until done.

88 Replace the kohlrabi with grated chayote, white or red radish.

Drumsticks in Red Chilli Sauce

Makes about 5 to 6 helpings

You require the following:

8 drumsticks cleaned and cut into 3-inch pieces [about 3 cups]

½ cup thick coconut milk

½ cup green peas

2 tablespoons Rob-e anar [pomegranate paste]

½ teaspoon jeera [cumin]

3 tablespoons oil

Salt to taste

Grind to a fine paste with water:

1 cup ground coconut

1 tablespoon ginger garlic paste

½ cup green coriander

1 teaspoon Parsee dhanajeera powder

6 red chillies [deseeded if you want less heat]

½ teaspoon turmeric

Heat the oil in a pot and add the cumin seeds fry half a minute then add the ground masala and continue to cook until a fragrant aroma arises. Add a little water now and then if the masala begins to stick to the bottom of the pan. Next add the green peas with a little water, season to taste and cook until the green peas are half done. Then add the drumsticks and the coconut milk simmer until the vegetables are tender. Finally, add the pomegranate paste and finish cooking. Serve hot with a sweet pickle, yogurt and a bowl of rice.

Roasted Capsicum with Tomatoes and Sunflower Seeds

For 4 or 5

Topped with a dollop of mascarpone

You require the following:

6 large capsicum 2 each purple, yellow and red

4 to 5 medium tomatoes [different colours look pretty]

2 or 3 stalks of celery

3 or 4 cloves garlic

2 tablespoons roasted sunflower seeds

3 or 4 tablespoons of olive or grapeseed oil

1½ tablespoons Asian lemon sauce or to taste

2 tablespoons chopped Kalamata olives

Salt and pepper to taste

Cut each capsicum equally in half lengthwise, retaining a portion of the stalk if you can. Gently remove the seeds and the core without tearing the walls, and dry off with a kitchen towel. Sprinkle the insides with a little salt and toss in a little oil, place in a roasting tin cut face down and roast in a moderate oven until soft but still firm. Meanwhile, chop the tomatoes, mince the celery and garlic. Add the olives and mix well, season with a little salt and pepper. Then add the lemon sauce and the roasted sunflower seeds to the mixture. Fill the capsicum halves with the tomato mixture, drizzle a little oil on top and pop back into the oven and roast until the tomatoes are soft. Serve warm with a dollop of mascarpone on top of each half.

Cook's note: There are so many varieties of oil available now, try nut oils such as pistachio and hazelnut.

English Vegetables

Ooty veggies were on the shopping list of every 'well to do' homemaker of the 60's and 70's. The Ooty market was where you could buy quality 'English Vegetables,' garden fresh asparagus, rhubarb, artichokes, Brussels sprouts, snap beans, scarlet runner beans, and yellow wax beans. This is where you got your parsley, flat leaved or moss curled, carrots that were the right colour and celery that was not only the right size but perfectly blanched. The fruit stalls filled with bull's heart and mangosteen, tree tomatoes and passion fruit, quince and persimmon, were fruit you were unlikely to find elsewhere.

The first mention of temperate fruit and vegetables grown in the Nilgiris was in 1821, in a report written by Assistant Surgeon General John Jones. The trees and seeds sourced from Bangalore were all grown in Mr. Sullivan's[89] garden at Dimhatti, where he had set up temporary residence until 'Stonehouse,' his permanent residence in Ootacammand was complete. The import of fruit trees, flower and vegetable seeds for the Nilgiris came much later, in 1831 and beyond[90].

The Ooty market was an absolute delight! The station Commanding Officer, Lieutenant Colonel Thomson first proposed its construction, in 1845. The market's foundation was laid in 1847, and many additions and alterations followed over the ensuing decades. Among them the European fruit and vegetable stalls, poultry and fish sections, and the 'meat hanging rooms'. Two sheds built and completed in 1904 for the sale of 'native vegetables' was a great success[91]!

The Ooty market was an absolute delight, but not all the vegetable stalls were equal! Anthony had his somewhere in the middle, and getting there was an accomplishment in its self. You had to sidestep baskets spilling over with produce, break through the sound barrier of a deafening babel of voices, and to negotiate a multitude of people, who like you, were all going somewhere. Dressed in fashionable drainpipes his black pointed shoes flawlessly buffed, a gleaming, slickly oiled Elvis puff, this man knew how to manoeuvre you with his persuasive sales talk! Anthony's Vegetable Stall was the best! This is where the Brussels sprouts were all the same size, the celery perfectly blanched, the artichokes so fresh and where there were more peas in a pod than elsewhere. When you finally left you knew that far more had been spent than intended, and painfully aware that you now had two coolies instead of the one!

89 John Sullivan the founder of Ootacammand, his residence Stonehouse was completed sometime in mid-1823.

90 Ootacamund - A History by Frederick Price published by Rupa & Co. 2002.

91 Ootacamund - A History by Frederick Price published by Rupa & Co. 2002.

20. My Family and Foogath

On our dining table, the dish of pumpkin foogath was always placed within easy reach of my mother and Granny Fergusson, and there is where it stayed - they loved it. My father, brothers and I shuddered at the thought of eating pumpkin foogath. Many, many years later when I discovered winter squash, I wished dad were around to taste my version of it! Winter squash responds wonderfully to being 'foogathed,' [my mother in law tells me, means 'to stir-fry' in Portuguese]. A foogath best described as a stir-fry with onions, a minimum of spice, ginger or garlic, and freshly grated coconut; start cooking 15 minutes before mealtime.

Cabbage Foogath

Enough for 4

Don't dismiss this dish too quickly; it can turn out really well with some effortless tweaking. Serve cabbage foogath immediately when at its best!

You require the following:

3 cups cabbage [Drumhead or Savoy are ideal]
100 grams white onion
2 or 3 bay leaves
2 tablespoons watermelon seeds
1½ teaspoons caraway seed or aniseed
1 tablespoon ginger garlic paste
2 long mild green or yellow chillies
3 tablespoons freshly grated coconut
2 tablespoons fresh coriander
2 tablespoons olive or grape seed oil
Salt and white pepper to taste

Roughly shred the cabbage, you don't want it too fine. Finely chop the onions and coriander, and grate the coconut. Keep the chillies whole or cut them into pieces. In a wok or frying pan on low heat, add the oil and caraway seed, watermelon seed and green chillies. Allow the spices to cook for 30 seconds but do not brown. Turn up the heat to medium, add the sliced onion and the bay leaves and cook three to four minutes. Now add the ginger and garlic paste, mix well into the onions and season to taste. Turn down the heat and add the cabbage a little at a time, mixing each batch into the onions. Keep the heat low, cover the pan with a tight-fitting lid and cook the cabbage for 3 minutes, or until the cabbage just changes colour. Remove the lid, let excess water if any evaporate, and add the coriander and coconut. Blend well, adjust seasoning and serve.

Cook's note: Use red cabbage as a variation; add an acidifying agent such as sumac or lime to the cabbage at the start of the cooking process helps to retain the colour of the cabbage somewhat. Using stainless cookware also seems to help in colour retention. I have used spiced watermelon seeds available from our farsan store in Belgaum. You can replace the watermelon seeds with roasted pumpkin or sunflower seeds or any other locally available nuts.

> A 'Farsan Store' stocks both sweet and savoury treats. You will find plenty of condiments, nuts, dried fruit, pickles and fruit leather here. It's a great place to shop because you never know what interesting things you can pick up and use in an unconventional way.

Foogath of Chinese Snake Beans

Enough 4 or 5

You can replace the snake beans with French beans, yellow wax beans or scarlet runner beans. Cluster beans also make a good foogath; tender young winged beans used 'whole' are also an attractive alternative.

You require the following:

500 grams red or black Chinese snake beans
200 grams red onions
1 tablespoon ginger
3 to 4 cloves garlic
3 or 4 spring onions
1 teaspoon black mustard seed
1 or 2 tablespoons Asian spicy black bean sauce
2 tablespoons freshly grated coconut
3 tablespoons vegetable oil
Squeeze of lemon juice
Salt to taste

Top and tail the beans and cut into pieces diagonally. Squeeze a little lemon juice onto the beans, mix well and steam until nearly done then put aside until needed. Finely chop the onions, mince the ginger and smash the garlic. Roughly chop the spring onions with a portion of the green. Heat the oil in a pan, add the mustard seed and allow them to crackle. Then add the onions, ginger, and garlic. Fry until the onions brown, but do not burn. Then add the spring onions and cook for 2 or 3 minutes, next add the beans, season lightly to taste. Finally, add a spoonful or two of the black bean sauce mix well and allow the beans to cook thoroughly. Just before serving, add the coconut and a squeeze of lemon juice if desired.

Pumpkin Foogath with Bibiya [or Pecans]

Enough for 5 to 6 guests as a side dish

Highly recommended for all pumpkin haters!

You require the following:

750 grams of winter squash or pumpkin [after cleaning]

200 grams red or white onions

1/3 cup prunes [ready to eat]

1/3 cup bibiya seeds[92], walnuts or pecans

2 bay leaves [*Laurus nobilis*]

½ teaspoon cumin seed

½ teaspoon Parsee dhanajeera powder

½ tablespoon ginger garlic paste

¼ cup fresh coriander leaves

2 tablespoons freshly grated coconut

¼ cup olive oil or any other vegetable oil of your choice

Salt to taste

Dice the pumpkin, sprinkle with a little salt, toss well to coat and steam the pumpkin until a little over half done. This saves on cooking time and can be done much ahead. Roughly chop the onions and prunes, and finely chop the coriander leaves. Heat the oil in a pan and add the bay leaves and cumin seed, on low heat fry 30 seconds. Next add the bibiya seeds fry a further 30 seconds, increase the heat to medium and tip in the onions and cook until they change colour to a light brown, lower the heat and add the ginger garlic paste, the

---

92 See page 286.

dhana jeera powder and the prunes, stir well and cook a further minute or two. Now add the pumpkin and still on low heat stir fry adding salt to taste. Sprinkle in a little water and cover the pan allow the pumpkin to cook until done, add the green coriander and the coconut mix well and serve hot.

Cook's note: You can vary the dish by using some colored capsicum or some of the more interesting chilly varieties that are not too pungent, such as Hungarian wax.

I like to use bibiya seeds because their dark nearly black colour contrasts well with the pumpkin. If unavailable near you, use any other nut of your choice; Walnuts are a great alternative as are pine nuts. Choose a nut with a strong flavour to give the pumpkin a lift. Try salted sunflower or watermelon seed.

My favourite pumpkin and winter squash – Waltham Butternut, Queensland Blue and the Hubbard's, green, golden or blue.

21. Rice

Coconut Rice with Lemon Grass and Szechuan pepper

Enough for 4 to 5

You require the following:

400 grams long grain rice

300 ml thick coconut milk

4 to 5 fat cloves of garlic

1 generous knob of ginger or galangal

120 grams red or yellow onions

¼ teaspoon Szechuan peppercorns [any species]

3 thin or 2 thick stalks of lemon grass

1 tablespoon finely minced lemongrass

3 or 4 whole dried red chillies [fresh if available]

½ teaspoon turmeric powder

800 ml water [or as required]

3 tablespoons vegetable oil of your choice

2 tablespoons ghee [optional]

Salt to taste

Some fresh green coriander to garnish

Steep the red chillies in hot water until soft and soak the rice in cold water for 30 minutes. Finely chop the onions, crush the garlic and thinly slice the ginger or galangal. Remove the hard outer leaves of the lemongrass stalks; retain only the white bulb and about 3 inches of the stem. Crush lightly to release the flavour.

In a heavy bottomed pot over medium heat, add the oil and the Szechuan peppercorns and fry for one minute. Next, add the red chillies and turmeric powder and fry for a minute more. Then add the garlic, ginger or galangal, minced lemon grass and onions and continue to fry until the onions turn a light brown. Now add the lemon grass stalks, drain the rice and add to the pot. Stir until well coated with the oil and spices, and then add the coconut milk, 500ml of water and season to taste. Bring the rice to a boil, then lower heat and cook until done adding the remaining water as and when required. Just before serving, remove the stalks of lemon grass, tip in the ghee and gently mix into the hot rice. Let the rice rest for ten minutes, then serve garnished with fresh green coriander.

The Tamilian Kuruvan with Zereshk

[Black Rice with Persian Barberries]

Enough for 4 or 5 persons

Serve with spicy grilled chicken, pork or vegetable curry and slices of lime

Kuruvan is a traditional non-glutinous variety of black rice grown in Tamil Nadu that is often used in the making of sweet dishes. You can use any non-glutinous variety of black rice or other heirloom rice such as Rosematta rice from Kerala, or the Rajamudi of Mysore. All traditional Indian heirloom rice is best pre-soaked and cooked in a pressure cooker. Heirlooms also require a little more water to cook them than modern hybrids, so add an extra half cup or so.

You require the following:

300 grams non-glutinous black rice

½ cup zereshk

¼ cup sugar

25 grams butter

Few strands of saffron

½ cup lightly roasted pine nuts

100 grams onions

½ cup onion leeks

4 to 5 garlic cloves

2 tablespoons oil

2 tablespoons mint

Salt to taste

Wash and soak the rice for 2 hours. Then pressure cook seasoned to taste with a little salt. You will need approximately 2½ cups of water. Meanwhile, rinse the zereshk under cold running water and tip into a small pan with the sugar, butter, and the saffron. Place on low heat, cook until the sugar has dissolved and the berries are soft and begin to glisten about 10 minutes. Ensure that they don't burn by adding a tablespoon of water if need be. Finely chop the onions, crush the garlic and thinly slice the onion leeks using both the white and green parts. Heat the oil in a large pan or wok and add the onions and garlic, season to taste and cook until the onions change colour to a nice medium brown. Add the leeks and cook until they soften, and then add the pine nuts. Turn down the heat and add the rice, mix well. Now add the berries, mint, and gently fold into the rice. Serve the rice on a large flat dish with the grilled chicken piled on top or around it.

Poor Man's Pulao

Enough for 6

You require the following:

500 grams short grain rice
100 grams green peas
100 grams potatoes
400 grams minced meat [beef or mutton]
120 grams red or white onions
4 to 5 plump cloves of garlic
5 cloves
5 cardamoms
3 bay leaves[93]
10 peppercorns
1 teaspoon cumin powder
1 teaspoon coriander powder
½ teaspoon turmeric powder
2 tablespoons ghee [optional]
¼ cup vegetable oil
1200 ml of water approximately
Salt to taste

Peel and dice the potatoes and finely chop the garlic and onions. Heat the oil in a large pot, add the cloves, cardamoms, peppercorns and the bay leaves, and brown lightly. Add the onion and garlic, and allow them to cook, stirring now and then until the onions change

93 If bay leaves are unavailable, you can use cassia leaves, in which case use two instead of three.

colour to a light brown. Next, add the minced meat, and brown along with the coriander, cumin and turmeric powders. Add two cups of hot water to the mince and cook until just about 3/4th done. Then dry out the mince, and add the green peas, potatoes, and the rice and mix well. Season to taste, add approximately 3½ cups of water and cook until done. Just before serving fork in two tablespoons of ghee if desired.

Mushroom Risotto Cooked with Marathi Moggu

Enough for 4 or 5

You require the following:
400 grams Arborio rice
200 grams fresh button mushrooms
30 grams dry wood ear mushrooms
1500 ml chicken or vegetable stock
75 grams butter
½ tablespoon oil
120 grams red onions finely chopped
4 plump pods of garlic crushed
4 or 5 medium-sized Marathi moggu or any other spice of your choice
1½ teaspoon garam masala
2 tablespoons Kasuri methi
Salt to taste

Soak the Kasuri methi in a bowl of warm water and set aside. Prepare the wood ear mushrooms and steep in a bowl of hot water for 20 minutes. Slice the button mushrooms and set aside. Lightly crack the Marathi moggu and heat the chicken or vegetable stock.

Place a heavy bottomed pan over medium heat. Add the butter and oil and melt slightly, and then add the Marathi moggu, garlic, and onions. Stir-fry until the onions change colour to a light brown. Next, add the mushrooms and cook until they are soft. Now add the rice, mix well and season to taste. Then add 500ml of the hot stock and continue to stir until all the stock is absorbed. Still on low to medium heat, add another 500ml of the stock and allow the rice to cook stirring from time to time until the stock is absorbed. Now add the garam masala, Kasuri methi and the remaining stock to the pot and allow the rice to finish cooking. The consistency of the rice should be soft and moist. Serve immediately with sliced lemon.

Herbed Soybean Pulao with Preserved Moroccan Lime

Enough for 3 or 4

You require the following:

200 grams brown rice

750 ml vegetable or chicken stock [approximately][94]

½ cup dry soy granules

½ cup green moong sprouts

½ cup garlic or onion chives

3 plump cloves of garlic

½ a large preserved Moroccan lime

1/3 cup cubed feta cheese

¼ cup celery

3 tablespoons vegetable oil of your choice

Bring the stock to the boil, add the rice and cook until done and then set aside to cool. Soak the soya granules in one cup of warm water for about 20 minutes. Drain, and then squeeze out as much of the water as possible. Meanwhile, chop the celery, garlic or onion chives, and smash the garlic, rinse and drain the moong sprouts thoroughly. Cut the lime into bite size pieces.

15 minutes before serving, heat the oil in a large pan or wok, add the garlic and toss on low heat until lightly browned, next add the chives, the celery and moong sprouts. Fry 2 or 3 minutes until lightly crisped and then add the soya bean granules and season to taste. Cook for three to four minutes more. Finally, add the rice and Moroccan lime and mix well. Tip into a serving dish, pile the feta on top and serve immediately.

Rice cooked with Sausage and Chives

Plenty for 5 healthy appetites!

You require the following:

250 grams fresh pork sausage[95]

350 grams short grain white or brown rice

94 You can use two small soup cubes instead of the vegetable or chicken stock.

95 You can choose a mildly spicy sausage for extra flavour. If unavailable, replace with pork mince.

900 ml water approximately[96]

200 grams onions

1 teaspoon pepper powder

1 teaspoon coriander powder

1 teaspoon cumin seed

½ cup chopped garlic or onion chives

100 grams tomato

1 or 2 tablespoons kudampuli molasses [*Garcinia cambogia*][97]

2 tablespoons vegetable oil

Sea Salt to taste

Boil the rice in approximately 900 ml of salted water until done. Remove from the heat and turn onto a large flat plate to cool. Meanwhile, thinly slice the onions and roughly chop the tomatoes. Place a large pan or wok on medium heat and add the oil. Next, add the onion and cumin seeds and cook 3 to 4 minutes. Then add the sausages, break up and mix well into the onions. Add the pepper and coriander powders and cook a few moments more. Then add in the tomatoes, cover the pan and allow the sausage meat to cook on low heat, adding a little water only if necessary. When the meat has cooked through add the chives and kudampuli molasses, and check for seasoning, adding a little salt if required. Cook a further 3 to 5 minutes then gently fold in the rice, and mix in the meat evenly. Serve nice and hot with a salad on the side.

Beaten Rice [Pohe or Rice Flakes]

Beaten rice or rice flakes come in three grades thin, medium and thick. Choose either the medium or the thick grade for the following recipes. It is crucial that pohe is rinsed very quickly under cold running water, and drained immediately, or it will disintegrate. Don't overcook the pohe because it tends to harden, all you need is about 3 to 5 minutes. Look for beaten rice in an Asian store near you [check the product date for freshness]. Always serve pohe immediately.

96 The quantity of water required depends on the variety and age of the rice, the amount given above, is just a guideline.

97 The kudampuli molasses gives a flavour that is unique, but if you don't have any, not to worry substitute with some rob-e anar [pomegranate molasses], which will prove to be a wonderful alternative!

Pohe, Green Peas and Bamboo Shoot

A hearty snack for 3 to 4

You will require the following:

250 grams beaten rice

100 grams red onion

75 grams sweet green peas

75 grams bamboo shoot

2 mild green chillies

1 sprig curry leaves

1 teaspoon black mustard seeds

1/4 cup rocket or garlic chives

2 tablespoons vegetable oil of your choice

A drizzle of Chinese chilli oil

Salt to taste

Put the green peas to boil in salted water until done, drain and set aside. Finely chop the onions, slice the green chillies and chop the rocket or garlic chives. Place a wok over medium heat and add the oil. Then add the mustard seed and allow them to crackle, followed by the curry leaves, onions, and chillies. Fry until the onions change colour to a medium brown. Next, add the green peas and the sliced bamboo shoot and cook for about three to four minutes, season to taste. Meanwhile, quickly rinse the pohe using a colander under cold running water, then drain thoroughly. Add the pohe to the wok with the rocket, mix in thoroughly and check again for seasoning, adding a little more salt if necessary. Drizzle on the chilly oil, heat through and serve immediately with slices of lemon.

Pohe with Sun-dried Tomatoes

Good for 3 to 4

You will require the following:

250 grams beaten rice

100 grams red onion

1 teaspoon cumin seed

4 cloves garlic

5 or 6 large pieces of sundried tomatoes in oil

1/3 cup roasted pine nuts

8 to 10 Kalamata olives

¼ cup fresh coriander leaves

2 or 3 tablespoons vegetable oil of your choice

1 tablespoon shredded kaffir lime leaves

Salt to taste

Finely chop the onion, smash the garlic, and roughly chop the coriander. Carefully remove the tomatoes from the oil and cut into pieces. Place a wok over medium heat, add the oil, garlic, and cumin seed and cook for 1 minute. Next, add the onion and cook until it changes colour to a light brown. Now add the pine nuts, olives, and the sundried tomatoes and mix well with the onions. Cook together for 2 or 3 minutes and season to taste. Meanwhile, using a colander quickly rinse the pohe under cold running water, and then drain thoroughly. Add the pohe to the wok in batches along with the fresh coriander and mix in thoroughly. For added flavour and a richer taste, drizzle on some of the oil from the sundried tomatoes. Finally, stir in the kaffir lime leaves and serve immediately.

Cooks note: The shredded kaffir lime leaves I use comes in a bottle and preserved in brine.

Paddy Fields Forever

Cruising down Highway 17[98] in an old Ambassador[99], when distances were measured in furlongs and miles, the paddy fields of Mandya district are a memory, a picture, that I have framed and stored away to enjoy forever. With no 'play stations' or phones to distract you, you watched as mile upon mile of brilliant green carpeting rolled out before you, interspersed with rocky outcrops, ancient and timeless stone temples, coconut groves, and decorous water birds socializing with lazy swamp buffalos wallowing in pools of mud. Alas, this once splendid stretch of asphalt is now home to colossal advertisement boards, featureless factory buildings, and ugly shopping complexes pretentiously called Plazas.

Many miles away at the Hermitage, we grow our paddy and every year we have the pleasure of watching the white-throated kingfisher flit and hover above that brilliant carpet of green. With the arrival of November's winter sun, the warm earthy aroma of the maturing crop wafts across the land. With sickles sharpened on whetstones, we harvest our paddy, stack it into ricks and allow it to rest until threshing time. In the not so distant past the threshing or 'mulni' was done at leisure on an enchanting full moon night perhaps. But no longer, the tractor has replaced the use of bulls and now anytime can be mulni time. The paddy harvest in recent years is synonymous with elephant time. When these hungry uninvited guests drop by to feast on the produce that men have so kindly and thoughtfully, sown, grown and harvested for them!

The paddy threshed and then winnowed to remove the chaff, is stored through many months to mellow and mature, then bagged before taken to town to be milled. Mastering the art of winnowing is a skill that appears straightforward and unsophisticated, but realistically takes years to perfect. To succeed, the bamboo winnowing trays must be an element of your childhood; watching your mother deftly throw up the grain separating the good from the bad with the flick of a wrist. As much as I tried, I failed, so with humble acceptance gave up the struggle, but not the enjoyment of hearing and watching other rhythmic hands deftly, seamlessly effortlessly working that deceptive bamboo winnowing tray.

---

98 The Bangalore to Mysore Highway.

99 During the sixties and seventies, the Ambassador was one of the few cars available in the Indian market. This limited choice meant, that when wanting to buy a car, the only decision that was of any consequence was to choose its colour.

22. The Millets

Kodo Millet, Broccoli and Cheese Bake

Good for 4 to 5

You require the following:

150 grams kodo millet hulled [millet rice]

250 ml hot water [approximately]

250 ml chicken or vegetable stock

200 grams tender young broccoli florets

100 grams mushrooms thinly sliced

5 or 6 spring onions chopped with a little portion of green

3 cloves garlic crushed

1 cup grated cheese of your choice

A knob of butter

Squeeze of lemon juice

200 ml single cream

Salt and pepper to taste

Lightly butter a baking dish and set aside. Rinse the Kodo millet in cold water, place in a pot, pour over 250 ml of hot water, and set aside for one hour. Later add the chicken or vegetable stock and cook on medium heat until all the liquid has been absorbed and the millet has cooked.

Meanwhile, blanch the broccoli florets in hot water for about 3 to 4 minutes, and then drain thoroughly. In a frying pan, add a little of the butter, and fry the crushed garlic. Add the broccoli, and cook with the butter and garlic, then tip into the baking dish. In the same pan heat the remaining butter, add the mushrooms and spring onions and stir-fry for 2 to 3 minutes until soft but still crisp. Add to the broccoli in the baking dish along with the millet. Mix all the ingredients together, season with salt, pepper, and sprinkle with some lime juice.

Put the cream and the grated cheese into a saucepan and blend well. Place on low heat and stir until the cheese has melted. Pour over the millet and broccoli and bake in a moderate oven for half an hour or until set. Remove from the oven, rest for 5 minutes and serve hot.

Foxtail Millet with Winter Squash

Enough for 5

You require the following:

250 grams foxtail millet [hulled/ rice]
750 ml chicken or vegetable stock
75 grams red onions
1 cup diced yellow winter squash
1 cup diced orange winter squash
1/3 cup raw monkey nuts [peanuts]
3 or 4 cloves of garlic
2 or 3 slices of smoked ham[100]
2 tablespoons Asian plum sauce
2 tablespoon olive oil
1 tablespoon butter
1/3 cup curled or flat leaf parsley
Salt and freshly ground pepper to taste

Rinse the millet and soak in just enough water to cover for two hours. Drain and then put to the boil with the chicken or vegetable stock. When the grains have cooked and all the liquid absorbed, remove from the heat. Set aside to cool, and then with the help of a fork fluff up and break up any clumps that might have formed, keep warm. Chop the onions; mince the garlic and the parsley. Slice the ham and set aside until needed.

Place a large heavy bottomed pan on medium heat. Add the butter, oil, and then tip in the squash and stir-fry a few minutes. Next, add the monkey nuts and season to taste with salt and pepper. Continue to cook on low heat until the vegetables are half done, then add the garlic and the onion and cook a further 5 minutes. If the squash begins to stick, sprinkle a little water to keep it moist. Add the parsley, and when the vegetables are cooked, stir in the plum sauce and the ham. Check seasoning, and remove from the heat. Tip the millet onto a large serving plate, pile the squash on top, and serve immediately.

100 Vegetarians can omit the ham or substitute it with tofu or panir.

Foxtail Risotto with Mushrooms

Good for 4 to 5

Serve with grilled lamb chops

You require the following:

200 grams foxtail millet [hulled/rice]

250 grams a mixed variety of mushrooms

5 to 6 young spring onions

100 grams red onions

4 to 5 cloves of garlic

1 teaspoon cumin seed

700 ml vegetable or chicken stock [approximately]

1/3 cup almonds

½ tablespoon rose peppercorns

3 tablespoons oil

1 tablespoon butter

1 or 2 tablespoons parsley

Sea Salt and pepper to taste

Rinse the millet and soak in just enough water to cover for two hours. Finely chop the onions, crush the garlic and roughly chop the spring onions including plenty of the green part. Slice the mushrooms, and skin the almonds by first soaking them in hot water for a short while. Next, slice them lengthways into pieces as fine as you can. Heat 1 tablespoon of oil and the tablespoon of butter in a pan, add the almonds and fry gently on medium heat, then add the cumin seed and the rose peppercorns and cook another minute. Tip in the onions and the crushed garlic and cook until the onions change colour to a medium light brown. Drain the millet and add to the pot along with the stock. Season to taste, bring once to the boil, and then allow the millet to simmer until done and all the liquid is absorbed. Meanwhile, heat the remaining oil in a pan, add the mushrooms and spring onions, and cook until done. When the millet has cooked, stir in the mushrooms and spring onions and the finely chopped parsley, mix well and serve hot.

Semolina of Little Millet

Enough for 6 to 8

You will require the following:

200 grams fine little millet semolina

1 tin evaporated milk [approximately 385 ml]

800 ml whole milk

200 ml single cream, [optional but very good!]

50 grams butter

1/3 cup sugar or to taste

1/3 cup dried currants

1/3 cup dried cranberries

1/3 cup raisins

Few strands of saffron

Fresh rose petals to decorate

Dry roast the semolina for a few minutes on low heat, about 3 or 4 minutes, the semolina should brown slightly. Tip the millet into a heavy bottomed pan and cool a little, then slowly add the evaporated milk, the whole milk, saffron and sugar and cook on a low heat until it begins to thicken. Now add the butter and the dried fruit and continue to cook until the millet reaches the consistency of single cream. Remove from the heat and cool, add in the cream and mix well. Turn the pudding into a serving dish and serve warm or at room temperature. Just before serving, decorate with the rose petals.

Post Script: If the semolina thickens too much on cooling, add a little milk to thin. When served it should be the consistency of thick cream.

Baked Millet and Apple Pudding with Rum Butter

Makes 6 Servings

If you like, soak the currants in a little rum before using

You require the following:

120 grams millet [hulled/rice millet]

300 ml water [approximately]

250 ml whole milk

2 large eggs

2 medium crisp, firm apples

1/3 cup dried black currants

½ cup sugar or to taste

¼ teaspoon ground cloves

¼ teaspoon ground cinnamon

A little grated nutmeg

100 ml cream

A buttered oven proof pudding dish approximately 7 to 8 inches square

Rinse the millet and soak for two hours in just enough water to cover. Drain and put to the boil with a pinch of salt and 300ml of fresh water. When cooked and all the liquid absorbed, remove from the heat and cool. With the help of a fork fluff up and break up any clumps that may have formed. Beat the eggs and the milk together, add the sugar and continue to beat until the sugar has dissolved. Peel and grate the apples; you should have one full cup. Add the apple, the millet and the spices to the eggs and milk and mix. Next, add the currants and the lightly beaten cream. Bake in a moderate oven for about 30 to 40 minutes or until the pudding's set and the top has browned. Remove from the oven, rest for 10 minutes and serve warm with the rum butter.

For the Rum Butter:

100 grams butter at room temperature

100 grams brown sugar

2 to 3 tablespoons rum

1 teaspoon lemon juice

Beat the butter until light and fluffy, and then add the brown sugar a spoon at a time beating the mixture well. Next, slowly add the rum followed by the lemon juice and beat well. Empty into a beautiful glass bowl and chill until serving time.

The Minor Millets

Rukmi is one of the few in the village who has memories of the cultivation and consumption of the minor millets, but unfortunately also associates this period of her life with poverty and famine. The cultivation of minor millets in our region was associated with Kumbir or the agricultural practice of 'Slash and Burn' now no longer permitted. The minor millets disappeared from fields and the rural diet a long time ago, but the past decade has also seen a decline in the farming of finger millet, the one minor millet that somehow continued to remain in favour and outlast all the others. Today putting rice or wheat in the lunch tiffin is viewed as progressive and modern, sadly eating natchna bhakri undoubtedly is not.

The minor millets are small-seeded grains borne on slender grassy stalks and are survivors in the real sense of the word; they have a short growing season, an extensive capacity for adaptation, and accomplished at withstanding stressful weather conditions and poor soils. Minor millets can grow without the addition of harsh synthetic fertilizers and are practically pest free and therefore without the need for offensive pesticides. These nutritionally rich grains are the answer to the food and ecological crisis that stares us in the face. It is crucial that the minor millets find their back to the dining tables across the world.

The Minor Millets are very versatile in the kitchen; each variety has its subtle flavour and texture, but the wonderful thing is that they are usually interchangeable and not necessarily recipe specific. Millets are gluten free, healthy to eat and at breakfast, an alternative to packaged breakfast cereal. Cook just like rice for lunch or bake with meats or veggies for dinner. Millet semolina is excellent in both sweet and savoury dishes. Make porridge, bread, and pancakes with millet flour.

English Name	Botanical Name	Kannada	Marathi	Telugu	Tamil
Foxtail or Italian millet	*Setaria italica*	Navane	Kango	Korra	Tenai
Little millet	*Panicum miliare*	Saame	Swan	Samalu	Samai
Proso Millet	*Panicum miliaceum*	Baragu	Vari	Variga	Panivarag
Barnyard Millet	*Echinochloa frumentacea*	Oodahu	_	Udalu	Kuthiraivally

Kodo Millet	*Paspalum scrobiculatum*	Harka	–	Arika	Varagu
Job's Tears	*Coix lacryma – jobi*	Kotti Beeja	Kasari	–	Katter Kuntihumani
Finger Millet	*Eleusine coracana*	Ragi	Natchni	Ragi	Ragi
Teff	*Emgrostis tej*	–	–	–	–

23. Odds and Ends

Taro [Arvi] with Bacon and Sundried Tomatoes

Good for five

Taro is the common name for corms and tubers of several plants in the family Araceae. Arvi is a variety of *Colocasia esculenta* and used mainly for its starchy corms. There are some species indigenous to the Western Ghats, some that grow underground and others high up nestled in hollowed out trunks of large trees. Some varieties of taro require an acidifying agent, tamarind or lime is the best to nullify the calcium oxalate present, which can cause itchiness in the mouth and throat[101]. If you like, replace the taro with yam in the following recipe. Try not to over cook the tubers or they will turn squishy, use a fork to test if they are done. They should give but still be quite firm. Better to undercook slightly rather than to overcook.

You require the following:

750 grams taro

200 grams red onions

75 grams bacon chopped

12 halves, sundried tomatoes in oil drained

5 cloves garlic

3 to 4 mild fresh red chillies [or dry chillies soaked in water]

1 tablespoon dried fenugreek [kasuri methi]

½ tablespoon black pepper powder

3 tablespoon oil of your choice

Sea salt to taste

Lime or lemon juice to taste

Cook the taro in water until just done. Cool, then peel the tubers and slice crosswise into thick pieces and set aside. Soak the fenugreek in a little warm water, slice the onions thinly,

101 The corms are inedible when raw due to the presence of calcium oxalate crystals. The cooking process negates the toxin.

crush the garlic and cut the chillies into large pieces. Place a pan over medium heat; add the oil and tip in the bacon. Fry until crisp, then remove the bacon from the pan and set aside. Next, add the sliced taro, season with salt and pepper and fry for a few minutes until lightly browned and crisp around the edges. Remove and set aside. Then in the same oil fry the onions, garlic, and chillies, next add the fenugreek, toss for a minute more and add the sundried tomatoes. Finally, tip in the bacon and taro, mix well and check seasoning. Add a generous splash of lemon juice remove and serve hot.

Papaya seeds: The next time you slice open a papaya don't throw away the seeds, rinse them under cold running water to remove as much mucilage as you can. Then tip the seeds into a wide mesh strainer and with the back of a spoon rub the seeds against the mesh to remove what remains. Rinse again and dry in the sun, then store in an airtight jar. The seeds are slightly bitter with a lingering flavour of papaya. To use, roast them lightly and add to a dry vegetable dish such as a foogath or a stir fry. Like the fruit, the seeds contain an enzyme that tenderizes meat, so marinate or cook mutton or beef with the seeds. You can also toss them on medium heat in little ghee or oil and add them to yogurt. Interesting rather than spectacular!

Curried Sheep's Trotters

Good for 4

Serve with white rice, papadums, lime and a bowl of tomato salsa

An old cookery book suggests that you use only the forelegs, no reason given. Carefully inspecting the trotters beautifully cleaned by our local butcher, I have been unable to differentiate between foreleg and hind leg, and have decided not to split hairs.

You require the following:

8 plump sheep's trotters, cleaned

200 grams red onions

½ teaspoon turmeric

1 or 2 tablespoons palm or brown sugar

3 tablespoons vegetable oil

1/3 cup green coriander

Salt to taste

For the masala:

1 tablespoon ginger garlic paste

1 tablespoon coriander seed

1 teaspoon cumin seeds

4 mild red chillies

4 cloves

3 Cardamoms

1" piece cassia bark

8 peppercorns

2 tablespoons Vinegar

Grind to a fine paste with the vinegar and a little water.

Finely slice the onions and fry them in the oil until brown, then add the turmeric and fry for a minute more. Add the ground masala and continue to cook on medium heat, adding the masala water [used to clean the grinder] as the mixture begins to dry out. Add the trotters and toss well with the masala, fry for a few minutes longer. Then add enough water and salt to taste, cook [preferably in a pressure cooker] until done. Open the pressure cooker, add the sugar and the chopped green coriander simmer a couple of minutes more and serve.

Cook's tip: Use dark vinegar, I use Kolah's sugarcane vinegar, but do try Balsamic or red wine vinegar.

Liver with Onions and Grilled Tomatoes

Enough for 5 to 6

The contemporary 'Nose to Tail' movement recommends 'no waste,' and cooking liver slots in very well with the idea. However, during the '60's and '70's, liver was in favour, and no movement or campaign was necessary to popularize it. At Krupalaya, the following dish called 'English Style Liver' served with fried onion rings, mashed potato and grilled tomatoes featured on the dinner menu. Liver was very popular in many Anglo-Indian homes. Do make sure that the liver is fresh, and that it is not overcooked.

You require the following:

750 grams fresh sheep's liver

4 large red onions

5 large tomatoes

1 tablespoon ginger garlic paste

1 tablespoon Parsee dhanajeera powder

1 teaspoon brown sugar

Salt and pepper to taste

Oil for shallow frying

Clean the sheep's liver by removing the outer transparent membrane and rinsing under cold running water. Slice into pieces, making sure that they are not too thick. Marinate the liver with salt, pepper, ginger garlic paste and the dhanajeera powder and set aside for 2 hours. Meanwhile, prepare the onions and tomatoes by thickly slicing them crosswise into rounds. A little before you are ready to serve, sprinkle the tomatoes with the brown sugar, salt and pepper and grill on both sides for 2 minutes. Next, heat the oil in a pan and fry the liver in batches until the slices are cooked but not over done. Remove and keep warm. In the same oil, fry the onions sprinkled with a little salt and pepper until the rings are soft and a nice medium brown. Assemble the dish by placing the liver on a large platter and top with the onions and tomato. Serve with mash potato and greens on the side.

Fish Roe with Ladies Fingers and Sundried Tomatoes

Enough for 4

Cooking and eating fish roe once again augments the 'Nose to Tail' movement and the conviction that nothing should be wasted or carelessly discarded. In India, the fish roe usually cooked includes skate [rahu], Indian giant herring [bhing], mullet, Indian shad [hilsa] and carp [rohu]. Around the world, it is usually the swollen red sacs of shad roe on sale. The smaller more delicate roe are delicious lightly sautéed in butter after dusting them with salt and pepper and dredging them in rice flour or polenta. The round pea sized roe of the catfish does well in a dry fry, cooked with plenty of garlic, onions, and tomato.

You require the following:

250 grams fish roe

200 grams small tender okra [Star of David if available]

150 grams onions

4 to 5 cloves garlic

1small know ginger

1 teaspoon Parsee Sambhar powder or any other available with you

1/3 cup sun-dried tomatoes in oil with a wee bit of the oil

1 teaspoon tamarind paste

1 or 2 teaspoons brown sugar

Salt and pepper to taste

3 tablespoons oil

Wash and dry the fish roe with kitchen paper [keep whole], then fry in two tablespoons of oil and remove onto a plate to cool. Then, slice the roe into pieces crosswise. Prepare the okra and slice into pieces about an inch long. In the same pan, add the remaining oil and on high heat fry the okra for 2 minutes, then lower the heat and add a little pepper powder. Continue to cook the okra until half done. Next, tip in the finely chopped onions, the crushed garlic, and thinly sliced ginger. Sprinkle in the sambhar powder and season to taste with a little salt. Add a tablespoon or two of water if the okra begins to stick. Next, add the sugar, tamarind paste and mix well. Then add the sun-dried tomatoes and cook for a minute more. Finally, add the fish roe. Mix gently, heat through, and serve piled high on toast.

A Dozen Brain Cutlets

Serves 5 or 6

A dozen brain cutlets were mandatory on a fishing trip, and munching on a cutlet sandwiched between two slices of bread confirmed that the day was turning out to be very agreeable! The following quantities will make a dozen cutlets. Enough for 5 or 6 people unless there are 'Iranis' present!

You require the following:

6 sheep brains

100 grams red onions

6 fat cloves of garlic

2 or 3 green chillies

½ teaspoon turmeric powder

2 or 3 eggs as required- well beaten

1 cup panko, crisp rice crumbs or bread crumbs [approximately]

2 tablespoons fresh green coriander

Salt to taste

Oil for shallow frying

Gently simmer the brains in water with the turmeric for about 8 minutes, drain well and cool, then clean the brains by picking off the membrane. Dry off the brains and mash with a fork. Finely mince the onions, garlic, coriander and green chillies. Add these to the mashed brains and season to taste. Beat a small egg and add to the brain, mix well and then form into cutlets. Set aside for two hours to rest, preferably in the refrigerator. When ready to serve fry the cutlets in hot oil by first dipping them in the remaining beaten eggs and then rolling them in the panko. Serve with hot parathas and lime.

Beginnings - Early Days at the Hermitage

A Bamboo Hut and Clay Pots

I started to cook when I was 24. David and I had just married and starting off on a new life and learning how to cook in order to feed ourselves was a part of this new experience! Sustainable agriculture was our brave new mantra and armed with very little cash, minuscule knowledge, but enormous enthusiasm; in September 1981, we bought this small but incredible piece of land in the jungles of the Western Ghats in peninsular India. We called our farm 'The Hermitage'. There were David and me, our beloved dog Gypsy, and Smoky our indomitable Siamese cat.

We lived in a thatched bamboo hut and my first kitchen functioned at ground level. Partitioned off at the back of our hut by a simple bamboo screen it measured 6 feet by 8 feet. When you move downwards and begin to work and live at floor level your worldview shifts dramatically. It is an experience that requires some adjustment. But it works the other way too; today in my 'modern' waist-high kitchen Rukmi and the other village women often move away from the counter top to sit on the floor to cut vegetables or clean through rice.

I sourced my down to earth rectangular clay stove from the local potter, the large ring in front had three long rafter nails driven into the sides as vessel supports. Two smaller rings on either side at the back were useful for simmering a stew or keeping food warm. Making our morning cup of tea wasn't exactly a labour of love, lighting a wood stove on a cold winter morning hardly ever is!

You begin by optimistically poking around in the ashes, hoping to find a few burning embers flickering away from the night before. You then begin to delicately stack the wood hopeful that it is nice and dry making sure to balance out the the size and getting the angles right; an overload will get you no more than rolls of smoke. The kindling is the ace up your sleeve, place it right and you will have your tea in no time.

Choosing the right wood to burn is a sensible idea; the Western Ghats has a vast range of hard and soft wood species suitable for an array of different applications. In the month of May, just before the onset of the monsoons, there is a mad scramble to collect enough dead wood to last through the wet season. Kindal *[Terminalia paniculata]*, awala *[Emblic myrobalan]*, and karambal *[Dellenia pentaozyna]* are all excellent types of wood to use in the kitchen, burning clean and bright and producing very little smoke. Nana *[Lagerstroemia lanceolata]* damin *[Grewia tiliefolia]* and kumbai *[Careya arborea]* are also good hard working woods but have the tendency to crackle and spark, and 'shooting stars' are not a very good idea if you live in a grass and bamboo hut! Splitting Jamba *[Xylia xylocurpa]* and madti *[Terminalia alata]* is simply too much work no matter how long you hone your axe. Rosewood tinder is unsuitable for the kitchen hearth. The beautifully grained purple wood does not burn well, producing copious amounts of dark highly scented smoke, while the soot that collects on the base of pots and pans is hard and stubborn, and near impossible to remove.

Following the example of the other women, I cooked our food in unglazed clay pots. Available in all shapes and sizes from the local potter they were baked in traditional ovens using the best hardwoods available, thereby resulting in excellent pots that didn't crack during the 'baghaar'![102] Today, you need to be a little careful in choosing your pots, making sure they are well baked and come from a reputable potter.

Cooking in a clay pot or 'chatty' gives the food a distinctive flavour and though there is nothing complicated about cooking in clay, there are a few things to bear in mind:

Clay pots are fragile, but if carefully handled will last a lifetime. They cannot withstand extreme or sudden temperature changes they will crack. Food can be cooked at much lower temperatures because heat retention is good, so begin cooking on 'low' and gradually increase the heat to 'medium' but never higher.

A new clay pot must be 'broken in' gently before you can begin to cook with it. Rinse the pot under cool running water and set aside. Heat water to just below boiling point and pour into the pot to fill it completely. Set aside to cool, do this for 14 continuous days at the end of which your pot is ready to use.

Use your pot on a regular basis slowly hardening and strengthening it. Soak your pot in water for 15 to 20 minutes every time you wish to use it to guard against cracking. Until you are fully comfortable cooking with clay use a heat diffuser on your stove top.

Do not use soap or detergent to clean your clay pot. I use wood ash with plenty of hot water and a stiff brush. For that stubborn stain rub in some sea salt, it should do the trick, but lime or a little vinegar will work just as well. Dry off your clay pot before storing it; any residual moisture will bring on mould, in which case wash with a solution of baking soda and water and scrub off with a brush.

Begin by cooking a simple dhal or vegetable stew in your clay pot, progress to rice and later to a fish curry. As the weeks and months go by you will notice that your clay pot takes on uniqueness and a character of its own rewarding you with some very tasty food.

102 The Baghaar: is an Indian cooking technique where spices and other ingredients such as ginger and garlic are fried in very hot oil.

Lemon Infused Jackfruit

Makes 4 servings

To cook with jackfruit you need to get hold of young unripe fruit, usually available in South Indian markets between February and May. There are dozens of jackfruit varieties, many of them nameless. Cook the unripe fruit of any variety as a vegetable. Choose firm, oblong fruit, measuring from 7 to 8 inches in length and approximately 4 to 5 inches in diameter.

To prepare the fruit, thoroughly rinse the jackfruit and with a large knife or cleaver chop the fruit into 6 pieces. Place the pieces of jackfruit in a large pan, cover with water and bring to the boil, lower heat to just below-boiling point and cook until the jackfruit pulp is tender, about two hours. Remove from the heat, drain and allow the pieces to cool. To prepare the fruit use a sharp knife and completely peel off the outer green rind, then carve out the inner core of the fruit either with a knife or by hand. This will leave you with just the flaky pulp, using your hands separate the flakes. For the following recipe, you will need two or three small unripe jackfruit.

You require the following:

2 to 2½ cups well packed cooked jackfruit pulp

200 grams red onions

2 fresh red, yellow and green chillies

1 teaspoon nigella seeds

1/3 cup roasted sunflower seeds or bibiya seeds

Small knob ginger or galangal

½ to ¾ of a large preserved Moroccan lemon

¼ cup fresh green coriander

3 tablespoons oil

Salt and pepper to taste

Heat the oil in a pan and add the nigella seed, finely chopped onion and ginger. Cook until the onions turn a medium-brown and then add the chopped chillies. Fry for a few minutes more then toss in the roasted sunflower or bibiya seeds. Cook for a further two or three minutes then add the shredded jackfruit pulp, a little at a time, mixing it well into the onions. Season to taste with salt and pepper. Cut up the Moroccan lime and add to the pan along with the finely chopped fresh green coriander. Serve hot with pooris or parathas.

Raw Cashew Kernels with Mince Meat

Serves 5

With the onset of spring the cashew trees bloom, and in no time at all, there are signs of bright yellow false fruit or peduncles emerging with their tiny olive green kernels attached. The immature cashew kernels harvested and cooked, about six to eight weeks after their appearance, is a well-loved treat in the South. Rural markets often have the kernels on sale, and in Belgaum, they come with a high price tag attached. Cleaning the immature nuts is really all that stands between you and a really delicious meal!

You require the following:

250 grams immature cashew nuts [shelled]

250 grams mince meat

100 grams onions

6 spring onions

½ tablespoon ginger garlic paste

1 tablespoon spicy Asian black bean sauce

½ a tablespoon freshly ground black pepper

1/3 cup well packed fresh green parsley

2 or 3 tablespoons of oil

Salt to taste

Finely slice the onions and chop the spring onions and the parsley. Place a pan on a moderate heat, add the oil and fry the onions until a light golden brown. Add the mincemeat and the ground black pepper and cook the meat until nicely browned; add salt to taste and the ginger garlic paste. Cook for a few minutes more, and then add a little hot water. Cover the pan and cook the meat until just over half done, then add the cashew nuts and the spring onions and finish cooking. Add a little more water only if required. Finally, add the spicy black bean sauce and the parsley, and check seasoning again. Cook for another 5 minutes and take off the heat. Serve with fresh warm bread or a paratha.

NOOSH -E JAN!

Cleaning Raw Cashew Kernels

Cleaning raw cashew kernels is tedious and make's you wish they came processed and conveniently available off the shelf. But unfortunately, they don't! If you want to enjoy this delicious ingredient you just have to do it yourself, and by hand! Or at any rate, persuade someone else to do it for you!

Choose raw cashew kernels that are about 1½ inches long and 1 inch across. They should be plump and 'give' slightly when pressed. The false fruit or peduncle [You will see the peduncle only if you are plucking the kernels off the tree yourself] should also be about an inch long, slim and pale yellow in colour.

To clean the kernels begin by removing the peduncle, then give the kernels a good rinse and dry off with a kitchen towel. Choose a sharp knife [Parbhi uses her sickle!] and oil both the knife and your hands with a liberal amount of vegetable oil. Hold the kernel upright with your thumb and forefinger, and split the kernel into two by first inserting the point of the knife and then cutting through. Now peel off the green outer skin of each piece. Drop the pieces of ivory into a bowl of cold water, where they must remain until you are ready to cook. Wash your hands and your knife in hot soapy water when done.

Udang Rang up Bercili [crispy prawn chilly]: This is a classic Malaysian condiment or sambal. Made from dried shrimp, chillies, shallots, oil, and garlic, it is mildly spicy, crunchy and very addictive. It is so versatile you feel lost without it. Use it in a salad dressing, in yogurt or rice. Very good with vegetables, such as ladies fingers, bitter gourd, and tomatoes, or weave it through your spaghetti or noodles. Available bottled, in an Asian store near you.

'Just in Time for Tea'

Teatime at Krupalaya meant lots of hot toast and butter, cheese, an assortment of jams, crunchy peanut butter, biscuits, and of course, that old time favourite the brownie. Fresh warm 'twists' were procured from Golden Age, the Irani bakery on Dhanvantri Road run by Behram and Minu. Delicious varkees and savoury biscuits from The West Coast Bakery opposite the Ooty market, and if we were lucky, delicacies from Poona sent by thoughtful relatives, Shrewsbury biscuits from Kayani's, or tantalizing wine biscuits from Royal Bakery.

Stacked one on top of the other in the storeroom, full of these teatime treats were umpteen biscuit tins. Some of the tins were as old as the hills, most of them with English Country scenes or portraits of British aristocracy. Seldom thrown away, empty biscuit tins were put to good use. Found all over Krupalaya including my father's office, filled with passports and gun licenses, newspaper cuttings, old photographs, seed packets, and medicines. My mother's collection of keys required a number of tins though most of the locks were either long gone or misplaced. The older more decrepit looking tins were given over to Raju for a coat of mostly green paint, and as good as they now looked, it usually also meant that the lids no longer fit.

Teatime ushered in a lot of visitors, the unfamiliar, the odd acquaintance, but also plenty of family friends, who dropped by for a chat. Among them, Dorothy Simonelli, wife of Carlos who was employed by the palace, Harold and Anne Devereux who at nearly 80 could still dance the night away, Caroline Parpia who sewed the most wonderful quilts. There was Barbara Van Ingen wife to Botha Van Ingen, son of Eugene, taxidermists who set up shop in Mysore in the 1890s.

Anna Berell, beautiful and charming, always found time to visit. Magnificently dressed, her headgear a brightly coloured turban with sparkling rhinestone, frock in a garden print, and stylish court shoes to match, would arrive exactly at 4. 30 and announce 'Just in time for tea. 'An educationist from Buffalo she brought down exchange students to the University of Mysore, one group in the late sixties, went renegade and took Mysore by storm, when they all turned long haired and barefoot, hippie and happy, and tripping all over town.

Yvette Shilla was occasionally in town. A friend of His Highness Jayacharmraja Wodeyar she stayed as his guest at Vasantha Mahal across the road. Yvette was French, buxom and blonde and a renowned dog breeder to boot. Her arrival at teatime, exquisitely dressed her two Chihuahuas neatly tucked into her large handbag, really took the tedium out of an otherwise unexceptional day.

24. Sheila's Sandwiches

I was convinced a long time ago that the 'method' my mother applied to rustle up dozens of yummy sandwiches was near perfect. Whether for a small garden party or for the tea stall at the annual fête held at the Holdsworth Memorial Hospital, they seemed to appear in no time and vanished just as swiftly!

What my mother did:

- Made up sandwiches spontaneously by raiding the store cupboard and using whatever was available on hand.
- Didn't think twice, trumped up plenty of motivation and experimented with conviction.
- All this backed by a firm commitment to harbouring no misgivings in hindsight!

Sandwich Spreads

Blend softened butter with honey or maple syrup and spread thickly on fresh white bread with the crust left on. Use with grated carrots, prunes, dates, or apple slices lightly caramelised in brown sugar and butter.

Replace peanut butter with fruit butter such as apple, lemon or prune. Create your own nut butter - chocolate and hazelnut or pine nuts and honey.

Blend softened butter with a little Asian sesame oil, a speciality salt and a teaspoon of black or white sesame seeds. Use with flaked tuna or crabmeat, or lightly cooked shrimp enveloped in rocket leaves or any other salad greens.

Blend butter with a little-grated onion or radish, your favourite herb, and celery or garlic salt. Use with leftover roast lamb or cottage cheese.

Grated cheese added to mayo or your favourite salad dressing with finely minced pickles, gherkins or spring onions, good with cucumber, tomato or sliced boiled eggs.

Chopped hard-boiled eggs, mayo, whole grain mustard or wasabi, bind together with a little cream. Use with salad greens, Chinese mustard, rocket, Osaka purple or silver beet.

Blend mayo with tahini and a generous pinch of garam masala and season to taste with a little salt. Use with your favourite vegetable fillings such as tomato, grilled aubergine, courgettes or cucumber.

With a little softened butter and mayo mixed together as the base of your spread, add any number of different ingredients:

Tomato kasundi

Orange marmalade

Asian yellow bean sauce

Chinese char siu sauce

Thai coconut flower syrup with a grating of fresh ginger root – super!

Sandwich Fillings

- Buttered bread, chunky peanut butter, raisins and slices of banana sprinkled with a little ground nutmeg or cinnamon.
- Buttered bread, with mayo, cream cheese and pineapple topped with finely chopped mint.
- Buttered bread, chopped dates, crushed walnuts, and your favourite cream cheese
- Buttered multigrain bread, wasabi, cream cheese, thinly sliced cucumbers and a little finely chopped parsley.
- Your favourite bread buttered, mayo with a clove or two of crushed garlic, microgreens, leftover grilled chicken or a slice of cheese.

Sandwich Making

Komala Bakery, on Sayajirao road, stood guard outside one of the entrances to Devaraj market, and facing Komala on the other side was Prabhat bakery, identical like two sentries. Both had indistinguishable shop fronts, identical glass fronted cases facing the road, their assortment of cakes coated in the same candy colours. Their warm crusty freshly made bread, loosely wrapped in white paper were difficult to tell apart, but Granny Ferguson's loyalty was steadfast and so Komala's bread labelled in blue, is what it had to be.

Venerable old bakeries set up generations ago still bake wonderful bread; scout around in your town or city for these often long forgotten establishments. For decades we drove past Akbar Bakery in Belgaum without a thought, relegating it to just a hole in the wall until we discovered their scrumptious brun pao. The range of commercially made breads that now swamp the market include more than just the standard white or brown, so do look around.

It is recommended that you use day old bread for sandwich making [easier to slice], but fresh bread also makes great sandwiches if you leave on the crust. Leaving on the crust also prevents the bread from drying out. For a sandwich iron, removing the crust will give a better fit. Use a sharp knife to prevent the bread from tearing.

To make up the sandwiches, line up matching slices of bread. Pair up the two slices that sit next to each other in the loaf. Soften the butter to room temperature and spread right up to the edge of each slice. Apply enough butter to both slices of bread; this prevents moist fillings such tomatoes from soaking in. After making up the sandwiches, wrap them up in a clean damp kitchen cloth to keep moist and fresh until serving time.

Sandwich Rolls

Makes 16 rolls

You require the following:
A loaf of fresh sandwich bread - 16 slices
125 grams butter at room temperature
16 tablespoons of your favourite sandwich spread
32 tender asparagus spears
16 thin slices of your favourite ham
Watercress or microgreens as required

Lightly steam the asparagus, set aside until needed. Using a very sharp knife remove the crusts from the slices of bread taking care not to tear them. Spread a generous layer of butter on one side of each slice followed by the sandwich spread. Place the slices of ham, asparagus spears with a few sprigs of watercress or micro greens on one side of each slice and roll up. Pin with a toothpick.

Post Script: Let a bit of the asparagus spears and some of the 'greens' stick out of the roll at either end.

Carrot Sandwiches

Makes 12 sandwiches

You require the following:

24 large slices of your favourite bread

2 cups grated carrots

1/3 cup nuts of your choice, such as bibiya, peanuts or pecans

¼ cup dried currants

150 grams butter

1 or 2 mild green or yellow chillies [optional]

½ a cup mayo

¼ cup sour cream

Dash of wasabi or horseradish sauce

Salt to taste

Bring the butter to room temperature and spread generously on one side of the 24 slices of bread, and set aside. Add the roughly cracked nuts, the currants, and the finely minced chillies to the carrots and mix in well. Mix the sour cream and the mayo together with a dash of wasabi or horseradish sauce, season to taste with a little salt. Tip in the carrots and mix well, check seasoning and divide the mixture evenly between the 12 slices of unbuttered bread. Spread the filling upto all four edges and top with the remaining 12 slices. Take on a picnic or a train journey.

Cook's note: Finely grated raw carrots tend to clump together and make it difficult to mix in other ingredients uniformly, so add the carrots a little at a time into the mayo mixture.

Toasted Eggplant Sandwiches

Makes 2 Sandwiches

I first made these sandwiches for a good friend and a regular guest at the Hermitage. Wolfgang had just arrived for his usual one-week stay, but too late for lunch, and too early for dinner!For a snack, I decided to trust my instinct and picked up the slices of fried brinjals left over from lunch. David was horrified, but the plate came back empty!

You will require the following:

4 large slices of bread

3 tablespoons softened butter

4 tablespoons mayonnaise

3 tablespoons tomato or red pepper relish

2 tablespoons grated cheese

4 lettuce leaves, rocket or greens of your choice

6 round slices of eggplant*[103]

1/8 teaspoon turmeric powder

¼ teaspoon cumin powder

¼ teaspoon pepper powder

Salt to taste

Oil to fry

Coat the slices of eggplant with the turmeric, cumin and pepper powders, season to taste with a little salt and set aside for 10 to 15 minutes, then shallow fry in a little oil on both sides until cooked and lightly browned. Set aside to cool. Meanwhile butter the four slices of bread followed by the mayo or sandwich spread on two slices, and the relish on the other two. Layer a few of the greens on the two slices spread with the relish, then arrange the slices of eggplant touching all four edges with an overlap in the centre. Top with the grated cheese, the remaining greens and the last two slices of bread.

Spicy Tomato Sandwiches with Water Cress

Makes 2 sandwiches

4 large slices of brown or multigrain bread

3 tablespoons butter at room temperature

2 or 3 tablespoons of homemade or store bought pesto

2 or 4 slices of cheddar cheese, depending on size

1 large tomato

2 tablespoons watercress or mustard microgreens

Salt and pepper to taste

A few drops Chinese chilli oil

103 You must be the judge on the number of slices depending on the size of your eggplant.

Slice the tomato and gently toss in half a tablespoon of hot butter on low heat for half one minute, sprinkle with a little pepper and salt. Remove from the heat and cool. Butter the 4 slices of bread on one side, followed by a generous layer of pesto. On two slices, layer the slices of cheese so that the bread is well covered; next add the slices of tomato and the watercress. Dribble on a few drops of Chinese chilli oil and finish with the remaining slices of bread.

Dearly Loved Boman Mama and Nergis Fui

My Brother Kairus

Above Colonel Jerry Rue and my father
On the Left: Nergis Darashah, Kay Fernandes, Colonel Rue and Colonel Mistry

25. Baking

Cinnamon Coffeecake with Crumble Topping

Makes one 8" cake, enough for 6 to 7

You require the following:

50 grams butter brought to room temperature

½ cup granulated sugar

2 large eggs

1 teaspoon rose essence

1 cup self-rising flour

½ cup dairy sour cream

1 cup dried fruit – dates, prunes, currants and cranberries

1 round cake tin 8" to 9" in diameter and at least 2½" deep, buttered

The Crumble Topping:

You require the following:

¼ cup brown sugar

4 tablespoons quick cooking oats

½ teaspoon cinnamon

½ cup walnuts

50 grams butter

To make the crumble topping roughly chop the walnuts and add the brown sugar, rolled oats and cinnamon powder together. Cut the butter into the mixture, and with your fingers blend all the ingredients to resemble the texture of breadcrumbs.

To prepare the cake:

Preheat oven to 175°C, beat the butter and the sugar together until light and fluffy. Then add the well-beaten eggs. Prepare the dried fruit, cut up the larger ones and toss with one or two tablespoons of the flour. Add alternative spoonfuls of flour and dried fruit to the beaten eggs and butter mixing thoroughly after each addition. Finish by gently folding in the sour cream and the rose essence. Pour into the cake tin and level off the top using a spatula. Cover the surface of the cake batter with the crumble topping and pop into the oven. Bake 40 minutes or until the cake has risen. Test by inserting a skewer into the centre of the cake and check if it comes out clean. Remove from the oven and cool. Turn out the cake and cool further until ready to serve.

Delightful Carrot Cake with Cream Cheese Frosting

Serve at tea time, for a family of 6

Decorate with edible flowers

You require the following:

400 grams grated orange carrots
2 cups self-rising flour
1 cup granulated sugar
1 cup brown sugar
2 teaspoon ground cinnamon
½ teaspoon grated nutmeg
1 cup pine nuts or walnuts
300 ml refined vegetable oil
50 grams butter
4 large eggs
1 teaspoon salt
2 round cake tins 8″ to 9″ in diameter and at least 2½″ deep buttered

Preheat oven to 175°C, grate the carrots [medium grade] and in a pan gently heat the butter, taking care not to let it burn. Then add the carrots and fry, stirring constantly until they turn colour, about 5 to 8 minutes. Set aside to cool. Break the eggs into a mixing bowl, and beat them well, all the while pouring in the vegetable oil in a slow steady stream. Continue to beat until well mixed. Now add the brown sugar and the granulated sugar and blend again. In another bowl mix the flour, salt, and spice powders. With the help of an electric beater fold the flour into the egg mixture, finally add the carrots and the chopped pine nuts or walnuts and blend again. Divide the mixture in two and pour into the cake tins and bake 30 minutes or until done. A skewer inserted into the centre of the cakes should come out clean. Remove from the oven and cool completely, and then frost the cakes.

For the Cream Cheese Frosting:

You require the following:

250 grams cream cheese brought to room temperature

500 grams finely powdered sugar

50 grams butter brought to room temperature

2 or 3 drops kewra or vanilla essence

Beat the cheese with the butter until light and fluffy. Gradually add the sugar, mixing all the time. Then add the essence and beat again until smooth and creamy. When the cakes are quite cool, sandwich the two cakes together, with a generous layer of the cream cheese frosting. Then proceed to frost the cake on top and down the sides. Decorate with edible flowers, cornflower petals intermingled with marigold.

Palm Jaggery or Palm Sugar: Palm sugar, aproduct similar to cane sugar jaggery, but obtained from the sap of the palmyra palm or the date palm, is first boiled and then dried out to a concentrate. A good substitute for white sugar, and widely used in the South to sweeten filter coffee.

Palm Honey: A natural sweet syrup very like honey, and prepared by concentrating the sap of the palmyra palm. Palm honey or 'Panam Paani' as known in Kerala, or what the rest of us might know as palm sugar syrup, has outstanding taste and flavour. It blends beautifully with Spicy Black Bean Sauce or Chinese Hot Pepper Sauce.

Coconut and Date Cake with Coconut Topping

Tea for 6 to 8

You require the following:

200 grams butter at room temperature

3/4 cup castor sugar

4 medium eggs beaten

1 cup freshly grated coconut

2 cups self-rising flour

1/2 cup Iranian dates finely chopped

125 ml thick coconut milk

Butter the cake tin and preheat the oven to 175°C. Tip the chopped dates into the flour and set aside until needed. In a mixing bowl beat the butter and sugar together until fluffy.

Add the eggs one at a time beating well. Add a teaspoon of flour along with the eggs to prevent them from curdling. Then add the grated coconut and mix in well. Now add the flour a ladle at a time along with the coconut milk. Mix well and pour into the cake tin. Bake until done, about 30 minutes. Remove from the oven and cool. Meanwhile, prepare the frosting.

For the topping:
50 grams butter
1/3 cup brown sugar
¼ cup cream
½ cup nuts of your choice
¾ cup freshly grated coconut

Roughly grind or pound the nuts but do not powder them. Add to the coconut with the sugar and mix well. Then add the lightly beaten cream and cut in the butter. Mix all the ingredients together using your fingers. Pile on top of the cake and level down right to the edges. Place under a warm grill until the frosting turns a light brown, but making sure it does not burn. Remove from the grill and cool. Serve warm or at room tempreture.

Orange and Spice Short Bread

Makes one large 8 to 9 inch round shortbread

Perfect with a glass of hot South Indian Coffee!

You require the following:
275 grams all purpose flour
60 grams finely ground rice flour
200 grams butter softened
100 grams castor sugar
1 teaspoon grated orange rind
¼ teaspoon ground cloves
¼ teaspoon ground cinnamon
¼ teaspoon grated nutmeg
Pinch of salt

Tip the butter into a mixing bowl with the castor sugar and beat until light and fluffy. Sift the rice flour and the all-purpose flour together with the salt. Next, add the spice powders and the orange rind to the flour mixture and mix well. Work the flour mixture into the butter and knead into soft dough. Roll out into a circle about ¼ of an inch thick, pinch all around the edge and turn onto a baking tray, and bake in a moderate oven for about 20 minutes or until the shortbread is done. Remove from the oven and cool, cut into wedges and serve.

Cook's note: Reduce grated orange rind to half if you prefer a milder flavour

The Incident of the Salt Cellar

My brother Kairus was a bon vivant and our family recognized from very early on that he truly loved his food. Nevertheless, that did not stop my grandmother from intermittently reminding him that 'his eyes were bigger than his stomach'. The cuisine did not matter, as long as the food was flavoursome and well cooked, however, he did have a favourite breakfast - the 'Full English'. The early years in boarding school, therefore, were trying, to say the least. During one term, a bout of mumps sent him to the school hospital. If that wasn't bad enough he found the hard stodgy idli's served for breakfast deeply depressing, but inescapable nevertheless. One morning,desperate to circumvent them, he pushed a small rusty piece of metal he found lying around into one of his idli's, which he then proceeded to show to authority in the form of Nurse Sangamithri. She wasn't amused. Neither was Colonel Nazir the school doctor, who gave Kairus an earful and finally put to an end to his dreams of a 'Full English'!

On a family holiday to Sikkim in the late'70's, the then Governor of Sikkim BB Lall graciously invited us to dinner at Raj Bhavan[104]. In 1975, the institution of the Chogyal had been abolished, and Sikkim was formally inducted into the Indian union. BB Lall was the first Governor of Sikkim India's 22nd state. It was a momentous occasion for all of us; not only were we going to dine with the Governor, but also were to do so, in one of the most beautiful official residences in the country. Built by J. Claude White, Assistant Political Officer to the British Government in 1888, this beautiful gabled mansion was perched on top a hill with a panoramic view of the Kanchenjunga range. However, the icing on the cake was our police escort, outriders with flashing red lights, sirens and all!

We were quite a crowd, my parents and siblings, Noshir my father's brother and two cousins Meherab and Kayandokth, and of course Nergis Fui. My father who was really chuffed at the invitation wasn't going to let a bunch of unruly children ruin his evening. Kairus the youngest and always prone to some misadventure or the other was duly warned not to fidget and to finish all the food on his plate. But sometimes no matter how hard you try things just don't go the way you want them to. The first episode played out when Kairus decided he wanted more salt in his soup. Unfortunately, the saltcellar he chose had a badly fitting cap and with his vigorous shaking fell and drowned in his bowl of soup, with half the contents of the bottle following thereafter. To make up for the loss of his entrée he took a very liberal helping of the mains that followed! The spread at dinner was excellent, and

104 The Governors residence.

we all tucked in, finally the dessert arrived, stewed fruit with a large pot of whipped cream. Kairus was delighted and took a generous helping of fruit followed by an enormous helping of cream. The poor lad was in for a nasty shock the fruit was wonderfully sweet and soft but the cream skimmed off yak's milk was horribly sour, unfortunately, by this time, my mother had him under the scanner, and he had no choice but to eat it all.

Granny Fergusson's Melting Moments

Makes 12 to 14

This is Granny Fergusson's recipe handed down to her from her mother. Scrumptious! Very delicate, so handle with care; best baked in non-stick muffin tins or at least remember to grease your regular tins well.

You require the following:

185 grams corn flour

185 grams butter at room temperature

85 grams castor sugar

1 teaspoon baking powder

2 large fresh eggs

½ teaspoon essence of your choice

Cream the butter and sugar until light and fluffy, and then add the two well-beaten eggs. Mix and add the essence. Sift the corn flour with the baking powder and gently fold into the butter and egg mixture. Grease 12 to 14 shallow muffin tins with butter and half fill with the batter. Pop into a preheated moderate oven and bake until done with the tops lightly browned, about 20 minutes to half an hour. Remove from the oven and cool, then gently prise out of the muffin tins.

> Chinese Five-spice powder: There is no rule that says to use it in Chinese cooking alone. Fragrant and with a distinctive colour of burnt bricks this is a spice blend of star anise, fennel, clove, cinnamon and Sichuan peppercorns. Use it to flavour Kebabs, barbecued meats, and stews. Like all spices buy in small quantities and store in an airtight container.

Moist Almond Cake with Almond Frosting

Enough for 6

You require the following:
175 grams self-rising flour
175 grams butter at room temperature
175 grams castor sugar
100 grams almonds
Few drops almond essence
3 large eggs
1/4 cup milk
A pinch of salt
One buttered 8 or 9-inch spring form cake tin, pre heat oven to 375° f

For the frosting:
50 grams butter
50 grams castor sugar
50 grams almonds roughly crushed
3 tablespoons milk
3 tablespoons all-purpose flour

Grind the almonds to the consistency of fine breadcrumbs. Beat the butter with the sugar until light and fluffy, then add the eggs one at a time and beat again. Next, add the flour, the salt, and the almonds and fold into the mixture. Add a few drops of almond essence and beat again. Then add the milk a little at a time to thin the batter. Turn into the buttered cake tin, level out the top making a slight depression in the centre so that the cake rises evenly. Bake the cake in a moderate oven for 30 to 40 minutes, or until just done.

Meanwhile, prepare the frosting by first gently melting the butter, then add the roughly crushed nuts and mix well. Next, add the flour, the castor sugar and the milk and mix. Remove the cake from the oven, then carefully spoon the frosting onto the cake and spread it out evenly; return the cake to the oven and cook a further 10 minutes until the topping has set. Cool completely before serving.

Serve with a cup of hot lemon grass tea!

Chocolate Raisin Squares

Makes 12 squares

Very very tasty if I may say so myself!

You require the following:

400 grams condensed milk [1 tin]

40 grams dark chocolate

100 grams raisins

120 grams butter

120 grams self-rising flour

120 grams quick cooking oats

100 grams sugar

A pinch of salt

A greased cake tin measuring 7 x 7 inches

Break the chocolate into pieces, and empty into a pan along with the condensed milk. Heat over a pan of hot simmering water until all the chocolate has melted. Remove from the heat and set aside to cool. Add the raisins to the chocolate and condensed milk mixture. Bring the butter to room temperature, tip into a mixing bowl with the sugar and beat until light and fluffy. Mix the flour, oats and a pinch of salt and add to the butter and sugar mixture. Combine well and then divide the mixture into two. Layer the cake tin with one-half, pressing down with a potato masher or your knuckles, making sure that that the layer is level and smooth. Pour in the condensed milk and chocolate and top with the remaining flour and oat mixture. Once again, press down gently to level it out. Pop into a moderate oven and bake for 30 minutes or until done. Remove from the oven and cool before cutting into squares. Makes an excellent pudding served warm, with a pot of cream.

'The Old Baby Belling'

At Krupalaya, our 'Old Baby Belling' sat on a table in a corner of a large, rather cheerless room leading off from the breakfast room. The practical and useful 'dooley,' [with its legs standing in bowls of water to keep out the ants] stood opposite. There was also a refrigerator, a cupboard full of linen, a 'dumbwaiter' crammed with antiquated crockery, and an old ceramic water filter filled in another corner. There was a lot of baking done at Krupalaya, and so our Baby Belling was a venerable and very important piece of equipment in our household, so much so, that even when it had long past its prime we hung onto it for dear life.

During the 60's and 70's, kitchen equipment like so much else was hard to come by, and what little was available was hardly inspiring. My mother was a genius at procuring second-hand bits and pieces mostly from expat's on their way home after a 4 or 5-year stint in India. Unfortunately, quite a few of these gadgets turned out to be white elephants in the true sense of the word. In the early 60's, one of the first to arrive was a three-legged, top loading washing machine on wheels, it was a novelty that nobody knew how to use. Keeping abreast with the changes in power distribution in the city of Mysore, palace records show that Krupalaya was one of the first royal properties to move from an energy rating of 110 to 220 volts in September of 1950. [105] Nevertheless, we had very little success with the two magnificent General Electric cooking ranges bought off Dr. and Mrs. Edwards. Every time they were used, all the fuses blew and Krupalaya was plunged into darkness!

There were triumphs, of course, the food processor made a big difference, and the juicer was used quite frequently, the steam iron daily - but without the steam! Cupboards filled with kitchen tools and cooking accessories, cake tins and loaf tins, holiday decorations, linen, crockery, and cutlery - something's old and something's new!

105 Source: Palace Maramath Department, Divisional Archives Mysore.

26. Fruit

Baked Mango Pudding

Enough for 6 persons

You require the following:

½ cup cream

1 cup Greek yogurt or hung curd

3 generous pinches of cinnamon powder

¼ teaspoon grated nutmeg or powered acacia seed

1 or 2 tablespoons charoli [more the better!]

½ a cup castor sugar or to taste

2 cups sweet mango pulp [approximately 4 or 5 large ripe mangos]

Beat the cream until smooth and no lumps remain. Strain the mango pulp if necessary to remove any 'strings.' Lightly beat the yogurt to a smooth consistency and add the cinnamon powder, grated nutmeg or acacia seed, and the castor sugar. Add the cream to the yogurt and mix well. Combine all the ingredients and pour into an ovenproof pudding dish. Place the pudding dish in a larger pan, fill the pan half way up with water [bain-marie], and bake the mango pudding in a moderate oven until set. Can be served at room temperature but tastes best lightly chilled.

Cook's note: You can over bake this pudding making it shrink and discolour, so keep checking and remove as soon as it sets.

Custard Apple Basundi

5 to 6 helpings

You will require the following:

1250ml whole milk, preferably buffalo milk

2 cups of custard apple pulp [4 or 5 large fruit]

One third cup sugar or to taste

1/4 teaspoon nutmeg

1/4 cup mixed nuts and raisins

6 Iranian dates

200 ml thick cream

Pink or red rose petals to decorate

Pour the milk into in a heavy bottomed pan and bring to the boil just once, then simmer the milk until the quantity reduces to a little less than half. It will begin to thicken and change colour, stir gently be careful not to let the milk burn. Scrape off the milk solids that accumulate on the sides of the vessel back into the milk. Now add the sugar, and continue to thicken the milk. Then add the nutmeg and the assorted dried fruit. Cook for a few minutes more then remove from the heat and cool. Meanwhile, extract the pulp from the custard apples. Add the pulp and the chopped dates to the lightly beaten cream. When the basundi has cooled, mix all together, turn out into a serving dish and chill. Serve decorated with rose petals.

Minted Papaya Cream with Coconut

Serves 4

You will need the following:

400 grams papaya

3 tablespoons mint cordial

60 ml thick coconut milk

Sugar to taste if needed

Juice of 1/2 a lime

4 tablespoons fresh grated coconut

2 tablespoons roasted dhania dhal

Cut and clean the papaya, then chop into large pieces, papaya skin is bitter so make sure that you remove it all. Puree the fruit with the thick coconut milk, sugar, and the mint cordial, until creamy and smooth. Then add the lemon juice, mix well and chill for an hour or two. Just before serving, separately dry roast the freshly grated coconut and the dhania dhal. Divide the papaya between 4 glass bowls, top with the roasted coconut and dhania dhal and decorate with a sprig of fresh mint.

Granny Fergusson's Banana Fritters

Enough fritters for 4

The one thing that my family cannot abide, are fritters perfectly formed and held together by an overuse of flour. The recipe below will not make you the best-looking fritters but they taste wonderful. Keep an eye on the heat; add the batter to hot oil, then lower to medium. Sometimes the edges might burn a little, but they taste even better!

You require the following:

4 medium bananas

1 large egg

1/3 cup all-purpose flour or fine rice flour [approximately]

1/3 cup castor sugar or to taste

¼ cup raisins, black currants or any other dried fruit

¼ cup charoli

A little grated nutmeg

Oil to shallow fry

Roughly mash the bananas with a fork; you don't want it too smooth. Beat the egg well, add the sugar and continue to beat until the sugar has dissolved. Then add the bananas, dried fruit, and nutmeg and mix together until well blended. Now add just enough flour to thicken the banana mixture. Heat the oil in a frying pan, and do a test run, by dropping a spoonful of mixture into the oil. If the fritter forms with a few 'frills' around the edges you are doing well, otherwise add a little more flour. Drop in a small ladleful of the banana mixture for every fritter, and do no more than 4 at a time. Once the fritter has formed, turn over and fry the other side. Keep beating the banana mixture every now and then, as you cook. Serve warm with a pot of cream and slices of lime.

The Nanjungod Rasbale

An old Mysorean will lapse into a state of wistfulness if you mention the Nanjungod Rasbale. Once so omnipresent in the state of Mysore, this wonderful little banana is really difficult to find now. Other heirloom varieties, though wonderful in their own right are being passed off as the Nanjungod. It was the only banana that ever graced the table in Krupalaya, with my father knocking back 5 or 6 at a sitting. With an amazing shelf life of 12 to 14 days, it has a sweet unique flavour, and an irresistible and distinct aroma when fully ripe. Badly hit by Panama wilt the Nanjungod Rasbale is now facing extinction.

If you are ever in this part of the world and want to delight in its exquisite taste, stop by at Nanjungod on National Highway 212 to Calicut. Turn off the highway onto R. P road and ask for the railway crossing. There you will find the Government Boy's Middle School, and right opposite a tiny cigarette stall where you will also find a bunch or two of the incomparable Nanjungod Rasbale.

Mulberries and Mascarpone

4 to 5 generous helpings

You will require the following:

4½ cups sweet juicy mulberries
100 ml single cream
1 tablespoon lemon juice
200 grams mascarpone
Castor sugar to taste
Shortbread or oatmeal biscuits as required

If you are very particular you can snip of the tiny green stems of the mulberries with a pair of scissors as close to the fruit as you can, or just leave them on like I do. Place 4 cups of the fruit in a bowl and chill in the refrigerator for an hour or two. Using a fork, lightly crush the remaining ½ cup with castor sugar and the lemon juice, and chill. Bring the mascarpone down to room temperate, then add the lightly beaten cream and mix well, then chill. Just before you are ready to serve, swirl the crushed mulberries into the mascarpone and cream mixture. Reserving a few fruit to garnish, in individual glass bowls layer the fruit with a layer of mascarpone and cream, followed by a layer of roughly crushed shortbread or oatmeal biscuits. End with a layer of mascarpone and cream. Garnish each bowl with the reserved fruit and serve.

27. Cool Summer Drinks

Cucumber and Wasabi Lassi

Enough for 4

You will require the following:

300 grams thick well-set yogurt
500 ml cold water
500 grams cucumber
2 tablespoons fresh mint
2 tablespoons coriander
1 teaspoon cumin powder
1 teaspoon black pepper powder
1 teaspoon finely ground ginger paste
2 teaspoons wasabi or to taste
Rock salt to taste

With a fork or wire whisk beat the yogurt until smooth. Add the cold water, whisk again, and chill until needed. Finely chop the mint and coriander. Chop the cucumber into large pieces and blitz in a food processor until smooth. Add the spice powders, ginger paste, green coriander and one tablespoon of the chopped mint and blend again. Then add to the yogurt and season to taste with the rock salt. Finally, add the wasabi and chill until ready to serve. Pour into tall glasses and top with the remaining mint.

Minty Strawberry Lassi With Indian Black Salt

Makes 3 medium sized glasses

You will require the following:

400 grams strawberries
300 grams well set thick yogurt

250ml cold water

Castor sugar to taste

1 tablespoon finely chopped mint

A generous pinch or two of Indian black salt

3 to 4 tablespoons pomegranate pearls to garnish

Clean the strawberries and chop them roughly. With a fork or wire whisk beat the yogurt, then add the cold water and beat again. Put the strawberries and yogurt into a food processor with sugar to taste, and blend well. Add the chopped mint and chill until ready to serve. Pour into glasses and top with the pomegranate pearls. Finally, sprinkle with the Indian black salt and serve

Cook's note: The sharpness and intensity of Indian black salt is hard to replace, but if unavailable use any other specialty salt available with you.

Water Works

When David and I first moved to The Hermitage in 1981, we didn't bother to boil or filter our drinking water. It was wonderful as it was straight from an underground spring. In 2004 when we started our guesthouse, we started filtering it, surprisingly nothing changed, and our water is just as sweet and tasteful as ever. On a hot summer's day or after a long jungle walk, a jug of water tweaked with a little lime juice and chilled in the refrigerator is a super thirst quencher. Below are some of the things we do with our water at the Hermitage, you can keep topping up the jug of water as it empties through the day:

Mint: Add half a cupful of lightly crushed mint leaves to a jug of water, chill. Grow apple mint, spearmint or black peppermint in your garden.

Holy Basil [Tulsi]: Steep the leaves of the holy basil in warm water then chill in the refrigerator.

Mixed Herbs: Your choice of herbs, rosemary, thyme, marjoram or sage, crush and add to a jug of chilled water.

Crimson Water *[Caesalpinia sappan Linn.]*: Known as pathimugam in the state of Kerala, it is the heartwood of *Caesalpinia sappan*. Well known for its medicinal properties, a chip or two of this attractive redwood boiled in three litres of water for 8 to 10 minutes turns it a pleasing shade of red. Leave the chips in the water as it cools. Serve chilled with cubes of ice made with the same water.

Vettiver Roots *[Vetiveria zizanioides]*: Steep a handful of vettiver roots in two litres of warm water for a few hours or overnight. Strain and serve chilled with a squeeze of lemon juice.

Crushed fennel: Dry roast some fennel seeds. Cool and roughly crush the seeds, add to your drinking water and steep for a few hours or overnight, strain and chill.

Japanese preserved ginger: These wonderful slivers of pink used in sushi are also great in a jug of cold water, use whole or roughly sliced into pieces.

Chilled Rose and Watermelon Crush

[Makes 3 tall glasses]

You will require the following:

800 grams red or yellow watermelon [after cleaning the fruit]

½ tablespoon finely ground ginger paste

2 or 3 tablespoons rose or rhododendron syrup or to taste

1 tablespoon crushed mint.

1 tablespoon tukmaria [basil] seeds

Castor sugar to taste [if required]

Ice cubes

Place the chunks of watermelon in the refrigerator to chill. Cover the tukmaria seeds with cold water and allow them to swell. Just before serving, put the watermelon in a food processor with the ginger paste, rose syrup and sugar, and blend until smooth. Put a little of the crushed mint into each glass with a few ice cubes, and pour the watermelon juice on top. Drain the tukmaria seeds through a fine sieve and spoon on top of the watermelon juice. Chill for a further 10 minutes or serve immediately

Tukmaria [Basil] seeds: You rarely see basil seeds other than in Falooda, swimming in a tall glass of pale pink, rose flavoured milk. They do put in an appearance in the cuisines of Iran, Afghanistan and Indonesia. These tiny black seeds usually harvested from the Holy Basil [*Ocimum sanctum]* and Hairy Basil *[Ocimum canum],* are transformed when soaked in water. With little or no flavour of their own, but their unique jelly-like texture with a crunchy centre can be a wonderful contribution to your kitchen creations. Use in a smoothie, a glass of chilled herbal tea, fresh lime juice, a cocktail, or like I do in yogurt.

Blushing Pink Buttermilk

Serves 4 or 5

You require the following:

1 litre buttermilk, homemade or store bought

250 grams beetroot

2 tablespoons rob- e anar [pomegranate molasses]

6 to 8 large slivers of Japanese preserved ginger

2 or 3 cloves garlic

1 or 2 tablespoons castor sugar

1 tablespoon chopped mint

Indian black salt or any other speciality salt to taste

Chill the buttermilk until ready to use. Pressure cook the beetroot until done, cool, peel and puree in a blender. If necessary, add 100 ml of the buttermilk to make the task easier. Add the rest of the ingredients and puree again until nice and smooth. Stir the puree into the remaining buttermilk and mix well, check seasoning and chill until serving time.

Tutti Frutti

Most of us have ice cream memories that revisit our childhood, and growing up in the 60's in Southern India 'Ice Cream' memories usually implied 'Homemade'. Ours was hand cranked by Das or Krishna in an old wooden 'war horse' of a bucket that belonged to Granny Ferguson. I would watch, as they slot in the metal canister full of wonderful ingredients, load the wooden bucket with rock salt and cracked ice, and while they took turns laboriously cranking the handle, I listened to their interesting gossip. Made and later stored in the refrigerator in a beautiful midnight blue enamel container, the ice cream was usually served at lunch; my father calling for it to be removed from the refrigerator half way through the meal, so that it was just the right consistency when served later. I have that wooden bucket now, mostly retired but still capable of churning out delicious ice cream and a bucketful of memories.

Das' rich creamy dark chocolate, vanilla and coffee, maybe staid and old fashioned compared to the exotic ice cream concoctions of today but nevertheless how eager we were for a scoop! There were, of course, commercial ice creams to be had, Tutti Frutti mottled with brightly coloured candied fruit, Cassata - an ice cream and cake concoction topped off with glazed red cherries, pale pink strawberry, or a slice of pista, the colour providing identification more than anything else.

There are more than a thousand reasons why you should consider homemade ice cream over a commercial brand. That is the number of artificial ingredients, most of them unhealthy and some positively dangerous, that can be used to produce a carton of store bought ice cream. A long list that includes stabilizers, emulsifiers, artificial flavourings, and colourings; the ice creams may also contain artificial sweeteners and chemical preservatives, with some brands nothing more than a chemical concoction with no 'ice cream' in them at all.

Making ice creams at home helps you avoid dodgy ingredients such as Polysorbate 80, Potassium sorbate, or the Mono-diglycerides. When you cook, you can choose what goes in and what stays out. Natural wholesome ingredients are all that you need, milk, cream, and fruit inexpensive and easy to find.

For successful homemade ice cream, the cream is an essential ingredient and you cannot replace it, so do be prepared to use it! The cream should be thick but not too heavy or oily or flecks of cream will riddle your ice cream. Homemade ice cream stays fresh 3 to 4 days, and just so that you know, sugar tastes less sweet when it freezes and use alcohol in small quantities – too much prevents the ice cream from freezing and setting.

Use an ice cream machine to make the following recipes in which case follow the manufactures instructions. Alternatively, to set ice cream just your refrigerator will do! Pour the ice cream mixture into a container and place it in the freezer, allow the mixture to set partially. Remove it from the freezer and beat it well, repeat the partial freezing and beating process two or three times, this ensures that the ice cream has a smooth creamy texture.

28. Desserts - Ice Cream and Puddings

Avocado and Roasted Monkey Nuts

Enough for 3 or 4 kith and kin

Serve with warm peanut sauce

You require the following:

2 cups well-packed avocado pulp [2 large or 3 small avocados]

3/4 cup thick cream

120 grams fine castor sugar or to taste

1/2 cup thick coconut milk

1/2 cup monkey nuts [peanuts] roasted

Peel, stone, and mash the avocados to a smooth pulp.[106] Beat the cream until smooth and no lumps remain. Add to the avocado along with the castor sugar and the coconut milk. Mix well and then chill. Dry roast the monkey nuts until nice and brown. Remove from the heat and winnow off the skins. Allow the nuts to cool. Coarsely crush the nuts and add to the avocado pulp. Put into the bowl of an ice-cream maker and churn until it thickens. Next, transfer the mixture to a suitable container and place in the freezer until ready to serve.

For the sauce:

1/4 cup creamy or chunky peanut butter

1/4 cup single cream

1/4 cup mild honey

Mix all the ingredients together and warm gently on low heat. Serve warm with the ice cream.

---

106 A handwritten recipe in one of granny's recipe notebooks, suggests you use a silver fork!

Carrot and Walnut Ice Cream [with a hint of cloves]

Enough for 4 or 5 kith and kin

You will require the following:

250 grams sweet orange carrots

750 ml whole milk

300 ml chilled thick cream

100 grams walnuts

120 grams castor sugar

2 or 3 bay leaves

Few strands of saffron

1½ tablespoons corn flour

1 tablespoon black sesame seeds

½ teaspoon clove powder

Add the grated carrots to 500 ml of the milk, along with the saffron and bay leaves. Place on medium heat and stirring every now and then, cook the carrots until soft and the milk thickens slightly. Take off the heat and cool. Remove the bay leaves and blend the carrots until smooth. Put the carrot mixture back into a pan, add the remaining milk, sugar, and corn flour and cook on low to medium heat until the custard thickens. Remove from the heat, cool once again and then chill. Beat the cream and add to the chilled carrots with the clove powder and sesame seeds. Next, add the roughly chopped walnuts. Churn the mixture in an ice cream machine until done. Freeze in the refrigerator until ready to serve.

NOOSH –E JAN!

Chocolate Ice Cream with Hazelnuts

Enough for 5 to 6 modest helpings!

Make this at home, and you will never touch store bought chocolate ice cream again

You require the following:

4 large egg yolks

200 grams dark chocolate

250 ml thick cream

1 tablespoon corn flour

½ a cup hazelnuts cracked

150 grams castor sugar or to taste

3 tablespoons Kahlua or Irish cream

1 tin evaporated milk [385 ml]

Break up the chocolate into small pieces or grate it. Add the chocolate to the lightly beaten egg yolks along with the corn flour and sugar and mix well. Slowly add the evaporated milk, and then place on low heat stirring constantly until the custard thickens. Remove and allow the custard to cool. Transfer the cooled mixture to a container and chill. Beat the cream until smooth and add to the chilled mixture along with the hazelnuts and liqueur. Churn in an ice-cream maker until it thickens. Then transfer the mixture to a suitable container and freeze until ready to serve.

Custard Apple Ice Cream with Toasted Coconut

Enough for 5 to 6 kith and kin

You will require the following:

2 cups custard apple pulp [Approximately 5 large fruit]

4 egg yolks

500 ml whole milk

250 ml thick cream

A few drops kewra essence

1/3 cup shredded coconut

200 grams sugar

1 tablespoon corn flour

2 tablespoons charoli nuts

Chill the custard apple pulp in the refrigerator until needed. With a little of the milk make a smooth paste with the cornflour and then add it to rest of the milk. Lightly beat the egg yolks with the sugar, and add to the milk. On very low heat cook the mixture until thick and smooth, then remove from the heat and cool. Add the nuts and kewra essence and chill. Lightly beat the cream and add to the chilled custard. Then add the chilled custard apple pulp, and churn in an ice cream maker until thickened, freeze in the refrigerator until ready to serve. Just before serving toast the shredded coconut on a griddle a golden brown. Either serve separately in a bowl or sprinkled on top of each individual serving.

Cook's note: The same recipe works with bull's heart and cherimoya.

Cold Storage

Not very long ago, a guest of ours with a very young child needed some extra disposable diapers. David promised to buy her some on his next marketing trip to Belgaum planned for a day later. His return late afternoon meant there was a mad rush to empty the car and get the mountain of shopping sorted out before it was time for our staff to go home. We all completely forgot about the diapers. Urgently required later that day, we looked high and low for them. We very nearly gave up, until we discovered the box in the refrigerator nestled among packets of tofu, bottles of salad dressing and the butter dish. Whodunit?

We had no electricity for the first five years of rural living, so when my father - in - law Austin surprised us one day with a generous gift of a kerosene run Electrolux refrigerator, we were thrilled. It was old and temperamental and David spent hours coaxing it to work. A flimsy metal flue hung down the back of the refrigerator and heated by a tiny flame encased in a delicate deep blue cylinder of glass; these two seemingly innocuous objects ruled our lives for a very long time!

Finally, there was the advent of electricity! New efficient pumps for the farm, power tools for David's workshop, and music, plenty of music anytime of the day. Shopping lists changed, candles and kerosene were struck off the list, and a brand new Godrej refrigerator arrived in our kitchen. Our diet altered, mango kulfi and chocolate ice cream put in an appearance, fresh meat for Gypsy and our freezer bulged with enough 'bangada'[107] to feed the five hundred. The day came when it was time to move out our old Godrej and replace it with something bigger! Nevertheless, the old thing that served us so long and so well is still here. Housed in the shed next to the tractor, it is a very efficient rat proof cupboard and protects a medley of David's health remedies for the crops we grow on our farm.

The latter part of the 1980's and through the early years of the 1990's, the state government implemented a major drive for the total electrification of rural Karnataka. Street Lights made an appearance in villages, pump sets installed, and many village homes were electrified. Later years have seen a severe shortage of power with power cuts lasting several hours. Although our refrigerator isn't redundant thus far, we never ever take our electricity for granted!

107 Indian mackerel *[Rastrelliger kanagurta]* commonly found in the Indian and West Pacific oceans. There was a time when its abundance made it a cheap and affordable protein for all. Previously sold per piece at less than a rupee each, now it is available only by the kilo and is no longer an economical ingredient in the rural diet of our region.

Nevertheless, there have been many days of celebration. The Government of India, The World Health Organization, and other agencies initiated The Pulse Polio Programme in 1995. All children under 5 took the oral vaccine and mass inoculations of village children were organized. The vaccines needed refrigeration, which meant an uninterrupted supply of power! So while the children got their 'shots,' we made ice creams and set jelly, spiked our drinking water with cubes of ice, and in celebration raised a glass of chilled beer to the World Health Organization!

Pomegranate and Rose Ice Cream with Star Anise

Enough for 4 or 5 kith and kin

You require the following:

1 cup fresh pomegranate juice [2 or 3 large sweet pomegranates]

150 grams castor sugar

3 tablespoons grenadine

2 or 3 drops essence of rose

300ml rich whole milk

300 ml thick cream

1 tablespoon corn flour

5 star anise

Put the milk into a pan, add the star anise and slowly bring to the boil, then lower the heat and simmer for 10 minutes. Remove from the stove, and allow the milk to cool. Meanwhile, extract the juice from the pomegranates and strain. With a little of the cooled milk make a smooth paste with the cornflour, and then add to the rest of the milk along with the sugar. Place the milk back on medium heat and cook until the custard thickens. Remove from the heat and allow the custard to cool completely. Remove the star anise, add the grenadine, pomegranate juice, and the rose essence and mix well. Chill in the refrigerator. Lightly beat the cream until smooth and lump free. Then mix with the chilled custard, finally churn in an ice cream maker until it thickens and sets. Refrigerate until ready to serve, decorated with fresh rose petals and pomegranate pearls.

Banana Ice Cream with Jamaican Rum and Allspice

Enough ice cream for 5 or 6

Serve the ice cream with a platter of sliced bananas fried and caramelized in butter and brown sugar, and dusted with cinnamon. Just a suggestion!

You require the following:

1 cup mashed bananas about 5 to 6 depending on size

500 ml whole milk

3 egg yolks

250 ml thick cream well chilled

150 grams castor sugar

1 tablespoon cornstarch

2 tablespoons dark Jamaican rum

½ teaspoon freshly ground allspice

Beat the egg yolks with the sugar until light and creamy, then add the corn flour and mix well. Slowly add the milk and the ground allspice into the egg mixture and whisk together. Tip into a heavy bottomed pan and cook on low heat until the custard thickens. Remove from the heat and cool. Next, add the rum to the custard, mix well and chill. Lightly beat the cream until you get a smooth consistency, and puree the mashed banana. Add the banana to the chilled custard along with the cream. Churn in an ice cream maker until it thickens, transfer to a suitable container and freeze until ready to serve.

Apricot and Fig Crumble

Enough for 6 people

The light brown, shriveled Hunza apricot the size of a marble grows wild in Central Asia in Afghanistan, Turkey, and extensively in the Hunza valley in Pakistan. The fruits dry on the trees before picking, and as a result, they are so full of flavour. Hunza apricots need to be well soaked before you can use them.

You require the following:

200 grams dried Hunza apricots

200 grams dried figs

100 grams sugar or to taste

2 1" sticks cinnamon

400 ml water

350 ml red wine

For the crumble:

100 grams all-purpose flour or rice flour

50 grams quick cooking rolled oats

75 grams butter

75 grams brown sugar or castor sugar

¼ teaspoon cinnamon powder

50 grams nuts of your choice[roughly crushed]

Pinch of salt

Thoroughly rinse the figs and the apricots and soak in the water until they swell about two hours. Then add the red wine, the sugar and the cinnamon to the fruit and set on medium heat to simmer until they are nice and soft. Remove all the fruit with the help of a slotted spoon put into a glass ovenproof dish and set aside. Then reheat the sugar and wine syrup until it reduces and thickens, there should be just enough syrup to top the fruit. Pour over the apricots and figs. Prepare the crumble by mixing a pinch of salt, the cinnamon powder, the oats, and your favourite nuts into the flour. Add the brown sugar, and using a knife cut in the butter. With your fingertips, mix the butter into the flour to resemble the texture of breadcrumbs. Cover the fruit with crumble and bake in a medium oven until the crumble is a warm nutty brown and the sugar syrup bubbles through. Serve warm or at room temperature with a pot full of luscious buffalo milk cream!

Post script: Just cover the fruit with the syrup, too much will drown the crumble and ruin it. If you like, reduce the quantity of water and add more wine.

Baked Almond Custard

Serves 4

You require the following:

700 ml whole milk [preferably buffalo milk if available]

250ml thick cream

100 grams almonds

2 tablespoons charoli nuts

1/3 cup sugar or more to taste

4 large eggs

A little grated nutmeg

Butter an ovenproof glass dish and set aside. Add the sugar to the milk and heat gently until the sugar melts completely, remove from the heat and cool. Beat the cream until smooth and no lumps remain, beat the eggs well, and mix the cream and eggs together. Grind the almonds and add to the egg mixture with the charoli and grated nutmeg. Now gently stir in the milk, mix well and pour into the glass dish. Sit the pudding dish into a larger roasting pan and fill half way up with water [bain-marie]. Bake in a moderate oven until the custard sets. Best served chilled or at room temperature.

My Frying Pan

The early eighties was a momentous time for the Indian Haus Frau with the arrival of non-stick cookware! In big city shops, you saw impressive displays, black pots, and pans with shiny red lids. My father-in-law bought me my first non–stick frying pan; I was so pleased I was able to overlook the red lid that really looked quite out of place in my green and yellow kitchen. They were expensive, these new arrivals and with Indira's merciless socialism still fresh in collective memory, they seemed terribly extravagant, but what a relief from all that aluminium and stainless steel!

My frying pan hung on a long twisted nail flecked with rust and hastily driven into my kitchen wall, the lid discreetly tucked away in a corner until needed. It was the spring of 1985; we decided to lay down the flooring of our home, which until then was nothing more than rammed earth thickly coated with a paste of cow dung. For work on the flooring to begin, we moved all our belongings out and haphazardly piled then up in the front garden, including my shiny new pan. No one gave much thought to our handsome Khillari[108] bulls Rama and Laxman who happened to be grazing nearby. On what turned out to be a dreadfully inauspicious day, one of them accidentally and I presume unintentionally, put a hefty foot into my brand new, shiny non-stick frying pan. That was the end of the pan of course, but I still have that obtrusive red lid, and though no longer shiny, it still finds a place in my green and yellow kitchen.

Nutty Bread Pudding

Good for 5 or 6

Bread pudding will probably always remain within the domain of the home kitchen, with a 'comfort food' tag, and therefore not suitable for a dinner party. Too bad, for here is a lip smacking bread pudding you can make at home with a lavishness that will actually make you worry about having a third helping!

---

108 The Khillari is a breed of cattle originating from Satara district in the state of Maharashtra. Farmers of the neighbouring state of Karnataka also favour this breed of cattle for farm work. The best specimens of the Khillari are raced at rural fairs, and are stabled and looked after by their owners like any expensive racehorse!

You require the following:

10 to 14 slices of day old white bread

500ml whole buffalo milk [preferably]

1/3 cup castor sugar or to taste

A few strands of saffron

200ml light fresh cream

1/3 cup mixed dried fruits, [currants, raisins, cranberries] or more!

1/3 cup mixed nuts [walnuts, hazelnuts, charoli] or more!

100 grams butter at room temperature

A little sugar to sprinkle the top of the pudding

Ghee for frying

A well-greased oven proof glass serving dish 8″ square and at least 2½ to 3″ deep

Add the sugar and the saffron to the milk place on medium heat and simmer until all the sugar has melted and the saffron infused in the milk. Set aside to cool. Meanwhile, prepare the dried fruit and roughly chop the nuts. Using a sharp knife remove the crusts from the slices of bread and cut in half. Lightly butter the bread on both sides. Place a heavy bottomed frying pan on medium heat and melt a little ghee, then fry the slices of bread on both sides until crisp and lightly browned. Next, do a dry run and check whether you have enough slices; they should fit snugly and fill ¾ of the dish. Remove and set aside.

Quickly dip the slices of bread in the milk and layer the bottom of the dish, then layer on some of the nuts and dried fruit, followed by a layer of cream. Finish with a final layer of bread. Tip in the remaining milk and cream to completely soak the top layer of bread. Sprinkle on a little sugar, and bake the pudding in a moderate oven for 20 minutes or until the top is lightly browned. Serve warm with a bowl of preserved whole figs, see page 246 for the recipe.

Postscript: The quantity of bread required will depend on the size of the bread available with you. When the bread is fried, the slices will shrink, so keep this in mind.

Crème Brule with Saffron and Palm Honey

Good for 5 to 6 with a sweet tooth

You require the following:

500ml fresh cream

6 large egg yolks

½ cup palm honey[109] [or use regular honey]

Few strands of saffron

2 tablespoons charoli

2 teaspoons palm sugar or brown sugar

Pinch of salt

Tip the cream into a heavy saucepan, add the saffron strands and on low heat bring gently to a simmer. Remove and set aside to cool. In a mixing bowl beat the eggs until thick and creamy, add the palm honey and a pinch of salt and beat again, a wire whisk is best. Now slowly add the cream to the eggs beating all the time. Lightly butter 5 or 6 individual custard cups and place in a roasting pan filled halfway up with water [bain-marie]. Pour the custard into the cups sprinkling the charoli on top and bake in a moderate oven until set. Remove and cool, then chill for 4 to 6 hours. Half an hour before serving allow the custards to stand at room temperature, sprinkle the tops with the palm sugar, and with a 'chefs blowtorch' heat the sugar until it melts and browns.

Frog Spawn with Iranian Dates on a Bed of Bananas

Good for 4

Our guests often tell us that the last time they ate sago pudding was when they were children, made by their mothers and grandmothers. This is a slightly different way of making sago and the brandy really makes a difference.

You require the following:

½ cup medium to large sago pearls

1/3 cup thick coconut milk

10 Iranian dates

½ a cup sugar or to taste

---

109 Palm honey or palm sugar syrup.

1¼ cups water

1/3 cup thick cream

2 or 3 Yelllaki or two Cavendish bananas

Generous pinch of salt

1 or 2 tablespoons brandy

Rinse the sago and drain, place in a bowl add the water and allow to soak for three hours. Meanwhile coarsely chop the dates into large pieces and put aside until needed. Tip the pearls and the water into a saucepan with a pinch of salt and place on medium heat, stirring all the while. As the mixture begins to thicken, add the sugar and lower the heat. Continue to cook the sago, and when the sago begins to change colour add the coconut milk. The sago will now begin to bubble and spit, take care. Next, add the chopped dates, remove from the heat and cool. When the sago has cooled, add the lightly beaten cream and the brandy. Slice the bananas and layer the bottom of a glass bowl, pour the sago on top of the bananas and allow the sago to set, serve at room temperature or chilled.

Cook's note: The fresher the sago pearls the better they cook. On long-term storage, the pearls tend to disintegrate, turning into a glutinous mass with a mealy taste when cooked. If you add the dates too soon, they will cook with the sago and change the colour of the pudding from white to brown. The taste of the pudding is a little different but just as good. Yelllaki bananas are one of the many heirloom bananas available in the South.

Cafe Sunrise and a Cup of Irani Chai

Cafe Sunrise, located at the busy junction of Jungalee Maharaj road and the road leading to The Bhandarkar Institute in downtown Poona was the quintessential Irani restaurant. Run by our dear friend Mehdi and before that by his father Mohammad Sadegh,the restaurant was set up by a group of five gentlemen in the mid-'50s. Originally, called Cafe Kazemi, which Mehdi tells me is a famous Persian surname, tracing its venerable lineage to the family of Prophet Muhammad's great-grandson Imam Musa al-Kazim. Irani restaurants have quite extraordinary names, some full of flamboyance such as Poona's 'Deccan Queen' and Cafe Paris, both sadly now defunct, the 'Light of Iran,' and the unfathomable 'Mocambo' in Bombay's Churchgate, the loyalists 'Britannia and Company,' 'The King George,' 'The Shah of Iran' and the well known 'Cafe Leopold,' in all probability the Emperor's namesake. Mohammad Sadegh bought out his partners' in 1959. He changed the name of his restaurant to Cafe Sunrise to celebrate the early morning sun that would rise over the River Mutta, its first rays striking the doors of the cafe at daybreak.

The Irani restaurant has always offered great value for money and nothing illustrates this better than a cup of Irani tea. In the mid-sixties, a cup at 'Cafe Sunrise' was just seven paisa. When Mehdi joined his father in January of 1980, a cup of tea sold at the grand sum of thirty-five paisa. In the early days, restaurant owners and their families survived on the sales of their tea; profit margins were respectable and sheer numbers did the rest. When Mehdi took over, he was selling six hundred cups of tea every day between 4. 30 and 6. 00 in the evenings. On a good day in 1984, when a cup was priced at ninety paisa he sold between fifteen hundred to two thousand cups of Irani Chai through the day.

Tea in Iran is always black and usually served in a glass. The chai offered at the Irani restaurants in India has been a home-grown innovation with rich whole milk playing a significant role. The prosaic but hardwearing white cup and 'sasaar,' yes, a colloquialism for saucer is also iconic, with tea drinkers often pouring their hot tea into the sasaar and noisily slurping it.

This is how Cafe Sunrise made their tea:

Rich whole buffalo milk was poured into a heavy pot and boiled, the heat lowered and the milk left to simmer until it thickened and changed colour to a light creamy yellow. The process was never hurried. Three litres of water were filled into a copper vessel called a 'hunda' and brought to a rolling boil. A hundred grams of tea, usually 'Golden Dust' a product of the Maharashtra Tea Company then added, and sweetened with 400 grams of granulated sugar. The tea simmered gently in the hunda for about twenty minutes and later transferred to a copper samovar from which it was dispensed. The samovar sat on a low flame that allowed the tea to continue its gentle simmer, a few litres of hot milk placed beside it. Both the 'hunda' and the samovar were intrinsic to good tea, both had a silver lining or 'kallai' that had to be well cared for, which meant that they had to be sent to the smithy at least once a month to be plated. The tea making never stopped until late at night, after the last moviegoer had his final cup of Irani chai. Then Cafe Sunrise would finally close its doors.

Cafe Sunrise opened for business at 7. 00 in the morning by which time the 'Chai Stand' was perfectly primed. One of the waiters out front loudly calls out an order for a cup of tea. One of the 'boys' picks up a cup, and with a ladle spoons in hot milk then opens the tap on the samovar and dispenses the tea, all the while constantly and effortlessly rotating the cup so that white and the black swirl together in unison finally reconciling into one .

The patron at his table gets his tea just the right colour, to drink and to savour until the very last drop, knowing that sadly some good things must end. Cafe Sunrise closed its doors forever in December of 2006.

Mulberry Clafoutis

Enough for 5 or 6

Serve with a pot of cream

In Mysore and surroundings districts, the mulberry tree is associated with the rearing of silk worms, and so here, the leaves have far greater value than the fruit. Our mulberry trees at the Hermitage laden with fruit are the territory of the red napped bulbul and the bulbuls' many forest friends. They feast here every spring and early summer, so much so that for the rest of us at the Hermitage, mulberry clafoutis is not always a foregone conclusion!

Your will require the following:

500 grams ripe purple mulberries

125 grams plain all purpose flour

125 ml whole milk

125 ml fresh cream

4 large eggs

150 grams castor sugar or to taste

Pinch of salt

2 tablespoons Grand Marnier [optional]

A dusting of icing sugar

Lightly grease a glass ovenproof dish 8" square and at least 2½" in depth. Rinse the mulberries under cold running water and drain thoroughly, but leaving them a little wet. Toss with some of the sugar and evenly layer the mulberries in the dish. Sieve the flour, salt, and the remaining sugar into a mixing bowl, make a well in the centre and pour in the well-beaten eggs. Gently mix into the flour, adding the milk a little at a time until you have a smooth batter. Beat the cream lightly and add to the batter along with the Grand Marnier. Pour the batter over the mulberries and bake in a preheated moderate oven for about half an hour or until the pudding has set. Best eaten warm with a dusting of icing sugar sprinkled on top and a pot of cream on the side.

Rose Petals: With so many colours to choose from rose petals are fine decorative accents. Where you source your roses from is important, those growing in your own garden are best, commercially grown roses may have pesticides and other chemicals used on them. On a recent visit to a florist, I was dismayed to discover that it is becoming common practice to spray not only roses but all the flowers on display with Attar, which is a Middle Eastern essential oil or perfume; I am still trying to get my head around this one!

The Bee Whisperer

It is the dry season, sometime in mid-April, and the three of us are sitting on the forest floor, ever grateful for the shadows, however meagre, shielding us from the sweltering midday heat. The amplified sounds of summer are all around us the relentless 'kutroo kutroo' of the white-cheeked barbet, the crisp dry rustle of leaves underfoot and the loud monotonous buzzing of honey bees above us. There are David and me, and Rama, a Hanbar from the wada[110] not far from Theregali. We sit and contemplate how to help ourselves to a portion of the honeycomb we cannot see but know is there, the presence of the bees high above us giving us ample corroboration. We watch as the bees disappear into a hollow half way up a large nana[111]. Midday is hardly the best time to harvest honey when the purposeful bees are, well the most purposeful! But Rama is exceptional with a very special gift, calm and fearless he can help himself to all the honey he wants, remaining unfazed by the angry bees buzzing around him, hundreds crawling up his bare arms, landing on his head or sneaking down his back. His gentle blowing eventually soothes and calms them down.

Our honey at The Hermitage has always been raw and comes with the true rural experience of spontaneous collection. It is gathered in delicate 'botanical' cups made then and there, by bending and twisting the pliant leaves of the phansoda[112] or karambal tree[113], and pinned together with splinters of dry lustrous stalks of grass. With a watchful eye on the lookout for a stray infuriated bee, you savour the golden honey right away, dripping from its translucent waxy comb into your mouth and down your chin.

Our honeybee is *Apis serana indica* the most predominant species found and domesticated in India and other parts of Asia. They play a major role in crop pollination and because of their relatively mild temperament are the most suitable for beekeeping. There is a smaller cousin *Apis florea* with a

110 The Hanbars are a community of people widely though sparsely spread in pockets over the region, with a very distinct culture of their own. Living in settlements called 'wadas' on the fringe of a village, or in a forest glade, they are nevertheless linked to the village nearest to them and play an active part in its cultural and social life.

111 Nana *[Lagerstroemia lanceolata]* a large deciduous tree with papery, ash grey strips of exfoliating bark. Found growing in forests with heavy rainfall. The timber has great commercial value.

112 Phansoda *[Butea frondosa]* or flame of the forest.

113 The karambal tree Dillenia pentagyna.

simpler lifestyle; they have smaller colonies, modest methods of construction and their dance steps are uncomplicated. Though unsuitable for commercial beekeeping, their honey is highly prized. The rock bees *Apis dorseta* are claustrophobic, they abhor dark enclosed spaces, preferring to build their magnificent hives out in the open on rock faces or giant trees such the Pyree[114]. Rural folk collect their honey too, but mostly at twilight when tempers aren't so elevated.

Flowers play a major role in influencing the soul and character of honey. The nectar is collected and mixed with the bees own secretions, which results in the distinctive flavour of different kinds of honey. While commercial beekeepers aim to control the flowers their bees can visit, natural or wild honey is usually from a wide cross section of species. Here, in the jungles surrounding us, bees have access to the jambul *[Syzygium cumini skeels],* kindal *[Terminalia paniculata],* and nana *[Lagerstroemia lanceolata]* among many others. Some flowers give the honey a hint of bitterness such as hela *[Terminalia bellerica]* and madthi *[Terminalia tomentosa],* ever present in the jungles of South India with its panicles of dull yellow-green flowers. Surprisingly, bees do not visit the striking ever so conspicuous flame of the forest. It is the sunbirds, parakeets, and monkeys who enjoy the orange flowers with their deep well of nectar.

Honey with high dextrose content crystallises in a very short time and here too flowers play a major role. In North Karnataka, the bees visit the abundant fields of sunflower, which to some extent causes the crystallization of honey. If your bottle of honey crystallises, stand it in a basin of hot water until the golden liquid reappears. Then break open some warm, crusty, freshly baked brun pao, top each half with butter, dribble on the warmed honey and savour your first bite.

114 The pyree or strangler fig.

29. Windfall – Preserving a Bountiful Harvest

Red Pepper Relish

About 5 bottles

You will require the following:

1500 grams bright red capsicum cleaned

500 grams juicy red tomatoes

400 grams red onions

1 small bulb garlic

2½ cups sugar

250 ml apple cider vinegar or any other light coloured vinegar

12 peppercorns

2 pieces of cinnamon 1 inch long

8 cloves

6 cardamoms

¼ cup rock salt or to taste

Chop the bell peppers into small pieces and set aside. Finely chop the onions, garlic, and tomatoes. Place all four ingredients into a heavy bottomed preserving pan with the sugar and spices. Heat very gently, stirring all the time until the sugar melts completely. Increase the heat and bring the mixture to the boil just once. Then lower the heat, add the salt and allow the relish to cook stirring every now and then. When it begins to thicken, add the vinegar and mix well. Continue to cook until the relish begins to set. Check seasoning once again, remove from the heat and cool slightly. Bottle the relish in sterilized jars, to extend shelf life process in a hot water bath.

Green Tomato Preserve

2 or 3 bottles

Green tomatoes such as Aunt Ruby's Green a large beefsteak tomato, or Green Zebra a yellow-green variety with darker stripes or Dorothy's Green tomatoes make good choices. If these and other green heirloom varieties are unavailable to you, use red tomatoes instead, immature red tomatoes will not be a suitable substitute. You can use brown sugar or dark vinegar but they will ruin the colour of the preserve.

You will require the following:

1 kg green tomatoes

250 grams sugar or a little more to taste

200 ml apple cider vinegar or the vinegar of your choice

50 grams fresh root ginger

8 to 10 mild green chilies

100 grams sultanas or raisins

1 tablespoon salt or to taste

Chop the tomatoes into pieces. Skin and thinly slice the ginger. Deseed the chilies if you like and chop into large pieces. In a heavy bottomed pan, mix all the ingredients together, and place on low heat. Cook the preserve stirring all the time, until the sugar has melted. Now increase the heat and bring the mixture to a boil just once, then lower the heat slightly. Cook the preserve until it thickens and sets. Cool and bottle in sterilized jars, then process in a hot water bath.

Cook's tip: The quantity of sugar to use will depend to a large extent on the tartness of the tomatoes, use a little more if you feel that the flavours need to balance out a bit more.

Preserved Moroccan Lemons [l'hamd marakad]

The lemons used in Morocco are old traditional varieties and sold as 'citron beldi,' distinguished by their colour, fragrance, and unique shape. However, use any variety of lemons, such as Eureka or Meyer. I use homegrown Tahiti lemons, which make an excellent preserve. Flavour and texture deteriorate over time so make frequently in small quantities. Best to have on hand always, you will need them!

6 to 8 large blemish free, ripe lemons

Sea salt as needed

The juice of 2 or 3 large lemons

Sterilized glass jars just sufficient to hold the lemons

Hold the lemons upright and using a sharp knife cut lengthwise into quarters about 3/4 of the way down, with the four quarters still attached at the base. Pack each lemon with the sea salt, try and push in as much salt as you can then close the lemon as tightly as possible. Start packing the glass jars with the lemons as tightly as you can, compress the lemons as you add them to the jar. Fill the jar with as many lemons as possible, leaving very little space at the mouth. Finally, pour in enough lemon juice to cover the lemons completely. Secure the jar and store in a cool dark place for about 3 to 4 weeks shaking the jar every few days. You can use the lemons straight out of the jar, [best] or rinse them to remove the excess salt. Dice into pieces and use in vegetable or meat dishes or slice thinly and use in salads or in yogurt.

Green Chilly Kasundi

Fills 3 medium sized bottles

You require the following:

750 grams fresh green chillies of your choice

500 ml mustard oil

50 grams mustard seeds

50 grams fenugreek seeds

20 grams dhania dhal

½ tablespoon devils dung [hing / asafoetida]

3 tablespoons sea salt or to taste

You also require a little extra hot mustard oil to top up the pickle after filling the bottles.

Chop the chillies into pieces one inch long, retaining all the seeds. Tip into a ceramic bowl and mix in two tablespoons of salt. Set aside for an hour, turning the chillies over every now and then. Meanwhile, dry roast the mustard and fenugreek seeds and roughly grind both. Dry roast the dhania dhal until crisp, and set aside until needed. Pour the mustard oil into a large wok on medium heat, and add the ground spices. Fry a couple of minutes. Next, add the chillies and the dhania dhal quickly toss over a medium heat for about 6 to 8 minutes or until just cooked through. Add the remaining salt and the devils dung and mix well, and cook a further 3 to 4 minutes. Switch of the heat and allow the pickle to cool for a short while, check seasoning and then fill in hot sterilized jars, making sure that the oil covers the chillies completely.

Cook's note: Try making the kasundi with fresh red chillies or a combination of red and green, looks nice! Yellow chillies are now available in some urban markets and are a great option as well. You can also add some garlic if you like 1 large or 2 small bulbs. Chop or crush the garlic cloves and add to the oil with the spices. For a kasundi with real punch use whole fresh cascabel chillies.

Tomato Kasundi

Makes 3 bottles

You require the following:
1 kg ripe but firm red tomatoes
75 grams garlic cloves
15 grams ginger
150 grams sugar
40 grams fresh red chillies
40 grams green chillies
2 tablespoons turmeric powder
20 grams mustard seed
40 grams cumin seed
250 ml vinegar
500ml mustard oil
3 tablespoons sea salt

Skin the tomatoes first, by plunging them into hot water and then cold, and chop into small pieces. Finely mince the ginger and chop the garlic. Chop the green and red chillies retaining all the seeds. Place a large wok or pan on medium heat and add 200ml of the oil. When hot add the mustard seed and allow them to crackle. Then add the cumin seeds and cook a minute more. Now add the turmeric powder, chillies, ginger and garlic and cook another minute or two. Then add the remaining oil and the tomatoes. Cook on medium heat, stirring every now and then, about 15 minutes. As the tomatoes begin to break down, add the sugar, salt, and vinegar. Cook for a further 8 to 10 minutes or until the tomatoes are soft, fully cooked, and the oil begins to rise. Continue to cook a few minutes more, then remove from heat and set aside to cool slightly, then while still hot fill in hot sterilized bottles.

30. Jams and Jellies

Cherry Tomatoes and Cloves

Makes approximately 3 bottles

You require the following:

2 kgs red or yellow cherry tomatoes, for better colour, don't mix them

1. 5kgs granulated sugar

2 lemons

12 cloves

4 cassia leaves or bay leaves

250 ml water

2 or 3 tablespoons Drambuie

If they are small, keep the cherry tomatoes whole; otherwise halve them. Squeeze out the lemon juice and with a pair of kitchen scissors cut each cassia or bay leaf into four. Place a pan on medium heat and add the tomatoes, the water, cloves and the cassia leaves. Cook the tomatoes stirring constantly for 5 to 8 minutes; however do not allow the mixture to boil. Lower the heat and add the sugar. Once the sugar has dissolved, add the lemon juice, increase the heat and bring just once to a boil. Then let the jam cook until it thickens and sets. Remove from the stove and cool. Discard the cassia or bay leaves, add the Drambuie, mix well bottle in sterile jars, and process in a hot water bath.

Carrot Jam with Almonds and Prunes

Makes three 400 gram bottles

Pile onto hot buttered toast, or lightly warmed onto vanilla ice cream!

You require the following

1 kg sweet carrots preferably orange or yellow[115]

700 grams sugar

100 grams almonds[116]

50 grams ready to eat prunes

750 ml water

2 lemons, the juice, and the grated rind

2 or 3 tablespoons Grand Marnier [optional]

Grate the carrots, blanch the almonds in hot water for a few minutes, skin them, and then slice thinly. Chop the prunes into small pieces and set aside until needed. Put the carrots and the water in a pan and cook the carrots for about 10 minutes. Meanwhile, grate the lemon rind and extract all the juice. Add to the carrots along with the sugar. On low heat, allow the sugar to melt completely. Once all the sugar has melted increase the heat and bring the jam to a boil just once, then cook just below boiling point until the jam begins to set. Then add the almonds and prunes and allow it to cook until the jam sets. Then remove from the heat and cool slightly. Add the Grand Marnier mix well, fill in sterilized jars, and process in a hot water bath.

Preserved Whole Figs

Makes about 2 large bottles

1 kg medium size green or purple figs

700 gram sugar

300 ml water

2 tablespoons lime juice

6 to 8 cloves

2" piece cinnamon broken up

1 or 2 tablespoons brandy [optional]

Choose ripe, unblemished figs, retain an inch of the stalks and wash gently under running water. In a ceramic or enamelled bowl, alternatively, layer the figs and sugar, cover the bowl and leave to macerate overnight. Transfer the figs and sugar to preserving pan or large pot, add the water, lime juice, and spices and set on low heat. Give the pan a gentle stir now

---

115 Try the striking bright orange Nantes.

116 You can use almond shavings or flakes if you prefer.

and then and allow the sugar to melt. Once the sugar has melted, increase the heat and bring to the boil. Then lower the heat to just below boiling point and let the figs cook. Once the syrup has thickened and the figs have softened, test to check if the preserve is setting. Then remove from the heat and cool slightly. Add the brandy and fill in sterilized jars, then process in a hot bath*. Serve with ice cream or a simple dessert that needs a bit of a lift.

*Cook's note: Processing in a hot water bath essential, the shelf life of this preserve is rather short. When helping yourself to a fig from the jar always use a clean dry spoon.

Spiced Whole Grape Jam

Makes approximately 4 bottles of 400 grams each

Grapes usually turn into jellies rather than jam. The following recipe produces an excellent jam, with a very long shelf life of more than 2 years.

You require the following:

2 kgs dark purple table grapes weighed in after cleaning

1400 grams granulated sugar

250ml water

12 cloves

4 one inch piece cinnamon

6 star anise

Juice of two large lemons

Thoroughly rinse the grapes, tip into a large bowl and with the help of a potato masher or the back of a large spoon lightly crush them. Add the sugar and allow the grapes to macerate for 4 to 6 hours, or overnight in the refrigerator. In a pan on low heat, add the grapes, sugar, water and all the spices and cook, stirring every now and allowing the sugar to melt completely. Once the sugar has completely melted, increase the heat and bring the jam to the boil just once. Then lower the heat to just under boiling point, and add the lemon juice. Cook the jam until it thickens and sets. When done remove from the heat, allow the jam to cool slightly then bottle in sterilised jars, and process in a hot water bath.

Royal Jambul Jelly

Fills 4 jam jars

The fruit of the jambul tree, also known as the Java plum or black plum *[Syzygium cuminii]*[117] begins to ripen by mid May. By the first week of June, the trees that grow wild in the surrounding jungle and along the country roads leading to Khanapur are full of luscious ripe fruit. You know when everyone has had more than enough, including the monkeys, when sacks full of the fat juicy fruit fall on the roads and are squished by passing traffic, leaving behind a purple jam of sorts!

The jambul is not suited to jam making but makes a delicious jelly. The method to get there can be a little tedious, but with a little care, there will be rewards. The pectin content of the fruit is very low, to help the jelly to set include 15 to 20% unripe fruit if available. To prevent the fruit and sugar syrup from burning, cook in batches of no more than half a litre, and cook quickly just below boiling point. You will find that the jelly sets in no time, is beautifully clear and a gorgeous deep purple.

You require the following:

2 litres of jambul juice [approximately 3 to 4 Kgs of jambul][118]

1½ kgs of sugar

4 small lemons

Rinse the fruit and place in a large vessel. Pour in enough cold water to cover the fruit and bring to the boil. Then lower the heat and cook the fruit until very soft. Remove from the heat and cool. Strain the juice through a fine sieve or a piece of muslin, but without squeezing or adding any pressure. Discard the pulp. Divide the fruit juice into 4 portions measuring 500ml each. Add 375 grams of sugar to each portion with the juice of one small lemon. Place on low to medium heat and cook the juice until the sugar has completely melted, then increase the heat and bring to the boil just once. Reduce the heat to just below boiling and cook the jelly until it sets. Repeat for the remaining batches of fruit juice and bottle in hot sterilized jars.

117 There is a related species *S. fruticosum* with a much smaller fruit that is not suitable for jelly making.

118 The quantity required will depend on the quality of the fruit; large fleshy fruit will, of course, give you more pulp.

Homemade Jams

Winter and summer are the ideal times to initiate a jam session but not so much the monsoons, though there is plenty of fruit available. The water content in the fruit is far higher this time of the year, affecting the sugar levels rendering them unsuitable for jam making. Reduced sugar levels affect the shelf life of a jam often resulting in mildew and spoilage. However, the other seasons bring in some unusual and delightful fruit that make excellent jam; in winter you have, the Cape gooseberry *[Physalis peruviana]* used on its own or combined with tomatoes or Rozelle *[Hibiscus sabdariffa]* that makes an excellent preserve or jelly. Summer brings with it the Carambola *[Averrhoa carambola]*, Passion fruit *[Passiflora edulis]*, and the Jackfruit. Making jam is easy; nothing is more heart-warming than a larder full of homemade jams and preserves made with good fresh fruit. Jam making hasn't changed much over generations, traditional methods are still in use and the practical advice is still very relevant. This is what I have learnt, sometimes the hard way!

You don't need any special equipment but a long-handled wooden spoon is convenient. A heavy bottomed aluminium pan works best, but make sure it is large enough; when the jam is on the boil it can spill over. A specialised wide throat funnel to fill the jam into bottles is a sensible buy.

Jam without commercial pectin requires a longer cook. To retain flavour and colour make your homemade jams in small quantities. Prevent the jam from burning and thereby affecting flavour by cooking in batches. I seldom use more than 2 or 3 kgs of fruit at any one time.

The ingredients you use must be the best you can find. Choose fresh, firm, unblemished fruit that is just ripe. Your jam will not set if you use overripe fruit.

Pectin, sugar, and acid are the three major players in jam making and all three must be present for success. Pectin helps the jam or jelly to set and is present in all fruit to a lesser or greater degree. Combine those fruit that contain very little pectin with other fruit such as apples and grapes that are high in natural pectin. If you so choose, there are commercial pectin products available that you can use as a substitute for natural pectin.

Guava jelly is so good to eat but because of its low pectin content, making it can test one's patience. Fully ripened fruit contains less pectin than unripe fruit, so when making guava jelly, ensure that 25% of the fruit is raw. This will help with a better set and shorten the cooking process.

Scum [I really dislike this word] raises to the surface as the jam cooks, and is usually removed; you need a slotted spoon to do this, by lightly skimming the surface of the jam while it simmers away. Reduce the scum considerably by adding a knob of butter. Leaving it in causes discoloration, and when the jam is cold forms a thick unattractive layer on the surface of the jam, but it does have loads of flavour. I have often ditched appearances in preference for taste.

To avoid jam from crystallizing in storage, start by gently heating the fruit and sugar until all the sugar has completely melted. Then and only then bring the jam to the boil.

To improve the shelf life of your homemade jams it is best to use sterilized storage jars. To help prolong the shelf life of your jam, process the filled jam bottles in a hot water bath.

Guard against overcooking the jam and in the process loosing the setting point. Test the jam every 5 to 8 minutes as the pulp begins to thicken.

To test whether your jam or jelly has set do one of the following:

1. Ladle a small spoonful onto a saucer and pop into the freezer for a couple of minutes. If the jam thickens you are ready to bottle.
2. Ladle a tablespoon of hot jam onto a plate and allow it to cool. Draw a line through the centre with the tip of a knife. If the two halves remain separate, you are ready to bottle.
3. Ladle a spoonful onto a saucer and allow the jam to cool. Move to the light and check the surface of the jam if a thin skin forms, you are ready to bottle.

Long Tong on the left

Rukmi Sous Chef at the
Hermitage on the right

Rama the Bee Whisperer
below left

Dependable Abbas
Below Right

The Waiters or in '60's parlance the
Bearers from Government House
Below: Ramu and Friends

Nergis Fui and Das, in the black apron
Below: Das, Patrick, Krishna Maria and Claire

Family and Friends

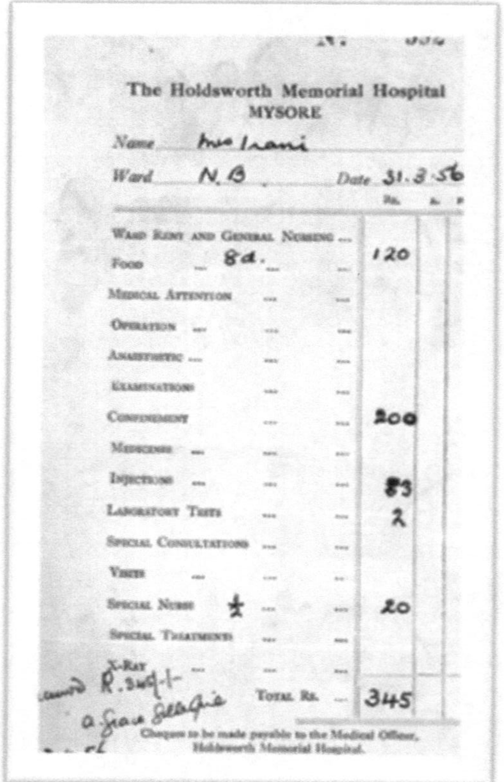

The Holdsworth Memorial Hospital
MYSORE

Name Mrs Irani

Ward N.B. Date 31.3.56

	Rs.
Ward Rent and General Nursing	
Food 8d.	120
Medical Attention	
Operation	
Anaesthetic	
Examinations	
Confinement	200
Medicines	
Injections	23
Laboratory Tests	2
Special Consultations	
Visits	
Special Nurse	20
Special Treatments	
X-Ray	
Total Rs.	345

R.345/-

Cheques to be made payable to the Medical Officer, Holdsworth Memorial Hospital.

My arrival on the 24th of March 1956 cost my parents the grand sum of Rs 345/00 at the Holdsworth Memorial Hospital

Cedric, Roman, dad, Prabhu Sanath Raian in the front and Puttamadiya on the extreme right

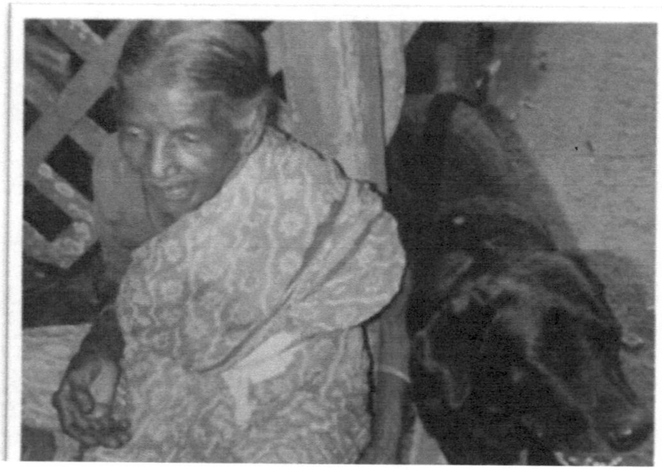

Louise with Winston

The Tamilian Cook

We found this photograph in an old Parsee Home.
The subjects are unknown, all it says
at the back of the photograph is:

'My Old Cook and his Family'

31. From your Garden to your Table

Homemade Sundried tomatoes

Why bother with store bought sun dried tomatoes when you can enjoy making your own at home. With our wonderful warm weather they can actually be sun dried!However, if you are not as blessed with dependable sunshine you can use your food dehydrator instead. Oven drying is not recommended for tomatoes because of the fruits high moisture content.

Choosing the right tomatoes for drying is the first step to ensuring that you are successful in your venture. The variety traditionally used is the oval shaped and very meaty Principe Borghese. However, unless you are growing your own these may be difficult to procure. The best fruit to use are firm full-flavoured varieties, with a high acid content. Choose ripe tomatoes that are thick walled, firm and heavy for their size. Tomatoes that are very sweet or low in acidity turn black on drying, and though still edible will not look very appetizing.

To prepare the tomatoes, first wash and dry the fruit. With a sharp knife [to prevent tissue damage and discoloring], cut the smaller fruit in half and slice the larger ones crosswise into slices half an inch thick. Drain the slices on paper towels for a short while.

If you are sun drying your tomatoes, put the slices on drying trays with protective netting and place them where the sun's rays are the sharpest. You need to turn the slices every 3 to 4 hours, so keep this in mind when you choose your spot. Move the trays with the sun, and bring them in at dusk. It will take you approximately 4 to 5 days to completely dry the tomatoes.

Drying your tomatoes in a dehydrator may take 8 to 10 hours; leave ample space between slices to allow the air to circulate. Near the end of the drying process check the tomato slices frequently; some will dry quicker than others, over drying will kill the taste of the final product. You will know the tomatoes have dried when they are leathery to the touch. Dried tomatoes can readily reabsorb moisture and lead to spoilage. Prolong their shelf life by packaging them securely in sealed bags or glass jars with airtight lids. Kept this way they should last 4 to 6 months.

Use the sundried tomatoes in stews and casseroles. For stir fries and other quick cooking recipes rehydrate your tomatoes. Soak them in hot water, chicken or vegetable stock for about 20 minutes. Reserve the soaking liquid and use it in your cooking.

You can also reconstitute your tomatoes in oil, to do this cover the tomatoes with olive oil, [I sometimes use Asian sesame oil] for 24 hours before you need them. There is the option of preserving your tomatoes in oil with some crushed garlic, red or green peppercorns and one or two of your favourite herbs. Store this awesome package in the refrigerator.

Rat Tailed Radish *[Raphanus sativus caudatus]*

I discovered rat-tailed radish rather late in my engagement with gardening but learnt soon enough that with very little care, an abundant harvest is forthcoming. So spare a little space in your veggie plot for them. In rural India, it is common practice to eat tender radish pods. However, the pods are usually conventional root-producing radishes allowed to run to seed. All radish seed pods are edible, but especially bred for their pods are varieties of the *caudatus* group. These 4 - 12" tapered purple or green seedpods are best eaten when young and tender, the older they get the more fibrous and tough they become.

If you enjoy the pungent tang of raw radish, then you will also enjoy the raw pods chopped and added to salads and garlanded by the edible pretty purple, pink or yellow flowers. Rat-tailed radish is an interesting addition to stir fries, a vegetable curry, or first steamed and then cooked as a 'foogath'. A good companion to couscous, do try the recipe on page 26.

False Coriander *[Eryngium foetidum syn E. antihystericum]*

Regularly added to the cook pot in rural India, false coriander also known as fitweed or perennial coriander doesn't seem to have found a place in modern urban cooking. Your herb garden shouldn't be without it! Not only is it easy to grow, but is also self-seeding. It is a tidy compact plant forming a rosette of narrow, saw-edged leaves and bearing small heads of greenish flowers. A word of caution though; there is a ring of spiny-toothed bracts surrounding each flower head so handle with care. It grows on a wide range of soils but for better growth requires good drainage.

Use the young tender leaves of *Eryngium foetidum* raw in salads, or chopped and added to yogurt. The older leaves with their razor-like margins are best cooked, and are delicious in soups, stews, and curries; remember to add them early in the cooking process so that they soften suitably. They are also wonderful used in coriander chutney or in a cucumber yogurt smoothie. Fitweed partners well with eggs, carrots, summer and winter squash. The flavour is similar but stronger than true coriander and can replace it for some outstanding flavour. I often make the following dressing to use on a fresh green salad or to lightly sauté vegetables.

Fitweed and Garlic Salad Oil

250ml sunflower or safflower oil

4 to 5 fat cloves of garlic

5 to 6 large leaves of mature fitweed [adjust this quantity to your liking]

Roast the garlic, cool and then slip the cloves out of their skin, crush lightly and set aside. Chop the fitweed into pieces, and on medium heat fry the fitweed in 3 tablespoons of oil for a few minutes until soft, remove from the heat and set aside to cool. Heat the remaining oil in a pan, and then cool slightly.

Tip the garlic and the fitweed with all its oil into a blender. Add half a cup of the remaining oil and blend well until smooth. Then tip in the rest of the oil and blend again. Store the oil in a jar in the refrigerator or a cool dark place for up to a week and then use as required, in salads or salad dressings, stir fries, and other vegetable dishes.

Microgreens

Microgreens are the seedlings of leafy greens, vegetables, and herbs. They are usually harvested when an inch or two in height and with a set of fully extended true leaves. The stage when seedlings are full of flavour and nutritionally at their best. Sprouts and microgreens are dissimilar, the methods and growth environment for each are very different. Unlike sprouts, plant the seeds for microgreens in garden soil or better still, a soil substitute such as peat moss or coco peat. Light conditions must be good, with plenty of air circulation and low humidity. Microgreens may need up to three weeks to mature, while Sprouts are eaten before the emergence of the first true leaves and are usually ready in two or three days.

What to plant?

To begin, delve into your store cupboard and make a selection from what you have on hand. Later broaden your repertoire with seeds sourced only from an organic seed supplier. You do not want some dreadful chemical lurking around in your salad. Finally the fresher the seed the better and quicker the germination, chances are that very old seeds won't germinate at all.

Herb Seeds - coriander, dill, cumin, and fennel, they will delight you with their swift arrival, all sourced from your store cupboard.

Amaranth's beautiful glossy wine-red seeds are also quick off the mark as are mustard seeds, alfalfa, and cress.

Follow up with basil, parsley, celery, rocket and chervil.

Fenugreek microgreens with their piquant, mildly bitter flavour are highly recommended.

Vegetable seeds can include the cabbage family, carrots, lettuce, spinach and radish. Asian greens, such as bok choy should also find a place on your list.

Avoid tomato micro greens they are toxic

Growing Microgreens

For better control over the growing environment raise your microgreens in containers rather than out in the garden. Any container will do as long as it has a depth of two or three inches. Improvise - I have used an old roasting tin, the lid off a defunct plastic barrel, an empty biscuit tin, and 'give away' plastic serving trays advertising Kingfisher beer. Drainage is important but you can always drill a couple of holes into whatever you plan to use.

Fill the containers with an organic potting mix or a soil substitute; lightly compact the soil and level off the surface. If you plan to use one variety of seed per container, then scatter the seed evenly over the surface and top with a layer of the potting mix completely covering the seeds. If you wish to plant more than one variety of seed per container, then using the back end of a pencil draw shallow lines about 1 ¼ inch apart along the length of the container. Thinly sow the seeds in the lines, and top with a layer of the potting mix. Water gently and place the container in a sunny spot where it will get at least 6 hours of direct sunlight a day. Do not let the soil mixture dry out.

To harvest the microgreens, [just before serving] use a pair of sharp kitchen scissors and snip them off just above soil level. Most seedlings will be ready within eight to ten days but some may take longer. You will easily recognize the first true leaves they look quite different from the cotyledons.

Include microgreens as a part of your everyday diet. Toss into salads, scatter on soups and pasta or pair them with eggs. Roll up a paratha [or tortilla] with a fat frankfurter smothered in mustard microgreens; layer them in a sandwich with cheese, ham or tomatoes. Sprinkle them on your pizza, sauté them to enliven a rice dish or add them to dips! Start with one tray and before you know it, you will be hooked for life!

Pumpkins and Squash - winter or summer

On our farm, some of the best pumpkins ever harvested have been from vines that have self-seeded on our compost heap. Nurtured by the bountiful South West monsoons we have, time and again received a splendid gift, a windfall of delicious perfectly grown fruit. Replicating this seemingly effortless cycle in our vegetable garden is anything but effortless!

Pumpkins, marrow, and squash – these are names that cause so much confusion around the world. Closely related and all within the genus *Cucurbita*, they fall into three different subgroups, *Cucurbita pepo, Cucurbita maxima and Cucurbita moschata.* The subgroup *C. Pepo* is the true pumpkin and includes both summer and winter squash. *C. moschata* originating from Central America has been cultivated for thousands of years and looks particularly different from the others, elongated or oblong instead of round, and tan instead of orange. This group includes my favourite the unbeatable butternut squash. The subgroup *C. maxima* is an enthusiastic explorer striking out in all directions and covering a lot of ground. The Queensland Blue belongs to this subgroup as do a number of winter squash.

In moderate climates, grow summer and winter squash throughout the year. Winter squash has a very long shelf life, hence the name [the ability to store well over the winter months]. Both require plenty of water to grow well and very hot summers can be unfavourable.

Summer squash loosely divided into four groups, The Crookneck, Straightneck, Zucchini, and Scallop, are picked when young. Unlike winter squash, which grows on vines, summer squash are bush plants, a delight in any vegetable garden with their striking leaves and flowers. Varieties of summer squash are interchangeable in a recipe, and because they require little cooking are great in stir fries, vegetable side dishes, or raw in salads.

Scrutinizing seed catalogues for winter squash is agonizing. They come in such an array of shapes, sizes, and colours, so attractive you want to grow them all. Substitute varieties freely and use in sweet or savoury dishes. Roast, steam or stew them, or puree them for soups. Toss them in butter or bake them in pies, complement them with walnuts and hazelnuts, raisins or cranberries, sprinkle them with sumac, acacia seed or hogweed. Most of all remember to save the seeds for another bountiful harvest.

32. Shades of Green on Your Plate

A number of exceptional, sometimes quirky, sometimes temperamental plants have made their way into my garden and then later onto our dining table. The following is a modest list of 'greens' that have found their space to grow somewhere at the Hermitage and at some point in time.

The Sweet Potato Vine

The sweet potato vine is always out of control, growing profusely in all directions covering every inch of ground available. I plant it within an enclosure to keep the spotted deer out; they fancy it and will eat through a patch in no time. Wild boar love the underground tubers. They will not spare you a thought when they use their tusks to rip out an entire row. Tender leaves and shoots are best for the cook pot. The older leaves can be steamed or stir-fried, but the older stems are too tough and fibrous best to discard them. The sweet potato vine is not very fond of hot weather, but during summer will do better in semi shade with plenty of water.

New Zealand Spinach

New Zealand Spinach also does a lot of travelling. However, you really shouldn't mind, because it is so versatile in the kitchen. Tender leaves are great in salads, stir-fries, and stews. The older leaves and stems do well as a soup in place of regular spinach. New Zealand Spinach is an excellent crop to grow in the hot weather when others have the tendency to 'bolt,' but keep in mind that it does require some shade and a regular supply of water.

Asian Morning Glory [*Ipomoea aquatica]*

Water Spinach

While used so extensively in East and South East Asian cuisine, it is relatively unknown in Indian cooking. *Ipomoea aquatica* is nevertheless seen growing wild on tank bunds, long green arms lazily stretching out and resting gently on the surface of the water, and always pointing in the direction of the wind.

Grow morning glory successfully at home by planting the seeds or stem cuttings [with a little root attached] in a large barrel filled with moist rich soil. If you run out of 'greens' for your salads, stir fries or soups, just walk out into your garden and head towards your Morning Glory.

Stir Fried Morning Glory

Enough for 2 or 3 as a side dish

You require the following:
3 cups of morning glory [leaves and tender stems]
3 to 4 cloves of garlic
2 or 3 fresh yellow or red chillies
2 tablespoons oyster sauce
1 tablespoons vegetable oil
1 tablespoon Asian sesame oil or Chinese chilli oil
A pinch or two of Indian black salt

Rinse the morning glory and drain well. Finely crush the garlic, chop the chillies into large pieces. Heat a wok or heavy-bottomed frying pan, add the vegetable oil, then tip in the garlic and chillies and cook for one minute. Next, add the morning glory and stir, coating it well with the oil. Then add the oyster sauce and when the morning glory begins to wilt, add the sesame or chilli oil. Season with a little Indian black salt and serve immediately.

Malabar Nightshade [*Basella alba and B. cordifolia*]

This tropical vine is a native and perfectly at home in hot weather when other greens, such as lettuce are either wilting or bolting! Nevertheless, it does love moisture, so water well and never let the soil dry out. The vine's greatest assets are texture and colour, and the ideal green to add to soups and stews towards the end of the cooking process. I have used it in dhal, sweet corn and baked it with macaroni and cheese. It also has a better shelf life than most other greens, staying fresh up to 5 days stored in a plastic bag in the refrigerator. A cutting will root in less than a week, but allow the plant to establish before you begin to harvest the leaves. Sunlight and good drainage will ensure a healthier plant.

Harbora Greens/ Bengal Gram Greens

When the post monsoon harvest gets underway in October and November, one of the first seasonal treats to enter local markets are bunches of fresh green Bengal gram sold at every street corner. After you have eaten the parrot green chickpeas, don't throw away the greens. Pick through the bunch getting rid of the hard stems, retaining the young tender ones and the leaves. I often use the greens in place of coriander finely chopped in scrambled eggs and omelettes. They are excellent mixed into salads, thrown into stir-fries, added to dhal, and cooked with potatoes. They have an amazing shelf life stored in the refrigerator; they will remain fresh for days.

Mustard Greens *[Brassica juncea]*

These peppery leafy greens frequently used in Japanese, Vietnamese and Chinese cooking are popular in Northern India, but not so in the South. It would be wise to include mustard greens into your diet on a regular basis to receive the fantastic health benefits they provide. These vibrant greens include an impressive number of varieties, are easy to grow and quick to mature. They have a milder flavour when young the most suitable stage for salads. With age, the flavour gets sharper and then the leaves are best steamed or sautéed. Enhance the flavour of mustard greens with a dash of Asian sesame oil, or if available the cold-pressed oil of the Niger seed.

Chinese Mustard Greens/Gai Choy

My favourite mustard green is gai choy, and if only all vegetables were as easy to grow. Broadcast the seeds, they will sprout with little care to give you a bountiful harvest. Water requirements are moderate, but bright sunlight essential and as with other mustard greens, the pungent flavour deepens as the plant matures. Harvest at all stages of growth for use in salads, soups, and stir fries. The yellow flowers sprinkled on top of your salad or randomly added to a dish of grilled fish will bring colour and compliments!

Osaka Purple

If you, like me are a cook on the lookout for colour the Japanese mustard Osaka purple really fits the bill; there is a Korean variety with deep red leaves, quite stunning! Quick and easy to grow, Osaka purple is a striking plant with dark purple leaves with a spicy peppery taste. Harvest at 4 to 6 inches for use in salads but allow the plant to mature for use in stir-fries, and for a longer lasting crop pick off individual leaves instead of harvesting the whole plant. You could occasionally have a problem with insects so you need to be vigilant.

Komatsuna [Japanese Mustard/*Brassica rapa var. perviridis*]

Japanese mustard or komatsuna is a delightful leafy vegetable, and belongs to the turnip family and though not as spicy as mustard it has quite a bite. The plants grow tall and have large deep green leaves, which you can use in salads and stir-fries. Use as you would spinach, in pasta or a vegetable bake. Komatsuna loves a moderate climate but is easy on other growing conditions.

The Drumstick Tree *[Moringa oleifera]*

A Native of the Indian sub-continent

The Moringa tree is visible everywhere in the South, on farms, in villages and provincial towns. The long pods that give the tree its name are a popular vegetable finding their way into soups, vegetable, lentil, and meat dishes. To cook the drumsticks knock off a bit at both ends, and with a vegetable peeler take off a sliver of the thick outer layer. Then using a sharp knife cut the pod across into 3 or 4-inch pieces. Tip the drumstick pieces into a pot of cold salted water, and bring to the boil, then lower the heat and simmer until just done. To eat, gently pry open the drumstick, and with a spoon scrape off all the pulp. Add the vegetable liquor to soups or stews.

Over cooked drumsticks fall apart and are not very appetizing to look at. You will know that yours are ready when they are semi-soft and change colour from a bright green to a light yellow. For a drumstick soup[119] cut the pods into larger pieces of 6 to 8 inches, so that they are easier to grip when scraping off the cooked pulp.

Moringa leaves are the new health food with a remarkable balance of complete proteins, antioxidants, vitamins, and minerals. Tender drumstick leaves can replace coriander, and finely chopped are an excellent garnish for any meat or vegetable dish. Try them on pumpkin soup, with lentils or chopped and mixed into mash potato.

The white wispy flowers of the moringa tree make an excellent side dish. Pick them fresh and discard any that are discoloured. The following is a recipe given to me by Mallamma, by Brother Raian's talented cook.

119 See page 190 for recipe.

Mallamma's Salver of Flowers

Good for 4 to 5 as a side dish

You require the following:

2 to 2½ cups well packed fresh drumstick flowers

2 medium red or white onions

1 large tomato

2 mild fresh red chillies

1 teaspoon coriander powder

4 to 5 cloves of garlic

¼ teaspoon turmeric powder

A generous squeeze of lime juice

2 tablespoons oil

Salt to taste

Rinse and drain the flowers, then with a pair of scissors snip off stems that are very long. Slice the onions and chillies, mince the tomato and smash the garlic. Heat the oil in a pan, add the onions and brown lightly along with the red chillies. Now add the garlic and continue to fry the onions for another minute or two. Tip in a cup of water and cook until the onions dissolve and thick gravy remains. Now add the tomato, coriander and turmeric powder and season to taste, cook until the tomato is soft. Next, add the drumstick flowers, check seasoning and add the lime. Serve hot as a side dish or as a snack with freshly made pooris.

Do other things with moringa flowers:

Add them to your sambhar or a dish of whole black lentils [whole masoor]

Fry them in ghee with cumin, garlic, and onions, and stir into your rice

The flowers are perfect for soups; try with carrot or spinach soup

Cook the flowers with garlic and onions and stuff your omelettes

A new topping for pizza, but first toss in butter

Stuff your poultry with onions, bacon, moringa leaves, and flowers

Add the flowers to a bowl of yogurt or to your pancake batter

33. The Store Cupboard

Grinding Masala's

For a fine silky masala powder, the ingredients you use must be crisp and dry; a red chilly should snap when broken in two. If it is a fine clear day, and you have time on your hands, sun the ingredients until they are warm to the touch. To roast the masala ingredients you need a tava or a griddle [preferably with a handle] and a clean dry kitchen towel. Roast each ingredient individually. Place the griddle on the stove and heat through, then switch off the heat and add the first spice. Hold the griddle firmly with one hand and crunch up the kitchen towel with the other and gently press down on the spice continuously moving it all around. The spice should brown lightly, but whatever you do, don't allow it to burn. Remove from the griddle and tip onto a plate to cool. Follow through with the rest of the spices. If you plan to make larger quantities, remember not to roast more than 4 or 5 tablespoons at a time.

Parsee Dhanajeera Powder

You require the following:

1 tablespoon coriander seeds

1 teaspoon cumin seeds

6 Kashmiri red chillies [or any other mild red chilly]

1 dry cassia leaf

½ teaspoon fenugreek seeds

½ teaspoon mace

One whole nutmeg

1" piece cinnamon

4 cloves

3 cardamoms

1 teaspoon poppy seed

Grate the nutmeg and set aside. Gently dry roast all the other ingredients separately. Dry grind all the spices together in an electric blender. Store the masala in a clean airtight bottle.

Parsi Sambhar Masala

You require the following:

300 gm dry red chillies

100 grams black mustard seeds

150 grams fenugreek seeds

20 grams asafoetida powder

20 grams cinnamon

20 grams cloves

20 grams black pepper

10 grams star anise

25 grams turmeric powder

100 ml vegetable oil of your choice

25 grams sea salt

Dry roast all the ingredients, except for the asafoetida. Grind all the spices together in an electric blender, then add the asafoetida powder and mix well, and store in a clean airtight bottle.

Grinding Masala's: The aroma of roasting masala ingredients may not be pleasing to all! An old cookbook of my mothers recommends, the husband should be out of the house, 'as the pungent odour of roasting red chillies causes a lot of sneezing and loose temper!'

Mysore Rasam Powder

You require the following:

250 grams coriander seeds

275 grams red chillies of your choice

1 tablespoon cumin seeds

1 tablespoon fenugreek seeds

2 tablespoons peppercorns

2 tsp mustard seed

8 sprigs curry leaves.

Dry roast the curry leaves and the chillies together, and each of the other spices separately. Grind all the ingredients together in an electric blender and store in an airtight bottle.

34. Chutneys

Green Coriander and Coconut Chutney

My generation grew up on chutney sandwiches; they put in an appearance everywhere, birthday parties, picnics and the food stall at the annual Mission Hospital fete. You can serve green coriander and coconut chutney with grilled fish, stuff an omelette with it, roll your pasta in it, or use as an accompaniment to sweet corn. Push the boundaries! Store in the refrigerator for no more than 2 days.

You require the following:
2 cups fresh green coriander or fitweed
1 cup fresh mint [spear mint]
1 teaspoon cumin seed
2 or 3 green chillies [or more if you like]
50 grams white onion
½ a cup of finely grated coconut
5 to 6 cloves garlic
2 teaspoons sugar
1 small knob galangal or ginger
Juice of one small lime or lemon
Salt to taste

Place a griddle on low heat and roast the coconut and cumin seed, then remove and allow them to cool. Roughly chop the coriander, mint, green chillies, onions, ginger, and garlic, and using a food processor blend all the ingredients until smooth. Use a tablespoon of water if required, season to taste with salt and a squeeze of lime or lemon juice.

Green Chilly Chutney

For the uninitiated, mix this chutney into a little sour cream, Greek yogurt or mayo to take away some of the heat, and use as a salad dressing. You can also select a milder variety of chilly or by deseeding them first. Store up to 3 days in the refrigerator.

You require the following:

12 long green chillies

4 to 5 plump cloves of garlic

½ teaspoon cumin seed

30 grams onions

1 tablespoon rice wine vinegar

¼ cup green coriander

¼ to ½ teaspoon of galangal or ginger

½ a tablespoon vegetable oil

Salt to taste

Heat the oil in a pan and lightly toss the whole green chillies, cumin seed and galangal for a minute or two, do not allow to burn. Then remove from the heat and cool. Roughly, chop the onion, garlic, and coriander, and blend all the ingredients to a fine paste including the remaining oil if any,season to taste. Serve the chutney in a small glass or ceramic bowl with taco's, corn nibbles or papri[120] as a snack, with a cup of tea.

Peppery Tomato Chutney

Does very well as a sandwich spread, mixed into pasta or with grilled fish, makes about a cup.

You require the following:

300 grams ripe but firm tomatoes

1 tablespoon balsamic vinegar

1 tablespoon brown sugar

1 tablespoon ginger garlic paste

1 tablespoon rose peppercorns

½ teaspoon clove powder

4 tablespoons olive or vegetable oil of your choice

Sea salt to taste

Cut the tomatoes really fine, heat the oil in a pan and add the rose peppercorns and cook for about 30 seconds, then add the tomatoes and cook until they soften and the oil separates. Now add the rest of the ingredients and continue to cook for another 5 to 6 minutes, check seasoning and remove from the heat. Serve warm or at room temperature.

120 Papri a well known North Indian snack made of gram flour.

Rukmini's Chutneyed Monkey Nuts [Peanuts]

If you like to eat food that is blistering hot you should try this one. Rukmini is from Theregali. She brings us a bowlful of this chutney after the groundnut harvest in October. Wonderful made with freshly harvested nuts if you can get them.

You require the following:

200 grams shelled monkey nuts [about a cupful]

75 - 100 grams green chillies [Rukmini uses half a cup of chopped chillies!]

1 fat bulb of garlic

75 grams minced tomato

2 tablespoons oil

1 teaspoon mustard seeds

Salt to taste, preferably sea salt

Dry roast the peanuts, remove from the heat and cool. Chop the green chillies into large pieces, then tip into a flat dish or large bowl and coat with a tablespoon of oil. Clean the garlic, and then chop before adding to the green chillies. Place a pan over medium heat and quickly fry the green chillies and the garlic for about 2 or 3 minutes. Remove from the heat and tip into the bowl of a grinding machine. Add the remaining spoon of oil to the pan and crackle the mustard seed. Add the peanuts, the tomato, and the mustard seed to the grinding bowl and season to taste with a little salt. Blend until you get a rough consistency, avoid a paste. Remove and store in the refrigerator until required. Delicious eaten with a naan, paratha or any Middle Eastern bread!

35. Dry Chutney Powders

Make and store these chutneys in a dry airtight container for up to three weeks. Sprinkle on vegetables, fish, eggs or salads, use in place of salt and pepper, folded into yogurt or in sauces and salad dressings.

Curry Leaf Chutney Powder

Makes a little less than 1 cup

You require the following:

8 sprigs fresh or dry but mature curry leaves

¼ cup gram dhal

4 to 6 dry red chillies

¼ teaspoon asafoetida (Hing)

½ cup freshly grated coconut

1 tablespoon coriander seeds

Salt to taste

Begin by dry roasting the gram dhal and when nearly but not quite done, add the curry leaves and roast for a minute more or until they crisp. Remove from the heat immediately and set aside to cool; dry roast the chillies and coriander seeds separately, remove from the heat and cool. Mix all the ingredients together and grind to a powder, store in a clean bottle for up to a month.

Chutneyed Monkey Nuts [Peanuts]

You require the following:

1 cup monkey nuts [Peanuts]

½ cup fresh coconut

1 or 2 tablespoons dried fenugreek leaves [Kasuri Methi]

1 teaspoon cumin seed

4 or 5 cloves garlic crushed

½ teaspoon minced ginger

2 or 3 green chillies chopped

1 teaspoon sumac, dried mango powder, or Persian lime powder

Salt to taste

Separately dry roast the monkey nuts, coconut, and cumin seeds. Switch off the heat and dry roast the fenugreek for just a minute. Mix all the ingredients together and dry grind, season to taste with a little salt.

Pistachio and Rose

Makes a wonderful ice cream topping

You require the following:

1 cup fresh pistachios

½ cup finely grated fresh coconut

2 tablespoons dry rose petals

1½ teaspoon fennel

½ teaspoon dried tarragon

A pinch of salt to taste

Dry roast the pistachios and tip onto a flat dish or plate to cool. Roast the grated coconut until it has just changed colour. Then add the rose petals, the fennel and the tarragon and roast for a further minute or two, remove and cool. Place all the ingredients into a blender, pulse just 3 or 4 times until the ingredients are just blended. The chutney should have the consistency of dry bread crumbs.

The Pansari

Were you to amble down Devaraj Urs Road in the heart of Mysore city, you will know that you are approaching K Govindaraja Setty and Sons by the fragrance that wafts towards you. If the fragrance does not guide you there, the nondescript storefront will. Surrounded by the superficial glitz of modern retail it sticks out like a sore thumb. Step inside and you know that you have come to a good place. Started in 1890, it's the fourth generation that now runs the family business; K Govindaraja Setty and Sons are herbalists.

You cannot mistake a pansari for any other store. Shop windows dressed with the dry crusty cowpats so necessary for religious ritual, gunny bags full of dry aromatic herbs, bottles of essential oils, cowries and beads, ropes of all kinds, luffas to slough off dry skin, and even a pallanguzhi, the Tamilian board game. The pansari is so rare and well hidden in the provincial towns and the big cities of Southern India, nevertheless, thankfully still in existence.

The long list of products available at K Govindaraja Setty and Sons includes and I quote, 'Items useful for pregnant ladies,' 'Items used for gastric trouble,' 'Garam masala ingredients' and 'Items Necessary for Grupravesham, Marriages, Homas, pooja and other ceremonies'.

On my last visit to the store, this is what I bought:

Indian black salt
A packet of fuller's earth
Liquorice root, about a quarter kilo for green tea
Frankincense
Ayurvedic bathing powder excellent for your skin
Vettiver root to make into a cooling summer drink
Red gundumani seeds[121]
Pure camphor crystals

121 Red gundumani seeds *[Adenathera pavonina Linn]* are one of those things that you may not really need but simply cannot resist. The brilliant red, biconvex seeds are enchanting, use them to make botanical jewellery, or fill up a clear glass bottle and put them on display. In the old days, goldsmiths used the seeds as unit weights to weigh gold, with each seed weighing four grams.

36. Souring Agents

Dry Pomegranate Powder

For many cultures across The Middle East, pomegranates are an integral part of the cuisine. In India, the powdered form has been dominant, with just a sprinkle adding that extra twist to a simple dish. Made from pomegranate pearls that have been sun-dried and ground into a fine powder, anar powder can be used as a souring agent in all manner of dishes; lentils and vegetables, chicken curries, biriyani, and kebabs, or even to flavour soups and stews. Try it in a smoothie, sprinkled on a fresh green salad, whole chickpeas, or on humus. Preparing the powder at home is easy, skin large ripe fruit, and sundry the arils for up to a week. Store the seeds in an airtight container, and grind to a powder as and when required. In my experience, the powder does not store well, so prepare in small quantities.

Postscript: The skin of the pomegranate should also be sun-dried and stored away; there can be no better remedy for an upset stomach. Simmer a piece of dried skin in a cup of water for 8 to 10 minutes and cool. Discard the skin and sip the tea three or four times a day or as needed.

The Case for Limes or Lemons

Limes and lemons are citrus fruits belonging to the family Rutaceae but their genus and species differ. Do the differences between limes and lemons, really matter in the kitchen? Lemons are larger than limes, and lemons are yellow while limes are green. The juice of both lemons and limes are fat-free, but lime juice has a higher nutritional value than lemon juice. Lemon juice, on the other hand, has slightly more citric acid than lime juice, giving it a sharper more acidic taste. So does it really matter, lime or lemon? A sensitive tongue could possibly tell the difference between the two, but for most purposes, I think either will do. Use fresh juice as much as possible rather than bottled, especially on salads.

Dry Mango Powder

Dry mango powder or amchur with its fresh piquant flavour is a souring agent used in both Northern and Southern Indian cuisine. It finds its way into chutneys, pickles, curries and dry vegetable side dishes. The colour is not a redeeming feature but texture is, as is the underlying aroma of mango. Use amchur to replace any other souring agent such as tamarind or sumac. Grilled chicken, lamb kebabs, pork chops, fish, salad dressings, steamed rice all benefit from the addition of a little amchur.

Persian Limes/Gard-e limu *[Citrus latifolia]*

To look at, dried Persian limes are pale ochre on the outside, jet-black on the inside and seldom of uniform size. They are hard, brittle, and lightweight, their flavour dark and complex. Dried Persian limes are simply impossible to ignore, and are one of a select few ingredients that hold a place of honour in my kitchen.

There are several ways to cook with Persian limes, remembering to pierce the lime with a fork before using. Slip into soups, stews or meat dishes; they are delicious in tur dhal too. Add the limes at the start of the cooking process; they need the time to impart their unique flavour to the dish. Pair them with saffron, cumin, fennel, or fresh herbs, and are excellent cooked with okra, eggplant, and pumpkin.

Powdered Persian limes [gard–e limu-omani] as the name suggests are limes that have been cracked open, seeds removed and ground in a food processor. You can do this at home, but do remember to remove the seeds they are rather bitter. Transfer to an airtight bottle, store and use as needed. Sprinkle on any number of dishes including potatoes, ladies fingers, and scrambled eggs.

Rob-e anar

Persian Pomegranate Molasses

I turn to 'Rob-e anar' that irresistible, deep ruby red syrup made from pomegranate whenever I find that the dish that I am cooking needs a boost. Used in Middle Eastern cooking, it has a sweet-sour flavour that is rich and unique. Have an inspired time adding it to marinades and vinaigrettes, even a dash to watermelon crush, yogurt or buttermilk. Add Rob-e anar to sauces and salad dressings, to honey glazed chicken and pumpkin soup or create your own cocktail with a dash of vodka and a slice of lime. It is great with sweet potato and glazed carrots, and I love the combination of 'Rob-e anar' with dried apricots and prunes in a meat-based casserole. Experience tells me an opened bottle won't last long, but do store in a refrigerator as long it does! If you wish to make 'Rob-e anar' at home here is the recipe:

8 cups of freshly squeezed pomegranate juice

The juice of 3 lemons

1/2 cup sugar [optional]

1 tablespoon salt or to taste

In a heavy bottomed pan on medium heat, bring the pomegranate juice once to the boil. Lower the heat, add the salt and lemon juice and simmer until the juice thickens. Stir occasionally to ensure that it does not catch at the bottom. When the juice has reduced and thickened remove from the heat cool, and bottle in sterilized jars.

Cook's tip: Add the sugar only if the fruit juice is not very sweet.

Sumac

The sumac of Middle Eastern cuisine is the dried fruit of the genus *Rhus* ground into a fairly course deep red or purple powder. With 250 species of shrubs and trees that grow all over the world, the plants with their pretty flowers can be a colourful addition to your garden. The fruits are crowded into compact clusters called sumac bobs, and for some inexplicable reason remind me of the precarious 'beehive hairdos' of the early sixties. [122]

Use sumac with its sour lemony flavour to replace other souring agents. Its sourness and astringency makes it suitable to sprinkle on stir-fried okra, creamed potatoes or glazed carrots. Traditionally, sumac finds its way on grilled meat dishes, such as kebabs, but you can also use it on chicken and fish. It can add some extra zing to curd rice and to fresh homemade panir. It has a long shelf life if stored away from light in an airtight container.

122 The beehive was an amazingly popular hairdo of the '60's and very suitable for the Indian woman's thick long hair. Worn by models, brides and mother- in- laws alike, the distinctive hive shaped pile of hair backcombed, and thickly lacquered with lashings of hairspray was a fashion statement all through my childhood!

The Tamarind Tree

As a child, there were warnings never to sleep under a tamarind tree, because you were certain to have nightmares. We have a tamarind tree growing in our front garden. While I use its fruit and tender young leaves in my cooking, the bougainvillea growing beside it, uses it as a dependable prop; and as a reward, when summer comes around, the tamarind tree is a cloud of splendid white bougainvillea flowers.

The fruit of the tamarind tree is sour, the pulp wrapped around large brown seeds and sheathed in a brittle grey-green shell. The leaves of the tamarind tree are also tart, their crisp green freshness adding an interesting note to salads or yogurt. Cook the fresh or dried flowers as a vegetable. Eat sweet tamarind, a variety from Northern Thailand out of hand, but you can also add the pulp to yogurt or combine it with mayo and peanut butter for a piquant salad dressing.

Tamarind is commercially available processed into a smooth ready to use pulp; I find it rather harsh. However, the pulp extracted from the natural dried fruit is subtle, mild and mellow. It is extra work but worthwhile. Blocks of raw tamarind fruit are available everywhere, place the quantity you require in a bowl, pour over enough boiling water to cover, and allow to steep for about 20 to 30 minutes. When cool to the touch, squeeze out the pulp; discard the seeds and strain through a sieve to remove tough fibre. Use as and when required, store in a jar in your refrigerator for up to a week.

The Garcinia's of the Western Ghats

Garcinia indica [Amsul] *Garcinia cambogia* [Kudampuli]

The Western Ghats is home to some exceptional plant species, and without a doubt, the Garcinia family is one of them. Amsul is the better known, but kudampuli is fast catching up, as its popularity spreads across the world as an effective, natural alternative to control obesity and cholesterol.

With the onset of spring, it is easy to recognize *Garcinia indica.* Pale pink leaves begin to emerge, quickly turning green tipped with red. The maroon almost purple fruit is the size of a lime. The skin of the ripe fruit is sun dried and has a marked presence in regional cooking; and utilized to flavour fish curries, lentils and in the preparation of a delightful summer drink called 'Sol Kadi'. Amsul's flavour is mild and understated, use it without worrying about how much is too much.

The fruit of the Kudampuli tree, on the other hand, is a dull yellow when ripe; and the rind when sundried a dull black. Plump and ribbed, the rind is often salted and smoked adding an earthiness to its flavour. The district of Coorg just north of Mysore is blessed with the presence of this small evergreen tree, here the juice of the fruit is extracted and slowly boiled down in a chatty[123] to a thick, black almost tar-like liquid. The Kodava's who love their pork add it to their curries.

Vinegar

Though the Indian palate has, a marked fondness for all things sour, vinegar hasn't much of a presence in Indian cuisine. Regional cooking utilizes it in pockets, such as Goa, Mangalore, and Kerala. Goa has a thriving home based industry where toddy from the coconut palm is made into vinegar. The process is a simple one; the toddy is first filtered through fine muslin into a ceramic jar or barni, then covered loosely and set aside for a fortnight. Thereafter, 3 or 4 pieces of broken clay roofing tiles are heated in a direct flame until red hot and then carefully dropped into the toddy jar. The jar is covered once again and allowed to rest. The vinegar is ready to use after a fortnight.

The Parsee community loves its vinegar and believes that the best vinegar comes from Valsad and Navsari, small towns in the state of Gujarat, which have been home to the community for generations. The most well known being Kolah's vinegar brewed from Sugarcane since 1885! Because it is fermented, vinegar has an indefinite shelf life. While synthetic vinegar will remain effectively unchanged over time, natural vinegar can change. Colour changes and sedimentation are the most noticeable, but these are cosmetic in nature and the product is still very usable.

Flavoured vinegar from the Home Kitchen

Fruit, herb and spiced vinegar are not only eye catching but also have a remarkably positive effect on the taste buds! For a smooth and mellow taste, use them in sauces, salad dressings, and marinades. With every bottle as unique as you, the inventor, it is the perfect gift for a relative or friend.

Choose mild light coloured vinegar but one with an acid strength of at least 5%. Vinegar with strong overtones will overpower and mask the flavour of the fruit or herbs. White wine vinegar is usually the preferred choice; Red wine vinegar is suitable for berry blends and spices such as ginger, garlic, and cloves. Asian rice vinegar and Goan coconut vinegar are valuable options; there are really no hard and fast rules!

123 A chatty is a clay pot, a term used by the Anglo-Indian's of my grandmothers' generation.

Berry Vinegar

Any of the soft berries, blueberries, mulberries, raspberries, or blackberries can replace the strawberries, and white wine vinegar can replace the red, ready in no time.

500 ml red wine vinegar

150 grams sugar

250 grams fresh sweet strawberries

Hull the strawberries, slice and place in a non-reactive bowl. Add the sugar to the vinegar and heat gently until the sugar dissolves; do not allow the vinegar to boil. Once the sugar has dissolved, remove the pan from the heat and pour the vinegar over the strawberries. With the help of a potato masher, mash the strawberries, cover and set aside for 48 hours, stirring the mixture every now and then. Strain the vinegar through a muslin cloth or filter paper and pour into a clean sterilized bottle. Store in a cool dark place and use after two weeks.

37. That Unusual Spice

Scouting around for unusual ingredients from across borders is a wonderful way to extend your culinary knowledge and to give your cooking an edge. The spices in the short list below can add new flavours, detail and interest to your food. Buy all spices in small quantities, and store in airtight containers.

Nag Kesar *[Mammea longifolia]*

Nag kesar are the dried flower buds of *Mammea longifolia* a handsome evergreen that is endemic to the Western Ghats of Southern India. They are similar in appearance to cloves and have a woodsy sort of flavour. Used extensively in Maharashtrian and Konkan cuisine, Nag Kesar is usually one among many spices ground into spice blends such as garam masala; it is rarely if ever used as a standalone. Well known in Ayurveda for its medicinal properties, it is often confused with another Ayurvedic element, the buds of *Mesua ferrea* or The Ceylon Ironwood tree, that are confusingly also called Nag Kesar. I use nag kesar whole, as you would any other whole spice in rice dishes, soups, meat stews and casseroles. I randomly combine it with black pepper, cassia bark, cubeb pepper and cardamom, and the results are often more than interesting, have a go!

Marathi Moggu *[Bombax malabaricum]*

The Red Silk Cotton Tree

In the hot summer months when this beautiful majestic tree is in bloom the scarlet, cup-shaped flowers, laden with nectar are irresistible to most birds, including the noisy drongo and that rascal the jungle crow. The little known Indian spice Marathi moggu are the odd shaped, dried, immature seedpods of the Silk Cotton Tree. Though used extensively in Chettinad[124] cuisine, in the rice dishes of Karnataka and in the preparation of various masala's, you will not find Marathi moggu on display in your spice store. Mild and without the heady aroma of a clove or cardamom, here nonetheless is a spice that is idiosyncratic and well worth adding to your store cupboard. I enjoy seeing it used whole in a bowl of tomato soup or in a mushroom risotto. Lightly crack the pods and fry in a little vegetable oil or ghee. Use as you would any other whole spice such as peppercorns, cloves, or cinnamon.

124 Chettinad cuisine: From that region of Tamil Nadu, known as Chettinad, the home of the Chettiar community, their food is spicy, aromatic and delectable, my daughter Katrina's favourite regional cuisine.

Rose Peppercorns *[Schinus molle]*

Rose peppercorns originated from the tropical French Island of Reunion in the Indian Ocean. They are not peppercorns but berries from the baies rose tree, a tall, quick growing, graceful tree with droopy branches and shiny green leaves. It flowers in summer, pendulous creamy clusters, followed by sprays of rose pink berries. Rose peppercorns are delicate so must be treated gently, but if you are looking for a slightly sweet peppery taste then look no further. Use them whole or crushed in a sauce, in yogurt or a vegetable stir-fry. Alternatively, pair them with your favourite cheese in a creamy bake. Rose peppercorns are one of those ingredients that are truly special, understated and subtle, but the catalyst to get creative in the Kitchen.

Long pepper *[Piper longum]*

Pippali

My first encounter with long pepper was not as a spice but as a home remedy for a nasty throat infection. Renowned in Ayurvedic medicine for its powerful medicinal properties, it is also a culinary spice of great merit. Though still used in traditional Indian pickles and many ethnic cuisines around the world, its use as a spice in most places has declined or been replaced by common black pepper.

Our small plantation of *Piper longum* is not easy to maintain. There are nocturnal creatures who relish not only the fruit but the leaves as well, among them are the Civet *[Viverra zibetha]* and the Slender Loris *[Loris tardigradus]*, many who make their home in the plantation, deep among the shade trees. The pepper is harvested [what's left of it!] when the slender pods turn dark, they are then sun dried until completely dry. Best stored in an airtight container in a dark cool place

Long pepper has a far more complex flavour than regular black pepper, sharp and pungent. It can be used finely ground or coarsely cracked, and is wonderfully complimentary to beef, pork, and mutton. Use it in kebabs, roasts, or when grilling meat. Buy your requirements from your local pansari or traditional grocery store, failing which you can order the spice online. Your supermarket is unlikely to stock it.

Postscript: For a sore throat, lightly dry roast 3 to 4 dry pods of long pepper on very low heat, then remove and cool. Pound the pepper to as fine a powder as you can, place in a small bowl and mix in a tablespoon or two of pure natural honey. Take a half teaspoon of the mixture every few hours or as needed. Works wonders.

Golpar *[Heracleum persicum]*

Persian Hogweed [often erroneously called garden angelica]

There are several species of hogweed endemic to the mountains of Iran. The tiny seeds of this perennial herbaceous plant are a spice in Iranian cooking, usually ground and sold as a powder. The character of this amazing spice is actually indescribable; you will know what I mean when you open a container of the stuff or sprinkle some on your roast potatoes. Traditionally paired with lentils, beans, and other legumes but especially so with pomegranate arils, you can go further and blend it in with your style of cooking. Highly recommended!

Cubeb Pepper *[Piper cubeba]*

Java Pepper

Cubeb pepper is easily recognizable by its attractive little tail. It is a relative of the common black pepper but has a far more complex flavour, slightly bitter with peppery undertones. It grows on the islands around Indonesia, in Sumatra and Java. Cubeb pepper has had a long interesting history, popular with the Greeks and widely used in The Middle Ages. Used mainly in curries and spice blends it is an interesting alternative to pepper. Cubeb pepper goes well with meat, especially pork, pork sausages, and lamb. Use in moderation.

Cassia Buds *[Cinnamomum tamala nees]*

The buds of the cassia tree,perhaps not as well known as the bark, are also used to cook with. Picked just before they bloom they are sun dried and used in spice blends and for pickling. With a milder floral flavour, you can use them in other creative ways, in a risotto for instance. Their warm spicy flavour enhances a dish of stewed apples or pears.

Szechuan pepper *[Zanthoxylum piperitum]*

There are over 250 species of the genus *Zanthoxylum* worldwide, of these the most predominant are found in China, Japan, and Korea. There are two Indian species *Z.limonella* and *Z.rhetsa,* the berries used as a spice in local regional cuisine. The differences between the berries in colour, [rust to a grey to a deep brown], shape, and size can be bewildering, but for most culinary purposes are interchangeable. The husk or pericarp is used, it splits open when dry. Discard the beautiful deep blue-black seed revealed within. Szechuan pepper [tirphal in India] is not for the fainthearted, it is strong, pungent, and can leave the palate with a numbing sensation. In India, it is restricted to the Western coastal belt and usually combined with fish and coconut resulting in some mouth-watering curries.

38. The Odd Ingredient

Wattle Seed [Family Leguminosae/Genus Acacia]

The Indigenous people of Australia have always had a long and close relationship with wattle seed eaten raw or dried and ground into porridge. While the seeds from most species of acacia are inedible, several species find their way into cooking pots around the world. We have our wattle too at the Hermitage. Every year I am ever so grateful for the beauty of the summer flowers brilliant against the dull reds and browns of a dry summer, but unfortunately, cannot collect and eat the seeds!

The unusual nutty or coffee flavour of wattle seed is complementary to ice cream, sauces of all kinds, biscuits, cakes and bread. Buy wattle seed that has been roasted and ground. Like other spices store in an airtight container and kept in your store cupboard away from heat and light.

My tin of wattle seed is precious, and the aroma that escapes when I open it is warm and pungent. It is remarkably versatile; use it to flavour fish or chicken. I sprinkle some on my mushroom soup; add it to whipped cream, tomato salad, or cucumber raitha.

Shiitake, Snow Fungus, and Cloud Ears

Handy Store Cupboard Standbys!

Living as I do in the interiors of rural India my store cupboard is my lifeline and what I have in it really matters! I call these mushrooms handy store cupboard standbys because if stored in airtight containers they have a very impressive shelf life. All three varieties are available dried and need to be soaked in hot water for 30 minutes. Snow fungus and cloud ears swell considerably too many times their size; therefore, very small quantities are required, ideal for a cupboard of moderate size!

Shiitake is a Japanese mushroom that grows on a hardwood tree called Shii. Robust and with a very distinctive flavour the mushroom's meaty texture is quite unique. Refrigerate fresh mushrooms and eat them within three or four days. Because of their texture, cook shiitake mushrooms a little longer than usual, but overcooking will toughen them so take care! The stalks are usually too tough to use, so discard them.

Snow fungus *[Tremella fuciformis]* looks very much like a natural sponge. In its dry state it is a pale yellow but when cooked changes colour to a translucent white. It has a rather bland flavour, but like a sponge, snow fungus absorbs plenty of flavour from other ingredients. Cloud ears *[Auricularia polytricha]* are dark brown almost black mushrooms that grow on dead wood. If the mushrooms are small keep them whole, otherwise, slice them into bite size pieces. The hard portion at the base of both varieties where they attach themselves to the wood they grow on is inedible, cut off with a sharp knife and discard.

Don't confine fungus to your Asian cooking use them as you would any other mushroom in soups, stew and stir-fries. Sautéed in olive oil and butter they are great in scrambled eggs and omelettes.

Kasoori/Kasuri Methi *[Trigonella foenum-graecum]*

Dried Fenugreek Leaves

Kasuri methi is a privileged ingredient in my kitchen because I simply cannot live without it. It is seriously addictive! Kasuri methi or dried fenugreek leaves gets its name from Kasuer in Pakistan, where it grows abundantly and is of the finest quality. In its dried form it retains the plants bitter flavour but with an aroma that is truly amazing. Perfect for curries, soups, and dhal where it can be added directly to the cook pot, preferably at the end of the cooking process. For drier vegetable dishes, soak it first in a little warm water. There is also the option of dry roasting the kasuri methi on a griddle for a couple of minutes to intensify the flavour. For a steady supply of kasuri methi, you need to go no further than your local Asian store they are bound to stock it.

So where do I suggest you begin:

Tomatoes especially sweet heirloom varieties

Does well with minced meat, egg curry, mushroom soup

With Potatoes, sweet potatoes and yams

Stewed fish

Rice and pasta

Or in your recipe for herbed bread

Niger Seed *[Guizotia abyssinica]*

Birds love Niger seed and in the main, large parts of the world have no other use for Niger seed other than in bird feeders. Which is a pity, because cold pressed Niger seed oil is an excellent dressing for a bowl of salad greens. A native of East Africa, the Niger plant is a "Survivor" much like the millet family, tolerant of a harsh environment, poor soil conditions, and low rainfall; this adaptability is what makes these plants so out of the ordinary and so fascinating. Widely grown in Africa and India, the black almost silky seeds with their smoky, nutty flavour should find a place in your store cupboard.

Niger Seed Chutney

Best made in small quantities and stored in an airtight container for up to two weeks.

½ cup Niger seed

2 sprigs mature curry leaves

3 or 4 cloves garlic

½ teaspoon cumin seed

1 teaspoon rose pepper

Sea or rock salt to taste

Choose a heavy-bottomed pan and on medium dry heat roast the Niger seed, until a warm nutty aroma wafts towards you, but don't allow the seeds to burn. Remove and cool, then add the other ingredients and dry grind to a fine powder. Use the chutney sprinkled on yogurt, on top of hot white rice mixed and a teaspoon of ghee, or on your favourite lentils. The chutney goes well with winter squash, carrots, tomatoes, or added to your salad greens; adds a twist to your sauces and dressings.

The Fox Nut *[Euryale ferox]*[125]

My kitchen counter has a display of fine looking old glass jars that once must have graced the counter of a sweet shop. The bulls eye's, barley sugar and turkey eggs have now been replaced with an assortment of dry chillies in vivid shades of red, offset by jars of brown speckled beans, beaten rice and fox nut. Also known as the Gorgon plant or makhana; the fox nut is related to the water lily, with large round leaves, thorny spines, and bright purple flowers that float on the surface of the water. When the dry edible seeds are roasted, they pop like corn and are the best way to eat them.

You should be able to pick up a packet of makhana from your local Asian store. Check the date for freshness; the makhana should be firm, crisp and odourless. Before you start to cook, remove any hard seeds that haven't popped. Do not wash the makhana, just pan-fry

125 Euryale is one of the names of the mythological Gorgons, the one with thorny hair. The name alludes to the thorny spines of the plant.

in a little oil or butter until they heat through and change colour to a light brown, season to taste. Eat them out of hand as a snack, with a squeeze of lemon juice or cook makhana as you would any other vegetable in a tomato or cream based sauce. Try this delicious desert:

Basundi of Fox nut

Enough for 4 - with no left over's!

You require the following:

1 litre whole milk [preferably buffalo milk if available]

250 ml thick cream

2 cups fox nut

50 grams pistachios

25 grams butter

1 teaspoon oil

Yellow rose petals to decorate

A few drops kewra or almond essence

½ cup sugar or to taste

Pour the milk into in a heavy bottomed pan; bring to the boil just once, then simmer until the milk reduces to a little less than half. Scrape off the milk solids from the sides of the pan into the milk as it reduces. This will take quite a while, but you only need to give an occasional stir. Meanwhile in a large wok or frying pan lightly melt the butter and oil and tip in the fox nut and fry until they change colour to a light brown, take off the heat and cool. Roughly pulp the fox nut, but not too fine, then add to the reduced milk along with the sugar and essence, and continue to cook until the mixture thickens. Remove from the heat and cool completely, add the lightly beaten cream and the pistachios and chill. Just before serving decorate with the rose petals.

Charoli *[Buchanania lanzan]*

The charoli is a large tree, a good 50 feet or more in height, and found growing in the deciduous and semi-evergreen forests of India and Pakistan. There is one growing very near the boundary of our land, it belongs to a community of Malabar squirrels. The tree flowers and fruits from February to May and during this time many visitors put in an appearance including the jungle crow and the Malabar grey hornbill. Village children, on summer break, spend their days collecting the fallen nuts. They are hard to crack, but with success reveal within the highly recommended soft, almond flavoured seeds.

Generally used in sweet dishes charoli are small, odd shaped and light to medium brown. However, don't hesitate to add them to celery soup, stir fried carrots, or to flavour meat. Replace the pine nuts in your next homemade pesto with charoli. You can lightly dry roast them for a deep intense flavour then grind them, and use to thicken sauces and batters. Mix into 'smoothies' for added flavour. Look for your supply in a local Indian grocery store or source online.

Bibiya, the Marking Nut Tree *[Semecarpus anacardium]*

During the 1960's, my mother spent many hours with an inkpot and scratchy pen, laboriously marking the 'effects' in my school trunk. The black indelible ink ensured, that I returned with my own skirts and shirts, and with all my socks in pairs! The ink, [dhobis used it as well to mark their washing], comes from the rind of the fruit of *Semecarpus anacardium*, The Marking Nut Tree.

Semecarpus anacardium is a deciduous tree 12 to 15 meters high and closely related to the cashew, and similarly, has a bright orange false fruit or peduncle, which is edible but very astringent. The true fruit or nut is black, lustrous and bitter. The oil extracted from the rind of the nut is an excellent lubricant for the wooden axle of a bullacart.

The kernel of the nut is edible, often mottled and ranging in colour from a deep dark red to black and with an unusual flavour. Toss it in ghee or butter on medium heat and add it to both sweet and savoury dishes. It goes exceptionally well with carrots and winter squash. When buying bibiya seeds check for quality and freshness and store in an airtight container, they can go rancid over time.

When Salt was Just Sea Salt!

My salt merchant's unpretentious depot is located in a gully in the old quarter of Belgaum city. To get there you have to plough through utter chaos, not a very enjoyable start to your day; but then consider the options, a packet of commercial salt full of additives off the shelf in a supermarket. At the depot, there are mountains of salt piled up on plastic sheets, great stuff, wonderful stuff brought all the way from the saltpans of Western India. There are many waiting patiently to be served, home cooks like me, restaurateurs, electricians who need the stuff to earth their wiring, farmers who add it to cattle feed, ice merchants, and street hawkers who sell their ice cream in push carts. Here salt is not only sold by the kilo but also by the shovel full!

To season food, it's best to use your fingers, and it is a far more tangible and dependable way of measuring salt - instinctively. With all the bad press that salt gets it is no wonder we tend to forget that the body actually needs it to regulate many of its functions. Sea, rock and other specialty salts with their unique flavour can turn the ordinary into extraordinary, so with 'moderation' your mantra explore the wonderful world of salt!

Sea salt: Natural sea salt is off-white, strongly holds moisture and is irregular in shape. Depending where it comes from, sea salt contains traces of potassium, calcium, magnesium, iron and other minerals, but does not contain any additives. Sea salt is an excellent all-purpose every day salt to use in cooking, and when finely powdered as a suitable table salt. There are specialty sea salts that include the hand-harvested French salt Fleur de sel and Maldon sea salt from England's south coast. Exotic black Hawaiian sea salt enriched with activated charcoal, or red Hawaiian sea salt infused with a natural mineral called "Alae" [volcanic baked red clay]. There is Italian sea salt or Sale Marino from the Mediterranean Sea along the coast of Sicily. Grey salt or Celtic sea salt is a premium natural salt with a distinctive flavour that gets its colour from the clay deposits in the saltwater pans from which it is harvested.

Smoked salt: Smoked salt is natural sea salt smoked over a wood fire allowing the flavour of the wood, [alder, hickory, apple] to be absorbed into the salt crystals. Smoked salts add an interesting flavour to grilled meat and fish. However like so much else, there is a 'shortcut' available, "smoke flavoured salt" which uses a flavoured additive instead. You choose.

Roasted salt: For over a thousand years, Korean monks have been preparing Juk-yeom. The monks collected sea salt from Korea's coastline they then filled sections of bamboo with it, sealed the ends with clay and baked the bamboo over fires infused with pine needles, one of my favourite salts to use with yogurt or to flavour buttermilk.

Kosher salt: A coarse salt that is milder than most other salts, and generally evaporated from brine. It is a pure natural salt with no additives and is a good salt for general use. As the name implies, it also means that the salt is "kosher" as outlined by Jewish law.

Flake salts: Often referred to as 'finishing salts,' and high on the premium list. As the name suggests they comes in the form of flakes rather than crystals, are delicate in flavour and excellent table salts.

Rock salt: Rock salt mined from underground deposits around the world is inexpensive and unrefined, it has multiple uses and available in different colours, shapes, and sizes. Indian black salt and Himalayan rock salt are two fine examples.

Indian Black Salt: If nothing else, the colours can simply floor you. They range from a muddy pink to a deep violet, but my favourite colour is an intense coal black. It has a strong flavour and a smell of sulphur due to the presence of greigite. Break free and use it in or on everything!

Himalayan Rock Salt: is available in delightful shades of white, pink, and red brought on by a unique blend of minerals found in underground deposits in the Himalayan belt. Said to date back 250 million years with the highest mineral content of any natural salt, it is prized for its colour, flavour and health benefits. Himalayan rock salt remains one of the most unrefined and untreated natural salts available worldwide.

In my book, there are no hard and fast rules about which salt to use where just do what your fingers tell you!

The Store Room

It had a bottle green door that didn't shut too well, nevertheless, the heavy bolt slotted in faultlessly and you couldn't help but notice the rather outsized lock. The 'Store Room' in Krupalaya, was a narrow rectangular space with two rows of stone benches running along one length, and a barred window at the end that looked out onto the garden. Located next to the breakfast room, it was one of the many pocket-sized rooms in this part of the house.

No one got to keep the storeroom key, other than my grandmother. The key was part of an assortment of other keys making up a rather heavy bunch. They were on my grandmother's person constantly, [like a badge to endorse her authority on all things household], or hidden away somewhere in her room when she was out of the house.

The two stone shelves were laden with glass bottles, jars, tins, and such like holding all manner of household supplies. Burnis[126] full of Nergis Fui's mango achar, her delectable carrot pickle, and her mango murrumba, all that unsurprisingly never languished very long on those stone benches. After the menu for the day's meals had been finalized, the storeroom was opened, usually just once, between 9 and 10 in the morning. A request for another opening later in the day, by the cook or any of the other servants, was not generally looked upon favourably. My siblings and I were not encouraged to enter this space but often sneaked in to grab a fistful of dried fruit.

The Store Room had a number of wooden rat traps, placed in strategic locations to nab that unsolicited visitor. The bait varied, and reflected the lifestyle of Krupalaya's occupants, from buttered toast and gooseberry jam, to stale chapatti's slathered with mint and coriander chutney or a piece of leftover roast chicken.

Every year, come December and the storeroom began to fill with an abundance of Christmas goodies, the first to go in were my grandmother's plum puddings. Made in mid-November, she believed 'they must hang for at least a month,' preparing the fruit for the puddings set the holiday mood. Gran's good friend Kay Fernandes dropped by to help make the kul-kuls, rose cookies, marzipan and a household favourite called 'dhol-dhol'. Dhol-Dhol, a sweet sticky halva made with coconut milk and 'puttu' rice, an heirloom variety of black Burmese rice, then only available in Madras. It is a Christmas delicacy enjoyed by the Anglo-Indian community and the Christian communities of South India.

---

126 Burnis are traditional ceramic jars used for storing homemade pickles.

The name of this delicious halva was a contentious issue between my father and grandmother, and one that was brought up every year at Christmas. It usually ended in a truce, but with my grandmother rather red faced, and my father the amused victor! In Dari[127], the ancient language of Persia and the language of my ancestors, 'dhol-dhol' is the term used to denote the male genitalia!

127 Dari is the ancient language of Iran's Zoroastrians and should not be confused with that spoken in Afghanistan and some parts of Central Asia. Belonging to Iran's North-western language group, Dari has two distinct dialects, those of the provinces of Yazd and Kerman. My ancestors came from Yazd, and the Yazdi dialect itself has around thirty variations!

39. What's in a Name?

To me, it really does matter getting the name right. I go to great lengths to identify a spice, vegetable or fruit, not only for the sake of identification really, but also because the process of getting there is so interesting. It is safest to stick with the botanical name though this can be rather 'cut and dried'. Once you have your identification, however, you can call it what you like. There are nonetheless, a few condiments wrongly identified, and others with a plethora of interchangeable names that can cause plenty of confusion. Here is a modest list:

The Bay Leaf vs the Cassia Leaf

Laurus nobilis Vs Cinnamomum tamala nees

The bay leaf is Mediterranean in origin and grown extensively in Europe, Russia, Central and North America. The mild gentle flavour does exceptionally well in soups, stews, and Mediterranean cuisine. The leaf used in Indian cooking and often erroneously referred to as bay leaf is from a large evergreen tree *Cinnamomum tamala nees* that grow in the Himalayan foothills. Also known as the Indian Cassia or tejpata it is very similar in appearance to the European bay leaf and in fact belongs to the same family Lauraceae. It has a much stronger flavour and does better in traditional Indian cuisine. My *Laurus nobilis* grows in a pot outside our front door - the best way to protect it from heavy monsoon winds. One of the trees we planted when we first moved here in 1981 was a *Cinnamomum Tamala nees,* now with a beautiful canopy and a safe haven for nesting leaf birds, and a rest stop for our other feathered friends such as the Tickell's Blue Flycatcher.

Cinnamomum vs Cassia

Cinnamomum tamala nees Vs Cinnamomum zeylanicum breyn

Cassia bark is thick, dark and with a rough surface and used in the preparation of spice powders. It also does very well in curries, meat and rice dishes. The dried flower buds of the cassia tree whole or ground, have a flavour similar to the bark. Another closely related species is *Cinnamomum zeylanicum breyn* a tropical evergreen distributed in Western and Southern India. In its wild state the tree grows to a height of 6 to 7 meters and this is the true cinnamon. Use cassia and cinnamon interchangeable. However, the latter does have a more delicate flavour and is preferable in deserts, cakes, biscuits and other baked goods, excellent with chocolate and stewed fruit.

Nigella or Onion seed?

Nigella sativa

You find nigella seed in store cupboards around the world, in Sri Lanka, India, and the Middle East. These intriguing, elegantly shaped matt black seeds have a bitter flavour that can be overpowering if not used with restraint. Nigella seed, also known as kalonji, and often erroneously referred to as onion seed, is probably because they look so similar. Nigella seed is a good companion to tomatoes; and with the addition of a little brown sugar, palm sugar or jaggery you can achieve a good flavourful balance. Use nigella seed in lentil and other vegetable dishes, or sprinkled over yogurt and salads. Day old rice can be returned to the dining table for a second run if cooked up with nigella seed. Temper some in a little oil or ghee, add a few of your favourite vegetables and herbs and mix into the rice!

Black Cumin or Bunium persicum?

There is no greater confusion regarding nomenclature than in the case of *Bunium persicum*, usually referred to as black cumin. Colloquial names include shah or shahi jeera, Kashmiri cumin and so on. In stringent botanical terms, *Bunium persicum* is no relation to cumin at all though it does belong to the same family - *Umbelliferae.* This down-to-earth spice with its unusual flavour is used extensively in India and Pakistan, and throughout the Middle East, and should be a favourite of yours. Most recipes recommend minimal quantities, perhaps shying away from its deep earthy character. I recommend that you use it freely in flavouring rice, meat or yogurt. Use it in place of cumin, or add a pinch or two to your scrambled eggs!

The Case of Caraway vs *Bunium persicum* [Black cumin]

Carum carvi Vs Bunium persicum

Caraway is a biennial growing up to two feet high with soft delicate foliage and in the sub-continent often loosely and erroneously identified as *Bunium persicum* or black cumin. Widely used in Europe, it is an integral part of German and Austrian cuisine, but caraway is more or less absent in Indian cuisine. So the confusion is quite mystifying.

Pair the brown crescent shaped seeds with onions and potatoes, carrots, cabbage, and turnips, or use in biscuits and cakes. Add it to your homemade cottage cheese or when you are stewing fruit, its delightfully sweet warm aroma goes well with all the meats and especially oily fish.

The Case of Anise vs Fennel

Pimpinella anisum vs Foeniculum vulare

A meal in an Indian restaurant usually concludes with a teaspoon of fennel seed to help aid digestion. In the 'districts' restaurants often give you your bill first, and then drop the change they owe you into a bowl of fennel before bringing it to your table! Fennel seeds are small, oblong and a delicate light brown or a soothing mellow green. Reputed for improving eyesight, they are delicious paired with fish, onions, cauliflower, broccoli and other members of the Cole family. Add them to pastries and confectionery, because they help in the breakdown of starchy foods. Fennel seeds are often mistaken for aniseed, small nut-brown seeds that are oval, and tipped at one end with a fine 'hair' known as a pedicel. With a warm, sweet, aromatic taste, similar to fennel, aniseed is also good for digestion. Use both in much the same way. Aniseed does not have much of a presence in Indian cuisine, but the confusion between the two can be partly accredited to the fact that both are called 'Saunf' in India.

Simply Homemade!

Weights and Measures

A weighing scale in the kitchen is essential; my kitchen scales are a simple 'common balance'. Countless shopkeepers also use them, all over South India. Antiquated perhaps, but my scales are so accurate that a few drops of water can register a difference.

To make it easier for you to cook, I have used weights and measures that I thought most suitable for a particular ingredient. Measuring out one tablespoon of ginger garlic paste is easier than weighing out 15 grams! The conversion tables given below should help you follow the recipes no matter where you live.

Dry Measure

30 grams	1 ounce
45 grams	1 ½ ounces
70 grams	2 ½ ounces
100 grams	3 ½ ounces
125 grams	4 ½ ounces
280 grams	10 ounces
450 grams	16 ounces
500 grams	1 pound 1 ½ ounces
700 grams	1 ½ pounds
1000 grams	2 pounds 3 ounces

Liquid Measure

5 ml	1 teaspoon
10ml	1 dessert spoon
15 ml	1 tablespoon
60 ml	¼ cup
85 ml	1/3 cup
125 ml	½ cup
180 ml	¾ cup
250 ml	1 cup

Oven temperatures

Centigrade	Fahrenheit	Gas Mark	
93	200		Low
110	225		
130	250		
140	275	1	
150	300	2	
170	325	3	Moderate
180	350	4	
190	375	5	
200	400	6	High
220	425	7	
230	450	8	
240	475	9	

Suppliers

There are of course many online stores where you can source your ingredients here is a short list that might also be of help to you.

Garcinia Cambogia, Sappan wood, Vattals, and Indian Spices

Lots of interesting things on this website, worth a visit

http://www.natureloc.com

South Indian Vattals and Papadums

Iyer's Food Products

www.iyersproducts.com

Mobile no. 093412 18087

Land Line: 080 23203539

For Seaweed and Sea Vegetables

They have a range of sea vegetables and much more

www.http://kalustyans.com/

For all Iranian Condiments including Golpar

http://www.sadaf.com/persian-foods/

www.http://persianbasket.com/

Indian Spices

This website has a huge range of Indian spices; including Marathi moggu, nag Kesar cassia buds and so on, you name it, and they seem to have it!

http://spicesonline.info/indian-spices/

Organic Palm Sugar, Coconut Sugar and Palm Jaggery

All available from http://ecobuddy.in

Liquid Jaggery

If you are ever driving down National Highway 4, and you are footloose take a diversion at Satara and buy some of Shree Gurudatta's liquid jaggery!

Organic Liquid Jaggery available in 300 gm, 500 gm, and 1 Kg packs

Jaggery & Agro Products Satara, Maharashtra

Mr Prakash Kadam

Satara Lonand Road, Near Wadhe Bridge, Khed, Malvi

Satara - 415003, Maharashtra, India

Mobile : +(91)-9767573157

Organic Heirloom Rice

Available at Pristine Organics Pvt. Ltd, heirloom rice such as Gowrisanna, Rajamudi, Ghandhasale, Kuruvan black rice from Tamil Nadu, including a wide range of other organic products.

www.pristineorganics.com

Udang Rangup Bercili Crispy Prawn Chilly

This marvellous condiment is also available online at the sites below. The Crispy Prawn Chilly that I love to use has the following name and address on it nothing more, High King Trading Malaysia 012 3662199. If it you find it in a store near you just buy it!

http://www.souschef.co.uk/

https://shop.waiyeehong.com

http://theasiancookshop. co. uk/

East Indian Bottle

Michelle takes orders for her homemade masala during January and February each year. She fulfils all orders by April.

Homemade East Indian Bottle Masala from Michelle Sampey

Email:mirellesampey@gmail.com

Phone no: +91 98209 20876

Address: 'Marionelle,' 81, Vakola, Market Road,

Santacruz East

Mumbai 55

Also available at:

Mark's Cold Storage

Phone no: +91 2655 1413, 2655 1409

Address: 2, Shahina Building,

Pali Mala Road,

Near Pali Market, Bandra (West)

Mumbai

Hibiscus, Rozella, and other Syrups

Naturellement

Udyogam,Auroville,TamilNadu India605101

+91 413 2622034

www.naturellement.in

Alfalfa Seeds, Brown Rice, and Brown Rice Flakes or Pohe

http://www.onahealthynote.com/

Parsee Masala Powders

For a wide range of masala's, including dhanajeera, and Parsee sambhar masala

www.mangalmasala.com

If you live in Poona or are passing through, you might like to pick up a full range of traditional Parsee masala powders from a small shop called P. S Chindhy next to the Fire temple on Sachapeer Street Poona 1.

Spicy Podi's

The first time I opened a packet of rasam powder made by Amirta Valli, I nearly swooned! The aroma was wonderful! Buy homemade masala's from Amirta at:

Rh-177, Ellis Nagar,

Madurai-10,

Tamil Nadu

Phone: +91 9500989422

Email: amirta0602@gmail.com

Morvarid Fernandez

For the past thirty-six years Morvarid, her Husband David, and Daughter Katrina have lived on an organic farm deep amid the jungles of the Western Ghats. Though agriculture has always been the family's mainstay, in 2003 they opened a guesthouse. Working in her 'Green and Yellow' kitchen, Morvarid cooks for the many guests from around the world who visit The Hermitage.

This book she has written draws on her experiences of living in a rural community, of forging a deep, unbreakable bond with the surrounding environment, and growing her organic food. Morvarid's family background, drawn from Zoroastrian, Irish, and Dutch ancestry gave her childhood a delightful insight into a melting pot of cultures, and this reflects in her cooking.

Morvarid loves dogs, and grows 'heirloom' vegetables; collects owls, glass bottles and anything that's old, and when she's not cooking spends her time doing needlework, craftwork, and gardening.

Modern Family!

Index